W9-BJD-998

When elephants fight
ants get killed.
— Cambodian proverb

WHEN ELEPHANTS FIGHT

Vannary Imam

A MEMOIR

A Sue Hines Book
Allen & Unwin

Copyright © Vannary Imam 2000

All rights reserved. No part of this book may be reproduced or transmitted in any form or by any means, electronic or mechanical, including photocopying, recording or by any information storage and retrieval system, without prior permission in writing from the publisher. *The Australian Copyright Act* 1968 (the Act) allows a maximum of one chapter or 10% of this book, whichever is the greater, to be photocopied by any educational institution for its educational purposes provided that the educational institution (or body that administers it) has given a remuneration notice to Copyright Agency Limited (CAL) under the Act.

First published in 2000
A Sue Hines Book
Allen & Unwin Pty Ltd
9 Atchison Street
St Leonards, NSW 2065, Australia
Phone: (61 2) 8425 0100
Fax: (61 2) 9906 2218
E-mail: frontdesk@allen-unwin.com.au
Web: http://www.allen-unwin.com.au

National Library of Australia
Cataloguing-in-Publication entry:

Imam, Vannary.
When elephants fight.
ISBN 1 86508 298 8.
1. Imam, Vannary. 2. Political refugees – Australia – Biography. 3. Political refugees – Cambodia – Biography. 4. Cambodia – Politics and government – 1975–79. I. Title.
325.21095960994

Text prepared with the assistance of Elizabeth Fulton Thurston
Cover and text designed by Guy Mirabella
Cover photograph courtesy of Bibliothèque nationale de France
Typeset by J&M Typesetting
Printed in Australia by Griffin Press

10 9 8 7 6 5 4 3 2 1

I dedicate this book to my mother. I have never known her to read a book, but every page I wrote, she was constantly in my heart

CONTENTS

Acknowledgements

When I undertook the task of writing this book, I felt there were many gaps in my knowledge. I relied on different sources. Milton Osborne's book, *Prelude to Tragedy*, gave me the background on the Cambodian economy, the traffic in rice and the decadence of the elite during the years before General Lon Nol overthrew Sihanouk. In Charles Meyer's *Derrière le Sourire Khmer*, I found further statistics relating to health and education. In John Pilger's works, namely *Heroes* and *Distant Voices*, I followed his account relating to the fall of Saigon and the difficulties of the new Communist government in Vietnam. He was among the first journalists who went to Cambodia after the fall of Pol Pot. From Adhémar Leclère I borrowed an anecdote relating to two young princes whose flesh were carved and fed to them by jail-keepers. Most of all, I owe much gratitude to Professor David Chandler, whose authoritative writings on Cambodia provided the backbone to my book. I leaned on his facts, his view on the history, politics and the men of power who shaped the destiny of my country. His influences are too many to pinpoint.

Details of my ancestry stretching back to the early nineteenth century came from oral history. My mixed background, full of cultural, religious, political and racial conflicts, the forces of which pulled the members of my family toward different loyalties, had given me the urge to find my own identity from an early age. I used to prefer the company of adults and suspected them of possessing a wisdom I could only guess at. My great grandmother, the Lady in White, whom I met as a child, was regarded as senile at that stage. She used to talk about the village of Tan Chau and two mysterious men. The first man was her grandfather. I was unable to find out more about him other than assuming that he must have been very wealthy and powerful, judging by the size of his escort on her wedding day, the size of the Lady in White's dowry and the importance she enjoyed because she was a bride who must be respected. Indeed I heard my own Grandfather Heng accuse the Lady in White's forefathers of soaking themselves in blood and being involved in piracy. The truth can be found more in a man's insults than in his flattery.

The second man I constantly heard about was called Number Four. The Lady in White never tired of telling me about her son's brutal death and his lack of a proper burial. It was my father who filled in the gaps relating to this character. My mother handed down to me the stories she had heard from Grandma Kim, Reama and Grandfather Heng's wet nurse.

The elders of the village of Prek Dek used to come and visit Grandfather Heng during my many holidays there. At night, they normally indulged in talking about the past. From them, I received a vivid and nostalgic description of life in this ancestral village through the generations. My oral sources were sometimes disparate, sometimes conflicting. I had to use my own judgement, at times my own imagination, to regroup them into a chronological order. I had to determine the likely truth and place it against the historical context of my country. Any unintentional mistakes and flaws must not reflect on my sources; they are my responsibility alone.

Although my mother furnished me the most useful link with the past, she was reluctant to touch on the period of her life that led her to meet my father and to explain the lack of communication between her family and his. I had to fly to Seattle in 1994 to meet for the first time some of my maternal uncles and aunts. It was Uncle Xuang who shed a lot of light on the past. I was warned that Grandma Nguen, then in her early eighties, would not consent to any interviews unless I played cards with her and let her win. Had real money been at stake, she would have accumulated from me a fortune.

I owe all of them a considerable debt. Directly or indirectly, they contributed to this book more than they could ever suspect.

I would like to thank Sophie Lance for seeing merit in my manuscript and encouraging me to pursue it. Without Elizabeth Fulton

Thurston, an editor and a friend, it risked remaining in its unpolished form, full of mistakes, and would have been condemned to collecting dust. Her guidance, her insight and her patience are integral in delivering the final version of the manuscript. Not enough can be said to thank her for her help.

It is my good fortune to have attracted the interest of Foong Ling Kong. I am grateful to her for her enthusiasm, her attitude for excellence and her insistence on getting personally involved in the editing process. Finally I am indebted to my publisher Sue Hines for the privilege of being on her list. Only with her approval and blessing will my work find its way into the world.

From the word go, my husband has been a consistent believer, especially during the many disheartening phases when I was tempted to give up. He was my sounding board and his companionship rendered writing a much less lonely process. He is hardly present in this book, but his role behind the scenes was vital. He was the one who challenged me to begin, continue and finish the journey into my past. For the five years while I wrote, I had to recall and relive all the unpleasant incidents I would have rather forgotten. Most days, I came out feeling drained, sick or numb, but Raafat was always there to mend me. Since I met him, he has always been there to pick up the broken pieces.

I would like to think of this book as my legacy to our three children. By the time they reach maturity and wish to visit the place where I was born, there might not be much left of my cultural heritage. Already, Angkorian relics have been removed and sold abroad; heads of thirteenth-century statues, pieces of bas-reliefs command high prices, the very reason which encourages the desecration of Cambodian temples.

Chan Sar Serei enabled me to go overseas and study. He was my angel of mercy. Australia gave me more than a scholarship. It adopted me and saved me.

Family Tree

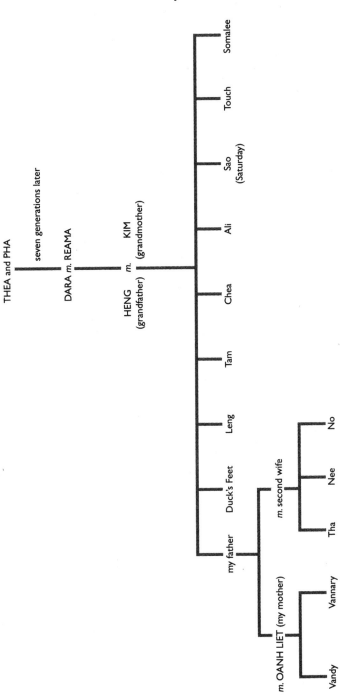
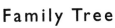

THEA and PHA

seven generations later

DARA *m.* REAMA

HENG *m.* KIM
(grandfather)   (grandmother)

Leng Tam Chea Ali Sao   Touch Somalee
Duck's Feet   (Saturday)

my father

m. second wife

Tha Nee No

m. OANH LIET (my mother)

Vandy Vannary

PROLOGUE

Today my name is Vannary Imam.

I borrowed the surname 'Imam' twenty years ago. It is an Arabic word and a title the Muslims give to their religious leaders. It belongs to the man I married and therefore denotes his heritage. My first name belongs to my heritage, which I believed I had left behind over thirty years ago.

One day in 1987, during a stay in Bangkok, I was quite conscious of not letting my thoughts wander toward the eastern sky. There across the border lay the country of my birth, Cambodia, an ancient land infamous for its killing fields. There lay a past that was full of tears.

For so long, I did not care to dwell on sadness and avoided situations which might evoke the tragedy that so affected my family and decimated my people. When my husband suggested Bangkok as our holiday destination, the place closest to my roots, I was embarrassed to express reluctance. Surely, after sixteen years of being away and having made a life elsewhere, enough time had passed for my hurt to heal? By that stage, I could even glance at old photographs of deceased relatives without much of an outburst of emotion. This convinced me I was ready to visit Thailand.

Every sound and every sight, the things I touched and tasted and the smell in the humid air during that trip conspired to give me the deceptive impression I was returning home. Thai food, generous with fresh herbs and fragrant spices, has the aroma of the meals my mother used to cook. The cityscape is dotted with the peaked roofs of Buddhist temples. The monks walking with begging bowls in the streets of Bangkok, whose chanting I could faintly hear at the hours when traffic eased slightly . . .

In Bangkok, I could not look upon the shadow of a temple or a saffron robe without remembering one particular head monk, Keo, who, a long time ago in Cambodia, gave to my grandfather Heng the name Vannary to be kept for me. This religious man always lived isolated from the world, and even my own father could not claim he ever saw him. Reverend Keo loved my grandfather like a son he could not physically have sired, and his teachings led Heng on a path to a set of choices that, in turn, prescribed the rules by which my family lived. He was a spiritual ancestor. My family did not actively practise Buddhism in the sense most Cambodians do, like going to temples, giving alms to the monks or hosting them at our home during certain religious occasions, but I do not think that my grandfather's mentor meant for Heng and consequently for us to do so. Keo's influence was deeper.

I remain a Buddhist. Therevada Buddhism, the state religion in Thailand and Cambodia, has imprinted its mark on me in more ways than I can describe. I have been exposed to foreign education and a few cultures, and have searched for alternative beliefs, through the Christian church to which my mother belongs, and the Islamic faith when I met my husband. In spite of all this, I still adhere to the fundamental principles of Buddhism I inherited from Grandfather, especially his fear of karma, his conviction that he was his own judge.

Grandfather Heng was an awesome figure in my childhood. He was either hidden behind a cloud of smoke from his pipe or half-drunk, mumbling curses, angry for no apparent reason and against no-one in particular. For all the terror he provoked in me, I also sensed a vulnerability. Though I was young, my intuition told me that a person must be tormented to drink so heavily. I was to find out more about him than met the eye.

It was me who had a dream in which he was dressed in a monk's robe. He descended to the riverbank where he sailed away in a dinghy; he looked so peaceful as I had never thought him capable and, bathed in the light of the rising sun, he gradually faded into the distant horizon. When I described to my mother what I saw, she looked at me strangely and forbade me to tell anyone else about the dream. I insisted that I had not made it up and wanted to know why it was such a secret.

'Your grandfather will not be with us for too long. If you talk about your dream, you might be seen as a carrier of doom.'

I kept quiet and really, my grandfather was as fit as a fiddle. A few days later, Grandma Kim sent word that he was not well. After the funeral two months later, under the guise of consoling her, I disclosed to her my dream.

'That he was a monk when he stepped in that boat meant your grandfather finally fulfilled in death the one wish he could not have during his life. His parents forced him to marry me, and they had the right to expect grandchildren from their only son.'

I was not aware until then that my grandfather had wanted celibacy. This revelation slipped out of my Grandma Kim's lips quickly and it was, among other truths and secrets in our family, not to be confided too readily.

Heng and Kim's marriage was an unusual arrangement and produced a new generation because Kim was Vietnamese. From my father's time onwards, all the members of my family, in various degrees, had to apologise for our mixed blood. In Cambodia, more than three centuries of intermittent occupation and humiliation by Vietnam have given rise to a deep national hatred. To the Cambodians, the Vietnamese are the hereditary enemy. Our family, living in that society, experienced many forms of discrimination. Whether they were overt, blunt or subtle, we were made to realise we were born with a sin, potentially a mortal sin, when the political climate swung against Vietnam. Then, the Vietnamese migrants in Cambodia bore the brunt of local wrath. There were, on and off, mass murders.

Things were more complicated for me since my mother is Vietnamese. This makes me only a quarter Cambodian, which was not an issue during my first few years of childhood. Although a tug-of-war must have existed—and it did in our midst—between my Cambodian great-grandmother Reama and her Vietnamese daughter-in-law Kim,

I was told by my mother, who wished to shield me from real life, that their conflict was either 'between in-laws, they normally don't get along', or it was put down to 'adults' affairs'. I knew later in my adolescence that it was partly based on racism.

I spoke both Cambodian and Vietnamese. They were indistinctly fused together in my mind, and I blended their words in the same sentence as if the two tongues were one. I started school when I turned four. Nothing prepared me really to defend myself against the attacks from a few children because I was Vietnamese. How they came to know makes me wonder today. I was not aware of what makes a person either 'Cambodian' or 'Vietnamese'. My complexion was a hint lighter than most and a hint darker than some, and I certainly could not differentiate.

Although once, I did ask my mother why the boy who lived not far from us was 'so' dark. She did not say he was Indian, she chose to answer my question with more questions: 'Why?' she repeated my question and seemed to stumble as she said, 'How can I know why roses are sometimes red and sometimes pink? Why are jasmines white? They are all flowers, aren't they?'

I concluded that my mother could not explain. I did not suspect that she did not want to, in order to keep me ignorant a little longer. She could not stop my visual ability to see a strong skin colour contrast, for instance, between the dark boy and myself, but she tried to spare me from acquiring too soon the abstract concept of race distinction. Children, unless they are taught, remain blind to racism.

However hard my mother attempted to protect my childhood innocence, I was to lose it rather quickly when I was a target at school. I began to make a broad distinction between Vietnam and Cambodia. I also began to comprehend more the irreconcilable differences that set them a world apart. Vietnam, a place I had never visited, tickled my curiosity because my mother so often spoke about it. And I tried not to allow myself to love it. I gave my loyalty to Cambodia because it bore me and it fed me, even when I was treated like its unwanted child.

My paternal uncle, 'Duck's Feet', made the opposite choice. He claimed to be totally Vietnamese and expatriated to France. He turned his back on Cambodia for nearly fifty years, but in his old age, dreamed of going back to see Angkor, to buy somewhere a small farm with a pond that reminded him of Prek Dek, our ancestral village. The nostalgic pull towards the place of birth is beyond most of our control.

In my own way, I tried to bury Cambodia when it became very painful to think about it. It was in Thailand that memories of my home and my country came back to life. The past imposed itself with a brutal strength that I could not dismiss. I was suddenly conscious that the money I spent in Bangkok as a tourist was more than what a poor Thai man could earn in a year. Across the border, a poor Cambodian was making even less. I shortened my holiday and booked myself on the next flight out of Bangkok.

Once back in Australia, the account I decided to write has taken me on a journey back in time, through several generations of my family and the history of my beloved Cambodia. It has also been prompted by the need to confront my past and to make some order out of the events in a heritage where chaos has prevailed for too long.

In writing, I have hoped to give you some insight to comprehend the incomprehensible—why my homeland was shattered and why many of my relatives and nearly two million of my race left their bones on the open fields and in ghost cities. Why some of those who survived are now scattered around the world.

One way or another, dead or alive, we fall victims. As they say where I grew up, 'when elephants fight, ants get killed'. I have chosen the first segment of this Cambodian proverb to be the title of my book. More than a tale of sadness, my story is a collective story of human survival against the odds.

On a subject such as this, my mind lacks the intensity of my heart. As James Joyce once said, I write with 'what is in the blood'.

Part One MUDDY ROOTS, LOTUS ROOTS

I

Township and Rice Fields

From its source in the Tibetan tableland, the Mekong River flows into Cambodia. Its offshoots, resembling tiny blood vessels on the map, represent the lifeline of my country. The wet season brings strong winds blowing northward, following the course of this river inland where it throws itself into a lake, the Tonle Sap, which forms a large natural reservoir full of freshwater fish, the main source of protein for the whole population. Swollen by the rains, the volume of the lake almost triples. In October, as the monsoon draws to a close, the winds turn southward and the lake begins to empty its excessive waters. The withdrawal of the floods leaves rich sediments.

Prek Dek, my family's native village, sits on the Mekong River, east of Chaudoc, one of the natural corridors for the Vietnamese who migrate to Cambodia. Because of its position, Prek Dek hosted a mixed population. It was never mixed, however, in terms of intermarriage. The Cambodians and the Vietnamese did not—and do not—mix. They segregate in two separate communities within an area; each ethnic group ignores the existence of the other.

Long ago, my ancestors dismantled their hut, put their belongings on a cart pulled by a bull. They made their claim on a vacant piece of land in Prek Dek. Here they reassembled pillars, planks and a thatched roof, and rebuilt their old home in a matter of days. Back then when a farm was deserted for three years and no taxes were collected, it could be re-occupied.

Rural life is tuned to the rhythm of nature, which is uncomplicated in times of peace. However peace was and would remain a wistful word in Cambodia.

The history of my family begins to take shape in the 1810s, more than ten generations before I was born, the time from which it can be recalled with some accuracy and the point I have chosen to begin. I start with the story of a marriage between two of my ancestors in the early nineteenth century.

The bride, Pha, short for 'Bopha', meaning flower, was not pretty. Her build was slender and her hips were too narrow to bear children. She was over twenty and considered an old spinster who had passed the prime of youth. It was a bonus for a woman to have dimpled cheeks; her complexion should be fair and her figure plump before she was looked on as beautiful. Apart from having none of these attributes, Pha's family had no assets to compensate for what she lacked. She was, however, strong; from the age of ten, from dawn to dusk, she spent the days in the rice fields, bent in half ploughing the fields to feed the other three members of her family.

Her story was typical of those who lived in villages. It spoke of survival and of selflessness from the moment her elder brother contracted poliomyelitis. He was the only son and was expected to carry the family line into posterity. Since his illness, the parents had become preoccupied with finding a cure. They took him to the temple for Buddhist prayers; they donated whatever they could afford in alms. They fed the poor while being poor themselves, in the hope that the active performance of these good deeds could reverse the cruel twist of destiny. Their son remained crippled. After they had exhausted all the conventional Buddhist suggestions and advice, they succumbed to sorcery. They carried him on their cart to other villages and far-off places, to wherever they heard of witch doctors. Each time, they dug deeper into their pockets. Before every trip, they unearthed their savings and their silver from their hiding spots, until there was nothing more to find. They had to borrow money and only gave up when usurers refused to lend. The couple returned to their farm and to their daughter who was left in the care of neighbours. What the farm produced only serviced the debts incurred by the fruitless pursuit of the son's miracle cure and little was kept to live on. Harassed by necessity, Pha's parents realised their last resort was to send her away to work for a rich family in Prek Neak Loeung, fifteen kilometres to the north of Prek Dek. They intended to bond her for seven years. To appease their guilt, they calculated that by the time Pha was freed, she would be twenty—still young enough to attract a husband and pick up the thread of a normal life.

The couple her parents went to see owned many servants and slaves, and certainly did not need an additional pair of hands from a thirteen-year-old peasant girl. But they were kind, and touched by the urgency of the situation. Acting on her impulse to do good, the mistress of the house said that she could use another maid. Pha would help an older woman polish the timber floor. The rich couple paid the seven-year fee in advance without attempting to bargain, and assured Pha's parents that they would look after her. Upon this, Pha's parents dropped their heads to the floor, muttered a profusion of blessings and, in typical Cambodian propriety, implored the gods, the *Tevodas*, to grant their benefactors long life, wealth and happiness.

Pha fitted quickly into her servant's role. She would not be seen standing up in front of her masters; she crawled the entire time even when she was not wiping the floor. In the old days, slaves and servants must move on their hands and knees when they were inside the main house. Her new keepers automatically assumed a parental role over her and she called them 'father' and 'mother'. They provided her with protection, while retaining the right to inflict terrible penalties when they suspected any wrongdoing. If suspected of stealing, the proof of innocence for an employee was nothing short of a miracle. The accused person had to hold a burning piece of steel or charcoal and walk ten steps. Another test was to dip the hand in a pot of boiling water to scoop an egg or swallow whole a steaming ball of glutinous rice the size of a fist. Local folklore was crowded with divinities that promised to intervene to save the innocent, but in everyday life, the very poor preferred to apply prudence.

Among the many other traps for young female servants, Pha's mother warned her against amorous advances. 'Poor girls,' she said, 'who consented to any males in the house where they worked, ended up destitute. They died in oblivion in the streets.'

Virginity was the most precious virtue a female could possess. Suitably impressed, Pha checked her conduct and kept out of trouble. Seven years were to pass, during which her master's eldest son was married. By the time Pha's bondage was about to expire, the youngest son was due to be ordained a monk in the season of rains.

When free at last, Pha walked back to Prek Dek, where she found her home leaning on the side, threatening to collapse at the first gust of wind. Her parents had aged threefold faster than the length of her absence. Rice-farming is backbreaking, and in their poverty, additional impositions had further arched their spines. Her parents could not afford to hire seasonal help, nor could they replace broken tools or tired work animals. Very often, her father had to pull the plough to give his scrawny old bulls a rest. Most rural folk scraped a bare living from an archaic method of planting rice, unchanged through the ages. They worked actively for twenty years until their strength failed them and retired at forty. Their twilight years began at this stage and they died at fifty-two, a stark set of statistics that is still relevant today.

Three years after Pha returned, her parents started to hint that she was denying them the pleasure of little children running around the house. They could not die in peace as she was still without a husband to care for her, but no suitor had approached them for her hand in marriage. Unbeknown to them, the youngest son of the family to whom she had been bonded was on his way to change their fate.

Thea had recently come out of the monastery. Compared to the stay of three wet months for the majority of young farmers, Thea's three-year stay in the monastery was longer than was required. He stated the reason for his ordination was to show filial gratitude to his mother. He wished the Neak Loeung community to envy her because she had brought up a respectful and loving son.

After he took off his saffron robes and left the monastery to resume his secular life, he revealed to his mother something that was not in keeping with the profile of such a dutiful son. He confided that he had always loved the bonded girl and intended to marry her. His mother stared blankly at him. When she could finally talk, she called for an exorcist, suspecting her son must be a victim of a terrible spell. She rushed him to the head monk to shower him with holy water. She adorned his wrists with silver amulets and placed an ivory statue of Buddha around his neck; she had his chest tattooed for further protection. Thea submitted to the rituals his mother deemed essential to remove the effects of magic love charms. When his mother finally understood that she was dealing with a phenomenon of the heart, she appealed to his common-sense. She painted a picture of poverty that he was sure to fall into if he married outside his township and below his class.

'You cannot survive among the rice peasants,' she warned. She drummed her hand on her chest and lamented: 'Why do you want to err from the comfortable path you were born into and return to the rice fields?' The most common prayer in Cambodia was to be spared from the mud.

Unlike the small village of Prek Dek, Prek Neak Loeung was a township where houses reflected its prosperity. They were imposing buildings set on cemented columns and roofed with corrugated iron or tiles.

The façades were carved with intricate leaf designs and they were built to last the test of time. Prek Neak Loeung was a trade centre where peasants came to sell their crops. It had a day market called a *psar*, a linguistic retraction from the Arabic word 'bazaar', which found its way into Cambodian vocabulary via our Islamic Malay neighbours. The town boasted historical significance; it used to link the river to the old city of Sithor in the sixteenth century. Blessed with the best soil in the country, known as *dey lobob*, these town people regarded themselves superior to the rice peasantry.

In this township community, Thea's mother occupied an exclusive place. Sole heiress to her parents' considerable fortune, she gave the bulk of heirlooms, slaves and properties to her husband when she married. A bride with a full purse and of noble origin, she enjoyed full authority in her household, but she was powerless to thwart the course of her son's destiny. After she had run out of arguments to talk him out of marrying Bopha, she resigned herself to fate. Faced with the task of escaping social embarrassment she decided to dress up Pha's ancestry. She concocted a white lie, claiming that Pha's forefathers had fallen on hard times and it seemed that their wealth dissipated through wars. The Cambodians were sympathetic to this kind of adversity, since sneering at someone's misfortune was believed to be a sin.

Thea's mother insisted the nuptial ceremonies take their full course of seven days during which time food was cooked and served around the clock. In her need to save face, she acted insensitively for at that very time Cambodia was in the grip of a horrendous famine. Inclement weather had set in, rains pouring down for months had flooded the whole countryside. Farther afield, the floor of the king's palace was rumoured to be two elbow lengths under water. He had to retire to the royal barge, and died from dysentery. Humidity rotted most of the crops and rice was very scarce—it could only be bought against the weight of silver and according to record, twenty kilograms of rice cost fifty-seven grams of silver. The annual harvest of 1817 was the lowest in living memory.

The house Thea's mother instructed to be built in Prek Dek for the newlyweds took two years to complete and respected sacred beliefs and superstitions. The size of the new house was indicative of Cambodian vanity to show off a wealth unscathed by the ongoing upheavals. Its front faced the morning sun for good luck. It was a two-storey house of brick and eighteen pillars (any multiple of three or four must be respected) supported the frame. A central staircase of five steps (even numbers are bad omens) led to the main entrance. Steel bars secured a large timber door. The ground floor was of a size that could accommodate relatives and friends and the whole population of monks from the local Buddhist temple. Five enormous divans were placed in a row; each one was made from one single trunk of precious ebony, each carved into its final shape without trace of joints or nails. An internal staircase allowed access to the second storey and a trapdoor sealed this upper level in the event of bandits' attacks. Round holes were drilled into the timber floor to enable sharp bamboo sticks to be thrown down. Outside on the wrap-around verandah, two rows of green glass bottles filled with hardened cement acted as decorations. These were in fact ammunitions against intruders. Under the tiled roof was a granary where provisions were stored for long sieges. Outside was moored a ten-metre barge, which would not rock against the waves when it cruised on the Mekong River. It provided a means of transport for Thea since he was about to live permanently in Prek Dek.

Thea planned to wean himself from his mother's financial assistance. He introduced crops to Prek Dek. Cornfields began to dot the landscape of his and Pha's farm. The white variety appeared first, and then the red variety was grown and sold. Soybeans were also planted, more land acquired, more workers hired. From the initial three hectares, a total of one hundred hectares were accumulated. In the next seven decades, the estate expanded but I was never told its exact dimension. My elders were not comfortable boasting while others had very little. In comparison to the average landholding, which seldom exceeded six hectares, our family's land covered a respectable size. In Prek Dek, it was known to be the biggest. In the context of Cambodia, our holding placed us among less than one per cent of those who owned over a hundred hectares.

2

Dara

Before its decline from the fourteenth century, the Khmer empire used to dominate most of Southeast Asia. The beginning of its end was closely related to the birth of a unified Thailand. By 1350, the Thais were gathered under one rule with a new capital in Ayutthaya, a hundred kilometres from the Cambodian city of Angkor Thom. By then, the Cambodian court was riven with internal problems and power struggles.

At the end of 1352, the Thai sent fifteen thousand troops to Cambodia. The Khmers resisted for a total of sixteen months, but by the end, anything of value was taken and ninety thousand captives dragged in chains to Ayutthaya. The Thais ruled Cambodia for five years. In 1357, they conceded defeat to a reorganised Khmer army, which fought to reclaim its capital and re-establish its monarchy.

In 1394, the Thais marched back into Cambodia with a vengeance. Deterred by the prospect of another lengthy war, they schemed to take Angkor by ruse. According to Adhémar Leclère, in his book *Histoire du Cambodge*, the Thais had to find a way to send some of their troops into the Khmer city. They staged a scene of corporal punishment, whipped almost to death six of their soldiers while making sure that the

Cambodians could see the flogging from the ramparts. Later that night, these beaten-up men came scratching at the gate, begging the Cambodians to let them in. They knelt in front of the Khmer king, whom they begged to accept their allegiance and claimed that they had been victims of unfair treatment. They were trusted to fight on the side of the Cambodians but during one major assault, they succeeded in unlocking the western gate and the Thais spilled into the besieged city. Angkor Thom surrendered. Seventy thousand prisoners were captured, among them court dignitaries, scholars, priests, soldiers and civilians. They were chained and forcibly migrated to Ayutthaya, where most of them became state slaves.

After another raid from the Thais in 1431, the Khmer king decided to abandon Angkor. Recent successive wars had prevented the maintenance of its sophisticated but fragile network of irrigation. The vandalised canals and reservoirs became breeding grounds for malaria. The king could no longer gather enough labour force to restore the hydraulic system since most of the villages had been decimated, its occupants killed or taken away to Thailand. Without workable irrigation and without the numbers, Angkor could not defend itself.

The Khmer capital shifted to where Phnom Penh is today. Already an affluent town, it sits on the confluence of two large rivers, the Tonle Sap and the Mekong, where its position made it easily accessible to merchants who came to trade. A distance of more than five hundred kilometres separated it from the Thai capital. For a short while, the Khmers enjoyed a period of prosperity.

From 1436 until the mid-1470s, the bickering between the king and his two brothers ended up splitting the country into three kingdoms. The area closest to Thailand sought the backing of the Thai king to defeat the other two. Relying on the interference of the Thais somehow became a precedent and a bad habit that future contenders would depend upon in order to ascend the Cambodian throne.

If the previous sieges at Angkor had been atrocious and damaging, the internal divisions of the civil war were a lot more damning. Never before did the people feel so deeply demoralised and confused. It was auto-genocide, a nightmare all too familiar to the Cambodians. After many foreign attacks, Cambodia was choked by its own hand.

From here onwards, constant divisions within the royal family weakened the once mighty Khmer kings, whose main preoccupation was to keep the crowns on their heads at all cost. As Thailand became powerful, so too did Vietnam begin to gather in strength and unity. Sandwiched in the middle of these two growing powers, Cambodia fought to survive. Its long-term prospects were grim.

In the eighteenth century it was reduced to serving its two neighbours when Europe's race to colonise the East reached its shores and changed the big picture. To compete with England, France believed Vietnam would give her the key passage to mainland China. Cambodia did not hold strategic importance although French travellers speculated that much natural wealth could be found on its lands. France took over Vietnam first and, very much as an afterthought, entered Cambodia and declared it a Protectorate in 1863.

My great-grandfather, Dara, was born around the 1880s, nearly two decades after Cambodia lost its autonomy. In those days peasants preferred to give children simple, single-syllable names. They were words of colours or of flowers for girls; they indicated the position of the newborn or were the first short, meaningless sound that came to mind. Infant mortality was high in villages, and it was feared that anything attractive would draw the attention of bad spirits. Quite against the trend, Dara's parents picked the word meaning 'star' for their son.

As he grew up, he remained their only child and his mother attended to him personally, a privilege that was rare among rural women who normally had to leave their infants to go out and grow rice. My ancestral family had by then distanced themselves from physical work and depended on others. Dara's mother preserved her youth and complexion into her old age. She did not have a wrinkle, her soft fingers retained the perfect shape of 'the thorns of the orange tree', which, to the Cambodians, were signs of beauty and ease of life.

At seven, Dara was sent to the temple school. More than teaching their pupils to read and write, the monks' guidance bonded a child to a Buddhist philosophy of life. But Dara protested and cried until his parents spared him the trauma of this early education. He locked his small hand into his father's large fingers and could not wait to inspect their properties. From a young age, he showed keenness in the land and his parents were delighted that this boy would do good to his estate. Scattered across the whole village, subdivided into small parcels, it was tended by twenty families, a mixture of tenants, contractual employees and descendants of Prek Neak Loeung servants from five generations before. Whatever the arrangements with these workers, Dara's father nicely called them members of his extended family. He was the 'palm', they were the 'useful fingers', and together they formed a hand. In his metaphor, he viewed his relationship with them as one of interdependence. He was eager to quote that half of him descended from bonded stock and perhaps because of this humble beginning, he was sympathetic to the problems of the peasants. They were always on the brink of starvation, having to meet with taxes or rent, regardless of whatever may affect their crops. Between illness and unkind weather, they never reaped enough to call any year a good year.

Villagers actively maintained the Buddhist church. In principle, the temples were not permitted to receive from the needy. In reality, the keeping of the monks, their food and clothes, the construction and upkeep of shrines weighed heavily on the shoulders of this poorest and largest class. Therevada Buddhism was more than a religion; its ancient roots had shaped a way of life. Together with the institution of kingship, they symbolised the two bastions of Cambodian life too sacrosanct to be criticised. It was blasphemous in those days to accuse either the Buddhist church or the Cambodian monarchy of being the sources of rural misery.

Dara's father was a devout Buddhist. His ambition was to accumulate good deeds rather than earthly gains. He used to say that his wealth was of the abstract sort that no pirate could rob from him. He repeated that in Karma's book, the recompense for a man's kindness would benefit three generations of his descendants. He hoarded nothing and gave generously. His wife cooked to feed the local monks; she made a point of getting up at dawn to begin preparing food for the monastery. Whatever the farms yielded, her husband shared and shared alike with their farmers and not once did he let them feel they were merely the recipients of his charity. These people reciprocated by offering him the best of their crops. They, too, believed that giving was good, and giving to a good man was better still. Both patron and workers were constantly competing against each other's generosity. During the weeks after harvest, the villagers sent carts of foods to his place to pay their due. Instead of unloading and storing more than his household needed to consume, Dara's father topped up these carts with fruit and vegetables he grew in his backyard. The carts went back and forth between his house and the workers' huts, each time they returned from their previous destinations fuller than when they left. This situation was resolved when they agreed to throw a number of banquets to use up the food. The whole Cambodian community was invited and in this small village, life could not have been closer to nirvana.

The big house was crowded on these happy occasions by women who came to assist Dara's mother to cook. She matched her husband in every good belief. They both took it for granted that their son would grow up and continue this family tradition of harmony and generosity.

When Dara turned twenty, his parents expected him to ordain. Statistics revealed that at any given time of peace in the Cambodian countryside until 1970, one adult male in every ten lived as a monk. Dara, who harboured bad memories of his short education at the monastery, did not wish to return. Before the wet season when ordinations normally took place, his parents had to remind him of this custom. They urged him not to miss the opportunity of becoming literate, since education was traditionally in the hands of Buddhist monks, as it had been from the end of the thirteenth century, when Buddhism gained full recognition with the ascension of the first Buddhist king. Popular legend has it that this Buddhist monarch was a young gardener who had a special talent for growing the most succulent cucumbers, which he took to the palace for the king to taste. The king loved them; he reserved the right to be the sole consumer and entrusted the gardener with a golden spear to guard his crop from thieves. One night, a sudden craving prompted him to go with no more than two female bodyguards to pick the fruit. The gardener mistook him for a common prowler, and in one blow of the spear he pierced the royal chest. The king died, leaving no apparent heir. In the search to fill the empty throne, dignitaries agreed to let the royal elephant pick a successor and lead the way. The mammoth was released from its palatial chamber and walked the streets. Draped in gold tassels, swaying its trunk from side to side, it thumped its way to a hut. In front of the gardener's door, the sacred beast knelt down. It was a sign that destiny had chosen the king's accidental murderer to wear the crown. He reigned under the popular nickname of 'King of Sweet Cucumbers'. From this time, the golden spear, which was the murder weapon, was kept in the palace and constituted a precious part of the Cambodian regalia that subsequent kings wore at their coronation. The King of Sweet Cucumbers admitted Buddhism as the official religion of his new court.

More than gaining literacy, Buddhist ordination marked the transition of a male adolescent into an adult; it was the closest the Cambodians had to the bar mitzvah. A man who had been a monk at some stage re-entered society with a prefix of honour attached to his name, similar to the title *hage* acquired by the Muslim pilgrims on their return from Mecca. Ex-monks earned recognition and respect. To dismiss the importance of this phase amounted to turning one's back on tradition.

Once Dara agreed to a pilgrimage, his parents went to great lengths and considerable expense to prepare the week-long rituals. His teeth were lacquered and on the final day, he was dressed in a new silk costume. Saddled on horseback under a large umbrella, a drum orchestra leading the way, his procession collected in its wake a number of other young farmers also about to be made monks, their relatives and friends. This elaborate procession, and generally all ordination processions, endeavour to simulate and commemorate a prince's journey many thousand years before. Back in the days when Prince Siddharta Gautama was still in the queen's womb, prophecy foretold the coming of her only heir who would not reign. It was predicted that he would go in search of spiritual wisdom to enlighten humanity. His parents undertook the preventive measures of confining him inside the immense palatial world as a child and brought him up totally ignorant of human miseries. Royal orders insisted that he should be alienated from signs of sickness, death, unhappiness or poverty. In this contrived surrounding where he luxuriated in idleness, his mind awakened slowly. By reflecting upon the birth of his children, his own adulthood and the advanced age of his parents, he determined the physical changes dictated by the years and discovered the cycle of life and death. At the age of twenty-nine he became acutely aware of those miserable human conditions his parents had tried in vain to conceal from him. Very reluctantly, his parents had to let him go into the world and follow the destiny for which he was born. They organised a gilded procession to send him off to his spiritual retreat in the forest.

Behind Dara, many men carried silver platters containing religious clothes, begging bowls, razors, prayer beads and flowers. In front of the eastern gate of the temple, the evil force symbolised by two men hired to wear hideous masks attempted to halt the party. After a symbolic fight between good and bad, the crowd slowly resumed its march toward the pagoda. They circled it three times to seal out evil. The ordination ceremony itself was brief and took place under the auspices of the head monk. At this point, hair got shaved and the new candidates changed into their togas.

Dara loathed the routine. Up at the crack of dawn, he had to start the novice's task of sweeping the floors. Grumbling to himself, broom in hand, he swished swiftly the leaf-strewn monastery ground. Every leaf that could hide insects had to be discarded from the walking paths. To step on, hurt or kill a living creature, however minute, was a major sin. The next chore of the day was to go begging with the monks. In groups of two or more they went from door to door to collect their food. Dara rated the meals in the communal dining hall insubstantial. Since he was advised to eat whatever was placed nearest and not reach too far to select what he liked best, he invariably settled on fruit. Alms givers spooned every imaginable dish into the same begging bowl. Stir-fried food, soup, casserole, dessert and fruit were thrown in together; consequently the meals were an unpalatable mixture of several courses in one. The monks were afforded fifteen minutes to eat twice a day and the last meal had to be consumed before noon. No solids could enter their mouths before the next mid-morning. The long fast between meals was hard for Dara to bear and the permanent sound of his rumbling stomach would remain his most distinct memory of his religious experience.

A friendship with a younger monk, Keo, made his stay in the monastery tolerable. Three years his junior, from a family that was large and poor, his companion opted to enter the order as an alternative to bondage. Because he joined when he was a child, his ordination was achieved at no cost to his parents. In his long apprenticeship, his role of an acolyte was no different from being a servant to senior monks. He and Dara got on well. When they went to recite prayers in private houses, Keo taught him that it was possible to sneak quick looks at the girls, by lowering the fan below the eyes and scanning the congregation for a pretty female face.

Three months came and went. Dara bade goodbye to Keo, who was

set to remain permanently with the temple. Alas, this great-grandfather
of mine walked away no wiser. Far from the contentment, the humility
and the Buddhist self-imposed poverty that he was supposed to absorb,
there was nothing that he valued more than security based on wealth.
No amount of exposure to Buddhist philosophy could sway the worldly
to the ways of a saint.

3

Reama

After Dara's ordination, his mother started looking around for a daughter-in-law. She emerged, however, from nowhere; a shadow of a girl with whom he fell in love from a distance.

Reama was orphaned at eleven after her pregnant mother had been gang-raped by intruders. Reama was saved by a fluke of circumstances—she had been sent with her visiting aunt to fetch a herbal concoction for her mother who had complained of a sudden ailment that night. When the pair returned, the noises coming from their hut indicated violence. They ran to seek help from a group of trembling peasants who, armed with farm tools and the occasional axe, made their way to the hut, only to witness a devastating scene. It was too late. The assailants, angry at finding nothing worth taking, had been swift and merciless. The villagers concluded that it was the work of pirates who signed their crimes with distinctive cruelty.

The farmers gave Reama's mother a proper Buddhist cremation. They also burned their hut. Local superstition held that the souls of those who perished in violence would never rest; they would haunt the place where they met their death. So, all traces of the violent crime must be wiped out. The dead, having nowhere to live, would be forced to travel to their new spiritual home somewhere else. Keeping the site intact for investigation was pointless; crime against the poor went unpunished. Officials only had time to apprehend those who committed sins against the king. Corpses hanging by their feet, disembowelled and dismembered, or decapitated salted heads stuck on poles could be seen around the city gates. They were the reminders of the existence of a law, but it served only the powerful.

Reama was adopted by the 'Mephom' of the village, who treated her like his own daughter. A peasant of modest means, he was elevated to chief of Prek Dek for being a strict upholder of Cambodian tradition. His two sons were monks for a couple of years. His real daughter and Reama were to follow another set of customs. Instead of joining the Buddhist clergy that excluded female ordination, the women had the choice of 'going into shadow'. A phase of retirement from the world, this period 'of going into shadow' lasted for a few weeks during which the girl was withdrawn from contact with any male presence, including her own father and brothers. In a segregated area of her house, she underwent a crash course of Buddhist education and of her role as a future wife and mother. This system combined the seclusion of a convent and the training of a finishing school. A symbol was displayed at the gate to alert strangers to respect the daughter's privacy and to advertise her coming of age. Older women in the household, relatives, mother, aunts or female servants attended to the young girl. In the village, they accompanied her to the river at nightfall to wash because the bathroom was the least private place. It consisted of a pot of water where people showered in full view from the street.

Reama and her adopted sister went into shadow together at the age of eighteen. Trudging home at dusk one day after visiting his farmers, Dara stepped on some excrement—a common occurrence in villages where adults relieved themselves behind bushes and children squatted anywhere. Shrieking and swearing to himself, Dara hopped on one leg to the riverbank to scrub his foot when he heard noises coming from a group of women upstream. One of them—Reama—removed her veil in readiness for her bath when she caught Dara watching her. Their eyes locked for a second but it was long enough for him to become infatuated with her. A fortnight after his chance meeting, he asked his mother to find out about the Mephom's family. The marriage broker was sent to his house to 'tie the knot'. She was received with courtesy but told that further negotiations had to wait until his daughters came out of their seclusion.

Like all Cambodian rituals, the end of the shadow period was complex, and included teeth-lacquering. A big party, more lavish than a marriage ceremony, celebrated girls' re-entry to normal life. Presents of gold, silver, money and silk were given in quantity to the girls, all the more to stress the importance of their re-entry because these gifts constituted their dowry when they eventually married. This occasion provided an opportunity for mothers with sons to choose their brides.

The go-between lady went back to perform the second of her three obligatory visits and the Mephom and his wife consented to lend Dara's parents 'the use of their paddy path and their front staircase'. In other words, they were willing to give away one of their daughters and they wished to know which one. Dara scratched his head and jested that he would have the prettier of the two. On the official level, his mother conveyed to the Mephom and his wife that the matter of choice lay in their court. They debated and nominated Reama.

After the village astrologer confirmed the compatibility of birth signs, the week-long wedding was deferred until the end of harvest to enable guests in the village to attend and to take into account days that were either for religious or superstitious reasons. They counted the holy uneven days of the lunar calendar, the ascending and descending moon, and a whole month during which the monks took their retreat. Given this formidable list of prohibitions, Dara was irate and amazed that any couple could find a suitable time to tie the knot in Cambodia. A suitable

wedding day was found, and set for eight months later. After the ceremony, it was understood that Reama would live at Dara's house instead
of the usual custom that expected the groom to move in with the bride's
family. The Mephom had waived the rule since Dara was the only son.

A traditional marriage is a visual treat in its entirety, colourful in its
costume, and symbolic in every word and gesture. In its last sequence,
wearing a multicoloured cape, heavily brocaded to resemble the scales
of the Nagas (serpent-like figures from mythical times) the bride leads
the groom into her room. He assumes the role of the freshly arrived
Brahmin Kambu on the Southeast Asian shores who meets a Naga
princess. They journey to her kingdom under the sea where her father,
the king of the Nagas, orders his maritime subjects to drink the waters
around the island from which the Realm of Kambudja appeared.

A crowd of women filled the bridal chamber to prepare Reama for
the wedding. They helped wax her clean from undesirable hair around
her face, her neck right down to her toes. On the morning of the
wedding day, the groom's party announced itself with the deafening
sounds of drums. The master of ceremonies leant the couple's heads
against each other while the elders called their household ancestors to
witness the union. A long set of rites was still ahead: the 'hair trim-
ming', the paying of respects to the locality's spirit, the prayers of the
monks and more. Crowded with many details, many changes of clothes,
one segment of the wedding merged into another, displaying the facets
of centuries' old tradition, centuries' old myths, with their glorious
stories of heroes, gods and goddesses.

In Reama's room, which Dara was about to share, they had their
first dinner together, of steamed rice and ripe bananas, with a fragrant
candle and three incense sticks burning. The elders advised them to
sleep with their heads to the south and for Reama to be on Dara's left.
Once the door closed behind them, they were alone face to face.
Outside, the music kept playing for their guests to feast and dance deep
into the night.

4

The Untouchables

Once married, Dara became head of the family estate. He made changes to fulfil his burning desire for wealth. His plan to develop the cultivation of mulberry trees did not, on the face of it, appear to clash with the way his family managed the farm. There was an existing mulberry patch from which his father used to draw a modest income.

The production of silk was a long, drawn-out process. The Cambodians grew the mulberry trees. They avoided breeding silkworms because the process involved killing insects and that was a Buddhist sin. The Vietnamese, who were not impeded by the same religious taboo, became breeders. The two races shared in common the reluctance to deal with one another. The Chinese made a good living by playing the role of go-between; they bought the mulberry leaves from the Cambodian growers to sell to the Vietnamese breeders. Then they bought the reels of raw silk from these breeders and sold them back to the Cambodian weavers.

Dara had the astute idea of bypassing the Chinese to increase his profits. He established direct contacts far and wide and invited his prospective clients, all of them Vietnamese, to come to Prek Dek to inspect the quality of his mulberry crops. He arranged for each buyer to pay him his annual fee in advance. This allowed them to mark the trees they wanted, and to come back and pick the quantity of leaves they needed at different stages.

The first Vietnamese on Dara's properties stood out from a distance with their cone hats. The sight of them sent Dara's father, Chan, into an unprecedented rage. He chased them away and ran home to rebuke his son. Dara justified his action by saying that he was insuring against the future, that the estate was subdivided in too many parcels to be profitable, and there were too many mouths to feed. While the family owned a lot of land, it generated no money. His father disapproved of the changes if they involved interaction with the Vietnamese. Their argument had no solution, when the nub of the problem lay, on the one hand, in Dara's greed and on the other in his father's racial prejudice. Cambodian society, which was never split in a clear-cut caste system— but one existed anyway—Dara's father classed the Vietnamese as 'Untouchables'.

The hatred Chan bore against the Vietnamese was commonplace in Cambodia. It dated back to 1620, when a Vietnamese princess came to the Cambodian court and was betrothed to King Chey Chettha II, who ruled from 1618 to 1622, and who loved her and honoured her with a proper title. Her father, the Emperor of Hué, sent an ambassador three years later who arrived with many gifts and one request. He asked his son-in-law to grant a Vietnamese civilian settlement in Prey Nokor (Cambodian literal meaning 'royal forest'), a region that was large in size and covered most of what is now the south of Vietnam where Saigon was founded. The Cambodians resented losing a big chunk of their country without an open war. They could not help but mistrust any subsequent migration by the Vietnamese.

Resentment and weariness deepened into hate at the turn of the nineteenth century when Cambodia sank to its lowest, serving two suzerains: Thailand on the west and Vietnam on the east. These two neighbouring countries were fighting one another over Cambodia. The Thais finished up annexing two important Western regions, Battambang and Siem Reap. The province of Battambang was rich and coined the 'rice bowl' for its capacity to yield enough rice to feed the whole population. It was also rich in precious stones; emeralds and rubies lay on its bare earth where people went to try their luck in the hope they would step on a sudden fortune. Shallow pits in the mining town of Pailin revealed a concentration of high-quality rubies, similar in value and beauty to those from Burma.

The other province that the Thais appropriated was Siem Reap. It was here that the Cambodian Empire once flourished and kings built the city of Angkor Thom, which boasted a population of one million. In an area with a radius of over one hundred kilometres, they erected numerous temples to outdo their predecessors, the most famous legacy being the temple of Angkor Wat. The biggest religious monument in the world, it is larger in size than the Vatican and like the Egyptian pyramids, was conceived as a tomb. Detailed studies by Eleanor Moron show that its dimensions are accurately proportioned, and relative to specific Hinduist concepts of space, astronomy and philosophy. By design and not coincidence, from its main western entrance, the sun can be seen rising directly above the tip of its central tower on 21 June, the first day of the Indian calendar.

For the Cambodians, losing the province of Siem Reap was like losing a link with their history. To make matters worse, the rest of their country fell under Vietnam's tight control. Putting in place the foundation for a permanent occupation, Vietnam installed in Cambodia twelve thousand of its troops, backed up by a contingent army of Cham mercenaries who were on its payroll. Vietnamese judges presided over the Cambodian jurisdiction. An influx of civilians from Vietnam came and settled in Cambodia, bullying local farmers out of their ancestral properties. Those who resisted were chased out of their homes and put on trial, punished by biased court rulings and publicly caned, some to death. A mass of villagers fled their homes and became refugees in their own country. All the provinces were renamed in Vietnamese. The Emperor of Hué sent further orders to 'Vietnamise' the local population. 'The barbarians', he wrote to his top man in Phnom Penh, 'had to be taught our customs'. One by one, the two most important cultural traditions of the Cambodian society were annihilated, starting with the monarchy. The king and his officials were made to wear Vietnamese ceremonial clothes and they had to bow publicly to a tablet bearing the name of the Emperor of Hué. Theravada Buddhism was abolished, Buddhist ordination forbidden, temples were vandalised and monks driven out of their monasteries by Vietnamese armed troops. Many rebellions broke out as a result, and were quashed. Vietnam often dispatched a force of many thousands of soldiers to crush a protest of a few hundred people. The regime took no prisoners; Cambodian villagers were accused of collaboration with the rebels, and were executed. Their fields were burnt. Their houses were looted. Their women were raped. The memories of this period remained bitter.

It should not have been a surprise to Dara that his father objected to dealing with the Vietnamese. To expect him to react otherwise was like expecting a Jew to forget the Nazis. Dara's father grew up with stories of abuse and victimisation. He made no excuse for his hatred and once amplified the strength of this feeling in a hypothetical situation. If he were, he said, to be faced with the danger of standing close to a deadly snake and a Vietnamese, he would kill the man first. Nothing was more preposterous than to hear his own son advocate reconciliation with the enemy.

Dara's father spent his remaining days in the monastery, and died in his sleep at the age of forty-five. Back then, the peasants said that extreme anger killed him. His jaws were locked so tight that his teeth chipped. Even by Cambodian statistics, he died young. Because he died with all his teeth in his mouth and especially because they were chipped, it was said that his spirit would come back to 'grind his descendants' good luck'. He did not make peace with his son before his passing. His widow retired in a hut away from the main house, in silent protest of the family discord. She shaved her head, conformed with the strict ten Buddhist commandments, and gave up meat and all worldly comforts.

Dara's plans were unaltered by his parents' reaction. The mulberry leaves were harvested and sold to the Vietnamese silkworm breeders as contracted. Once his mulberry trade ran smoothly, he handed the business to Reama and travelled up north to tackle the next ambitious project on his agenda. He took a team of woodcutters to the province of Kratie, where the Mekong River curves in the shape of an elbow, and proceeded to lop the dense and layered forests. Some of the trees reached a height of fifty metres. Other growth, which provided the lower layer, included the highly valuable species ebony (trayung), now protected worldwide. Elephants were hired to shift the trunks near the riverbank. Bolted in loose rafts, clusters of logs were floated downstream during the dry season when the course of the Mekong flowed to the south. In Prek Dek, the wood was steered to dry land where a big timber yard and a sawmill had been built.

For the next decade, Dara continued to deforest at a fast pace. He bought a ferry to tow the timber south when the currents of the Mekong were not favourable. He made the leap from landholder to entrepreneur. However, his financial success cost him his health, and he suffered from exhaustion. Kratie was the province most affected by malaria, which Dara contracted and suffered from regular attacks for the rest of his life. In his ambition to make money, he spent most of the year in the jungle with his men. He returned to Prek Dek only to negotiate timber transactions, which again kept him away from home.

His absence was equally punishing to his wife. Many years had passed and she stayed childless. She conceived several times but was unable to carry her pregnancies to term. The curse from Chan's death and other superstitious accusations from the community began to have an impact on her. According to old animistic beliefs, Dara's tree-lopping in Kratie rendered potent spirits that dwelled on those large trees homeless. They got angry and vindictive and snatched the souls of his unborn. Reama's miscarriages were the results of their anger. The fact that Dara did not donate to charity and had not brought his mother to live under the same roof with him invited social criticism.

After yet another failed pregnancy, Reama begged him to view her childbearing difficulties in the light of local superstitions. He consented to the astrologer's prescription and paid for a sequence of charitable deeds. The professional 'Achar' organised a ceremony, which had the purpose of dispelling bad spirits from the house. To aid his efforts, a school of monks came to recite prayers. The last and most important recommendation specified for Dara was to have his firstborn adopted out. He complied with most requests but balked at the last. Reama fell pregnant again. Before she miscarried, she returned to her bedroom to mourn in advance. She went into a deep depression and awaited for a bloodstain that would confirm her premonition. Dara softened and agreed to a symbolic adoption.

Reama suffered from severe morning sickness and was bedridden for the full term. At the end of 1908, a boy was born. He survived to become my grandfather.

5

The Silent Call

My grandfather was called Heng, for 'lucky'. The ritual of his adoption made him the symbolic son of Reama's adopted brother, Watt, and his wife. They were his official parents and he had to call his birth parents 'uncle' and 'aunt'. When he visited his adoptive family, he adjusted his spoilt behaviour, which he knew they would not tolerate. Frugality and correctness dictated their life; it complied with the rules of a very much alive and ageing Mephom who dominated in the background.

Dara and Reama's world revolved around the material wealth they created, and their business took full precedence over their son. They compensated with a throng of servants who catered to his every whim. After a series of miscarriages and a trying pregnancy, Reama could not breastfeed him, so she hired a Vietnamese woman who had lost her own infant to be his milk mother. He was kept on breast milk for a ridiculously long time, well into his sixth birthday, when he already had most of his teeth. When the wet nurse judged that he was ready to start on solids, he insisted that she cook and spoon-feed him until he was ten. She would blow on every bite of rice and check its temperature with the tip of her lips and run after him to beg him to swallow. His meals used to take such a long time that he spent most of his waking hours being fed; breakfast lingered into lunch and lunch into afternoon tea and dinner soon after that. Despite this Heng was all skin and bone. He was sung lullabies and rocked to sleep in the wet nurse's arms. When his weight and size exceeded her strength to carry him, she packed him in a hammock lined with a kapok mattress and still rocked him. She lulled him with Vietnamese poems. They were for the most part nostalgic verses that glorified heroes who died to free Vietnam in its long history of domination by the Chinese, and depicted the sufferings and sacrifices of Vietnamese wives widowed by wars. These songs prepared babies in the cradle to grow up and continue their fathers' struggles. In his formative years, Grandfather was fed a diet of Vietnamese patriotism, absorbing the culture of his country's hereditary enemy. In entrusting him to the wet nurse, his parents did not imagine her function would go beyond practical help and it escaped their attention that their son frequented Vietnamese classes. From nursery rhymes to epics, Heng wanted to learn more.

His wet nurse introduced him to two teachers who were retired toolmakers and unusual scholars. These teachers were born in Hué, where their father, Hong, had been a prominent mandarin in the Vietnamese imperial court from which they had to flee when their family fell victim to a political witch-hunt. In his haste to save their lives, their father took with him rare books, which he wrapped in waxed paper to protect them from the weather. He had been an influential man under the reign of Gia Long (1762–1820). Originally from a mediocre background of toolmakers, Hong benefited from the sacrifices of his family, who had the foresight to pay for his education. He sat for the exams to enter the service of the Emperor. In Vietnam, mandarins normally inherited their positions but it was also true that a few did win them by the degree of their scholarship, which allowed for some class mobility. The mandarin was loyal to his emperor but he could not predict that his personal backing of the legitimate prince to the throne would cause his downfall. Emperor Gia Long in his last years, instead of his rightful heir, chose Minh Mang, his fourth son by a concubine, to succeed him.

Emperor Minh Mang's ascension to power (reigned 1820–41) was irregular and his opponents were many. At the beginning of his reign, he was busy quashing a web of intrigues in his court, and persecuted many officials who escaped to the four directions of the wind. Disguised as a peasant, the ex-mandarin arrived in Prek Dek where he reverted to the family's old trade of toolmaking during the day. Every night, at the end of a long day's manual work, he gathered his two male children and imparted the knowledge he could remember. This private education was given in the old Vietnamese scriptures which were in Chinese characters before they were romanised by a French Jesuit priest, Father Alexandre de Rhodes. The social status of his two sons did not improve much, but the Vietnamese peasants in Prek Dek admired their literacy and sent their children to their informal classes. Given his precocious appetite for learning, my grandfather was their most favourite and regular student. He accumulated from them a wealth of knowledge, which was a rare form of Vietnamese erudition.

Reama realised too late that she was estranged from her son. Her solution was to dismiss the wet nurse. My grandfather stopped eating when the wet nurse left, and his parents became worried at his gaunt looks and fainting spells. His rejection of food, however, had the desired effect: his parents asked his wet nurse to return.

My grandfather's adoptive father (Watt) had observed the whole episode and proposed that the ten-year-old Heng attend the temple school. Nothing foretold that the education he was about to receive would put another form of distance between him and his parents.

Grandfather's initiation at the temple was presided over by none other than Dara's old companion from his days in the monastery. Keo had grown into a position of importance in the local religious hierarchy and, bound by his friendship to Dara, he gave special consideration to my grandfather. As time passed, he loved him like a son, and accelerated Grandfather to the study of theology and sacred texts. Heng aspired to follow his footsteps. The mentor doubted that Dara would endorse the call, and advised Heng on an alternative path that turned out to be more difficult than a life in seclusion.

His messages were not clear to Heng when he was young, but they could be summed up in one challenge—'to keep his hands as clean and empty as the day he was born'. It was to become the golden rule Heng would apply in his adult life.

At thirteen, Heng's mentor guided him to seek a secondary school education to experience other influences. At their parting, Keo's gifts were sheaves of papers he had himself compiled in separate volumes. During many sleepless nights he had hand-copied the temple's sacred books; some my grandfather had already learnt, the rest he had to read. They were the beginning of a private collection of literature he cherished.

Heng had a tough time convincing his parents to give him a higher education. They commended him for the standard he had already achieved and encouraged him to learn about the family's business. His further studies would be in Phnom Penh, a distance of 65 kilometres from Prek Dek, which meant he would not be able to commute daily. This would mean a physical separation that might alienate him from the life in the village. Reama suggested that he defer education for two years, hoping that the long delay might just dampen his enthusiasm for studying. If not, in two years, he would be more mature to board away from home.

Heng would not listen, and was determined to go. He went on a hunger strike. It finally seemed to his parents more sensible to let him leave with their blessings rather than give him a reason to disobey. Before the academic year was due to start in Phnom Penh, he had an obligation to familiarise himself with the farms. For the very first time, before he left his village, Heng had close contact with the workers.

The deprivation he saw appalled him. The national rice harvest in

1918–19 was catastrophic, but it was relatively unnoticed by my grand-father, who was too involved in his studies to pay attention to the wide-spread famine that did not afflict his family. He had not realised the devastation Prek Dek suffered and in particular the woes of his family's workers. Since the bulk of his parents' income derived from the mulberry and timber trade, corn and rice-farming were neglected. Nothing had been done to alleviate the hardship; no money was given to restore the production of corn and rice. The peasants in his estate needed to purchase an unusually larger quantity of seeds after plagues of insects interrupted the normal growth cycle. An old peasant told my grandfather about a wave of caterpillars undulating toward the river where they quenched their thirst and, like an indestructible army, raced back to the corn and rice, which they devoured. The peasants' attempts to save their crops were no match for the voracious caterpillars, which could be compared to a locust invasion. When there was not a leaf left on the lands, the caterpillars mysteriously disappeared.

In general, village life had never been easy, particularly since 1914, when not only higher but a greater number of levies were imposed to increase revenue. Even in 1918–19, with the failed harvest, taxes other than on crops still had to be paid by the peasants. While the Cambodian countryside continued to feel the pangs of a protracted famine, the cities only knew a brief setback that year. The boom they enjoyed in the twenties found its early momentum from 1914. It was fuelled by and depended on the additional revenue collected from the peasant. From the twenties, Battambang's development, which Thailand ceded in 1906, gave it a further boost. The capacity of this province to produce a considerable quantity of rice, the bulk of which was exported, enriched the French colonial bureaucracy and Chinese entrepreneurs. This period of prosperity contributed to show a more painful difference between poverty and wealth.

6

Phnom Penh

Heng cupped his chin in his hands and watched the Mekong meet the Bassac River. At this confluence, the boat made a turn to the south and landed in the capital.

In 1921 Phnom Penh had a population of fewer than one hundred thousand. It was one third of its modern size in area. Most of its western side was engulfed in swampy water; decades later more land was claimed from these permanently flooded zones. The Tonle Sap River contoured the city's eastern front where four boulevards ran parallel to each other from north to south. The longest of them was Boulevard Doudart de Lagrée. It continued to the north where it became Boulevard Charles Thomson, the name of a Governor to whom France owed much gratitude.

On 24 June 1884, Thomson sailed into the Mekong River with his fleet and summoned the Cambodian king to an audience. He intimidated King Norodom I into signing a new convention, which reduced Cambodia to total submission to France. If the king refused, he was made to understand that he would be seized and deported to another French colony, Algeria. Scared by the grim prospect of exile, the king gave his seal of consent.

This new convention introduced drastic reforms. Having subsidised Cambodia from the beginning of the protectorate in 1863 until 1884, France was getting impatient for the colony to become self-supporting, to pay for its colonial staff and other administrative costs. The administrators sent by France, known as 'French Residents' in Cambodia, were pressurised by their home office to revise their approach to achieve profit and to systematise their control. Those Residents of the earlier decades were being phased out; they had been romantically enchanted by the timelessness of Cambodia, by its beautiful past and its old civilisation. Some were primarily academics, who used their positions to do personal field research and write books. They deciphered chronicles, explored the Angkorian ruins and sent significant sacred artefacts to Paris. The fresh team that replaced them arrived with a commitment to manage the country like a 'business', and were reluctant to be seduced by culture.

After Charles Thomson's visit, Cambodia, although existing in name as a 'Protectorate', became in practice a true colony. From 1886, a French representative headed the Cambodian Council of Ministers. The management of the provinces and the collection of taxes were restructured. Forced labour of ninety days a year was enforced over the indigenous population. To be exempted, one had to pay annually four piastres per head. This brought the French constant annual revenue. Those who could not afford to pay provided a source of free workers. Ironically, while the French introduced the idea of forced labour, they also proposed to abolish slavery in Cambodia.

This item on their list of changes was the most publicised by the French. Hiding behind a worthy cause—the emancipation of slaves—France was able to justify its actions to the intellectuals in Paris that criticised its patronage of Cambodia. The government redefined its presence in terms of a civilising mission. The one important thing the French Residents failed to do was to explain clearly to the slaves what form of protection they would receive. After all, slavery meant work, which had guaranteed them survival in the past. In response to the grand but uncertain promise of freedom, the bonded men remained hesitant. They decided to stay loyal to the tradition they knew rather than risk venturing onto an uncertain path. Whatever choice they made, the underlying truth remained the same for the twenty categories of Cambodian slaves—they were pawns in a political game.

The king and the elite reacted swiftly to the abolition of slavery, and a rebellion of a national scale swept across the country. Slaves and masters, villagers and dignitaries joined forces to revolt against the French systematised control from 1885. The protest was secretly ignited and fuelled by the king himself, and lasted until the French realised that they should not underestimate the power that a king of Cambodia could still command. In the end, they had to work closely with him to restore law and order. As soon as he appealed to the masses and said that the colonials were backing down on their reforms, the rebellion subsided, but the two-year effort came at the cost of more than ten thousand lives.

The French were unable to show proof of King Norodom I's personal involvement in the revolt. The colonial administrators worked at emasculating his royal power and towards the end of his reign reduced him to a mere figurehead on an annual stipend of four hundred thousand piastres. His close advisers paid more loyalty to the French more than their king. He was relegated to a debauched life inside the palace with a complete harem and free provision of opium. Over one hundred kilograms of the drug was courteously delivered to his doorstep every year. Much to the frustration of the French, this recalcitrant king lived a long time. When he finally died in 1904, they ruled out his direct sons and gave the throne to his half brother Sisowath (ruled 1904–27), who had proved more compliant over the years. This prince had participated in quashing the rebellions. In April 1904, as he took the throne, Thailand ceded Battambang and Siem Riep. The return of these western provinces to Cambodia resulted from the efforts of the French Residents who let King Sisowath take the credit. In reality, his reign was utterly submissive.

Heavier taxes were imposed, and from the late 1920s the Cambodian peasants became the heaviest taxed in the French Southeast Asian colonies. The revenue collected funded modernisation—roads were built, electricity reached big cities, hotels and resorts were developed. The peasants paid the bills without receiving the advantages. They stayed primitive, uneducated and poor. If things did change for them, it was for the worse. An improved road system and communication allowed a more effective way to exploit them.

Overall, the Residents achieved what they set out to do. Cambodia became a prosperous colony. In the northern province of Kompong Cham, French-owned big rubber plantations, were sprouting. Rice production jumped; the French and a handful of Chinese entrepreneurs held the monopoly of its exports. The twenties boom brought a sudden migration of Chinese who, little by little, acquired a slice of the Cambodian economy. In 1930 Cambodia counted a population of a hundred and seventy thousand Chinese.

By and large the improvements which took place were directed to areas that did not benefit the indigenous population. For instance, little consideration was given to education. The five thousand temple schools, which provided minimal literacy, had been founded at negligible expense. More advanced education was limited to one school. College Sisowath remained for a long time the only place the French sponsored. Its maximum intake was one hundred and twenty students, most of whom were Vietnamese anyway. Admission to this institution was more accessible to the sons of Vietnamese civil servants who flooded the French bureaucracy. It was common practice for the Residents to prefer employing the Vietnamese who, in their opinion, could be more easily trained. The Cambodians were regarded as 'a lazy race that had fallen from the splendour of Angkor'. In Phnom Penh, Vietnamese students were predominant in the one school, which, ironically, had been created to benefit Cambodia.

College Sisowath was the place my grandfather imagined himself attending in the near future. On a rapid tour of Phnom Penh, he and his adoptive father lingered at its gate. The college was housed in what had previously been a palatial residence of Prince Sisowath before he was crowned. My grandfather had not been enrolled. Having left his village wearing loose black pyjamas and barefoot, he had other practicalities to worry about first. He had to purchase his first pair of sandals and buy fabric to make two sets of clothes to conform with city appearances. The tailor recommended safari shorts and shirts. With the practicality of a peasant, my grandfather opted for the shade of dark green, which would conceal stains. His colour choice and the tailor's suggestions produced an eccentric attire, a personal uniform that was his hallmark for the rest of his life.

He boarded with a family distantly related to the Mephom. Their house was situated on the west side, where dwellings were decrepit clusters of huts perched on stilts. The backyard flooded through lack of proper drainage; electricity and running water had not reached this neighbourhood. My grandfather offered to hire a man to carry water in fuel cans from the communal tap that was five minutes' walk away. His host was a gardener for a French Resident in the heart of the city and the wife supplemented his income by selling smallgoods, green vege-tables, fruit, and fermented rice sweets which she made herself. They scrimped and saved to bring up a family of four children. Their son by his very gender was privileged to go to the temple school, whereas the girls stayed home or squatted by the side of the streets to sell with their mother. The family received extra money from Prek Dek in exchange for their hospitality to my grandfather. They were extremely impressed by his ambition to study at The College and straightaway they could see a path of high officialdom stretching out in front of him. They were jumping ahead too fast with their assumption.

As it turned out, Heng encountered formidable difficulties to even pass the reception desk of the college. He was told to come back everyday with the vague promise he might catch the person in charge of enrolments. Their host confided that the way to get things rolling was to hand bribes to the right people. Grandfather's first-hand experience with the city administrative machine left him with a lasting anger against corruption, in those days an artform well beyond the grasp of two simple farmers. Ten days passed while they waited for the elusive enrolment officer. Heng went on waiting until the first week of classes began without him. It seemed that nothing else could be accomplished by staying in Phnom Penh. In the evening before he and his adoptive father were resigned to head back to Prek Dek, their host, eager to keep a boarder in his house, suggested they should approach his employer who could act in their favour. At the Resident's office, he was interviewed by his assistant. Grandfather's command of the Vietnamese tongue impressed the Vietnamese secretary who went to his desk where he banged out a short note on the typewriter, then disappeared into the Resident's private room from which he returned with a grin and an envelope that he put in Heng's hand. This letter of introduction with the Frenchman's autograph had the effect of a magic wand. It unlocked doors and carried the weight of a formal order to the college, which enrolled my grandfather instantly. He was to commence his classes the very next morning.

Heng continued to live at the gardener's house in Phnom Penh. By paying for his board, Reama and Dara expected their son would get regular meals. Like most Cambodian parents who placed their offspring with another family, they hoped that the head of that household would also automatically provide guardianship and some form of guidance.

Not much was really mentioned in my family about how well my grandfather was looked after in Phnom Penh. Heng never talked about it. As for Reama, she avoided referring to this period of her son's life during which she must have felt deserted. While she had reason to boast, she could not account for his stay in the city other than describing that her 'hair was getting grey in the five long years she waited for him to come back'. According to the wet nurse, Heng often returned to Prek Dek only to ascertain that his parents had not disposed of her service during his absence.

I can assume, in all likelihood, that those years had not been happy ones for my grandfather. It was during this stage that he got into the habit of drinking. He was a loner, and did not seem to have a single friend. Nobody emerged then or later on in Heng's life; nobody claimed that they had with him a relationship that dated back to students' days.

Yet my grandfather went to the same school with a group of men who were to become important political figures. He was among the first crop of Cambodians who were French-educated in the country, finishing at the highest level, the Brevet in the French system. At eighteen, he was still unclear of his purpose in life, and since he studied to please himself, and had no other plans, he let himself drift back to his native village.

7

Homecoming

When my grandfather returned to Prek Dek, his parents were in a hurry to find him a suitable bride.

Twenty years of business exchanges with the Vietnamese had convinced Dara to think well enough of this race. He admired their risk-taking and was particularly friendly with one Vietnamese family who lived in Tan Chau, a border village twenty kilometres south of Prek Dek, towards the Mekong Delta. They had been associated from the early days of his mulberry trade. Their silkworm-breeding enterprise depended on the supply of leaves from Dara; the Vietnamese were his biggest clients. Their silk-weaving operation was of a size that employed over a dozen permanent workers. Of Sino-Vietnamese origin, they migrated from the north of Vietnam to Tan Chau where they owned a property twice the size of Dara's. Their family compound counted three houses, their land stretched over one kilometre and hugged the river. They built their first and oldest house high above ground, to withstand the monsoon floods which were a yearly occurrence; it rested on unusually tall columns of such thickness that it took two grown men's full arm lengths to measure each of them. Adjacent to the house stood a large stable that housed their fifty buffaloes while most villagers owned only a pair. These animals tilled the fields and were used because they were more adaptable to floodwaters than cows and bulls. Two rows of bamboo groves fenced off the sides of the compound and toward the road in the front, which led to the centre of the village, two newer houses were added to accommodate the fast growing clan. From their fertile land, they produced two corn harvests a year, beans and soybeans, and the best quality of perfumed rice.

At the helm was a deceivingly frail patriarch. The spry old man was a moneylender. His terms were inflexible and both neighbours and kindred feared him. His wife died giving birth to their only son. She was remembered for her beauty and to the old man, she was irreplaceable. Since her death, he bought young virgins whom he used for brief periods before he tired of them. A few bore him children and stayed even though he gave them no right and no claim. But this was far more tolerable than being thrown in the streets. No longer eager to sire more bastards, he allowed virgins to satisfy his lust for only a fortnight and when they stopped screaming in pain at his touch and lay rigid in his bed, he got rid of them. He tendered them out to the next man willing to acquire a wife who was publicly known to not be a virgin. Normally some poor male who was already up to his neck in debt to the patriarch would come to his rescue. The patriarch forfeited the debt and recompensed him if he took immediate possession of the woman. Disposing of the woman in this hurried manner, the patriarch could disclaim his responsibility for any pregnancy. Virgins he still had to have; he thought they stimulated his strength and prolonged his life. He intended to live forever or at least as long as his money could buy him potency. He had no guilt in his heart and even less scruples in his dealings. Under his leadership, every relative near and far was gathered to live in the compound. They earned their keep and pooled their resources together to create an extraordinary wealth, which was the talk of the village and which, unfortunately, attracted bandits.

Thieving and random killings in and around the compound coincidentally ceased at the arrival of a lady who came to wed the old man's legitimate son. The patriarch who had arranged the marriage had his reasons for shrouding her background in mystery. He implied that she belonged to a family whose elders 'dealt with blood and sat with kings'. Haughty, unapproachable and very beautiful, the way she carried herself as she stepped down one day from a junk led to awesome speculation. She wore a white costume; her coifed hair was dotted with precious pearls and held up with gold pins. She gave a sweeping gaze around the area where she landed and was greeted with due ceremony and led to her quarters. Behind her followed her two personal maids and her five men, six horses and countless chests inlaid with ivory. This was her dowry; the bulk combined men, beasts, stocks and stones.

On the morning of her wedding, an elderly, imposing man galloped toward the compound with an escort of twenty horsemen. They pulled their reins to a halt in front of the gate, the stallions shuddered, the riders gave a glance inside, threw their heads back, then trotted in. The master sat by the side of the patriarch at the main table and his bodyguards spoke only among themselves. With a supercilious air suited to war chiefs, they talked in a foreign tongue, wore a frown and an air of disdain, which put them above the rice-growing Tan Chau crowd; they hurled orders or clapped for service. In the late afternoon, they thundered away, heading northeast, and did not return again. Only the bride stayed.

She rode most days across the fields, her five armed men right behind. Always dressed in white, mounted on her white stallion, she tucked under her arm an ivory cane, which concealed a long sword. She would sweep past the peasants like a flash of lightning; they stood and stared in awe. They were told that she regularly kept herself fit by training in martial exercises and her special artistry involved the use of the very cane she always carried with her. It was claimed that she could defeat five adversaries at once in combat. The village nicknamed her 'the Lady in White'. For many years, the bandit-free peace that reigned in the compound was attributed to her presence. Her fame outlasted her. Long after she vanished from the village and the compound, by the time I—one of her many great-grandchildren was born—the Tan Chau villagers could vividly recall the silhouette of her riding a white horse across the fields.

This woman towered over her husband who grew up with the constant assurance that he was the lucky heir. Disliked by his jealous illegitimate half-brothers and half-sisters and their mothers, he was once gagged, tied and left to perish in the hollow trunk of a gigantic tree. His father, having suspected the scheme, after long interrogation and terrible threats, discovered the hidden boy and delivered him from certain death. From that time on, he assigned two male servants to protect him. His son spent his childhood isolated. He was denied nothing, smothered by his father's love and shielded by his two guards. He grew up a wastrel. As a married man, he shifted his loyalty away from his father and existed in the shadow of his wife. His role was crudely reduced to continuing the legitimate line.

After one year of marriage, the Lady in White bore a daughter. Other male and female children were born in quick succession, so many they were merely known under the rank of their birth and not by their names. The Vietnamese custom called the first child 'number two', skipping the number one altogether to not tempt the gods. The second child was called 'number three' and so on.

This eldest granddaughter was the pride of the clan patriarch. Although his orders must be obeyed by all, he made exception to this first grandchild who, like her father, escaped the rigour of his authority. From the day Kim was born, without ever trying, she had a way of melting his heart. At thirteen, she was taught to take charge of the silkworm breeding and the silk-weaving, his second most profitable business after the money lending.

From their early stage of butterflies as tiny as half the size of a finger, incapable of flying, she imprisoned them in a room waiting for them to lay eggs. On the floor she laid clean sheets of paper, and protected the eggs against the attacks of rats, mice and cockroaches. Small worms two millimetres long hatched seven days later. Her duty was to send a worker to Prek Dek to pick the fresh mulberry leaves, which she rolled into cigarette shapes and chopped into fine strings. These she spread over the paper for the feeding. The worms grew fast and she monitored their attempts to crawl over the finely cut mulberry leaves. Those strong enough to successfully climb were the fittest; the rest she discarded and fed to the fowls. As the worms grew bigger, she transferred them over to cane baskets; she renewed their food four times a day for three days. Progressively she gave them thicker strings of leaves. At this point she proceeded with the second selection of the fittest and another transfer of the remaining worms to larger baskets. Like clockwork, on the twenty-third day, their size should have increased to five centimetres in length, their green bodies were plump and they fed themselves more avidly with whole mulberry leaves. She carried out the last selection the next day. She offered the good ones their last meal before they fell into a deep sleep, which she called the 'sleep of old age' during which the colour of the worms changed from green to yellow. On the thirtieth day, they woke up to weave. At this stage, she placed them on a vertical screen of thick smooth straws, spaced with a ten-centimetre gap. There, the worms wrapped themselves around the bars with the thread they secreted from their mouths, and enclosed themselves in their golden silk cocoons. Their hibernation had just begun. A week to ten days later, butterflies broke out. One per cent of the cocoons was left untouched to allow the cycle from butterflies to worms and worms to butterflies to begin all over again. The rest of the cocoons, with the chrysalis dormant inside, were plunged into boiling slippery liquid to loosen the silky thread, which was rewound on reels. The rolls of raw silk were then washed from the slimy water, beaten and dried in the sun. The colour dyeing and weaving completed the processing of the silk.

The silk alone generated twenty-five thousand piastres a year for the Tan Chau clan, more than twice the income of a French Resident in Cambodia. From the age of fifteen, the eldest granddaughter ran the silk workshop. Her dedication gave her grandfather reason to cherish her above the rest. But he deplored her 'light-headed nature'; by this he meant that she did not really attribute to money its true value. As she helped to augment the family's fortune, she siphoned to the needy what she could get her hands on. She was generous to a fault, which conflicted with her grandfather's ambition to hoard his wealth, the bulk of which he progressively buried underground. In the dark of night, he scoured for secret places on his land where he dug and deposited valuable parcels of stones, silver or gold. The tidbits he kept in circulation for his daily lending amounted to a handsome sum in any man's terms. He normally placed this money in between two slabs of ebony upon which he sat during the day and slept over at night. In spite of his vigilance, his eldest granddaughter Kim found his hiding place and pulled out what she could to give away to those who came crying poor. He gently scolded her because nothing that took place in the compound could escape his attention.

At nearly sixteen, Kim reached the full bloom of her youth and her ambitious grandfather entertained a possible match with Dara's only son. Both sides hoped to strengthen their business relationship and a marriage between the two families would combine their fortune in other investment areas. Since my grandfather spoke fluent Vietnamese, there seemed to be no obvious barriers of communication between the intended couple. Highly educated in comparison to the majority, and the only son to inherit from his estate, my grandfather was a very eligible man in the eyes of the Tan Chau patriarch.

During his business meetings with Dara, he had already dropped hints over the years. Now that my grandfather had returned home, the time was right for Dara to be more receptive to the suggestions advanced by the other party. Before the young people were aware of their elders' plan, their respective horoscopes were professionally consulted and arrangements were made to set a date for their wedding. Since the Cambodian and Vietnamese cultures differed in many ways, they arrived at compromises. The celebrations would take a whole week, ending with a banquet. The guest list was phenomenal. Tan Chau was further south on the Mekong River in relation to Prek Dek, so they had to hire a ferry for the whole week. In preference to small boats, which would have been a cheaper alternative, the ferry was a better means of transport because its wide platform minimised the risk of dampening the guests' ceremonial clothes. For seven days, those guests invited by the bride's side—more than three hundred—were transported across to the groom's Prek Dek house in this manner.

My grandfather was taken by surprise at the news of his own marriage. He was confronted a week before the ceremonies were to take place so it was almost impossible for him to back down. A last-minute cancellation would be a blunder with consequences he could not begin to enumerate. He knew that marriage was no small matter, and that he could not rely on a hunger strike, or a brooding mood to disobey his parents this time. He had no valid reason to oppose them.

'They have made a discerning choice for you,' his wet nurse whispered. She further teased his curiosity by rattling off the many virtues of his future wife.

The bride had no say. Kim was told by her grandfather to be ready for her new life in Prek Dek. Chests for her dowry were filled with new clothes, crockery and ten sets of matching dinnerware in keeping with Chinese custom. Her mother, the 'Lady in White', insisted on sending her off in proper style. From big items to small valuables, more than enough to decorate a house, for showing off to her new in-laws, they were stacked up on the ferry that morning. The bride was decked with jewels and clothed in red. She was en route to a man she had never seen.

At the end of 1927, my grandparents were joined in matrimony in the most lavish fashion. They were among the very few marriages that joined a Cambodian with a Vietnamese, a marriage that suited the ambitions of their elders. Love would come later. In most Asian cultures, one learns to love the person to whom one is married.

Dara's mother came out of her seclusion to attend the Cambodian religious phase of the wedding. She walked back into her shack without uttering a word and died quietly a few months later. Her funeral, which she had ordered to be small, brought an unexpectedly long procession of all the Cambodian peasants of Prek Dek. They were dressed in white, the colour of Cambodian mourning; they came to pay their last respects and to accompany her to the cremation site.

8

Mixing Oil with Water

After his marriage, my grandfather was asked to keep an eye on the estate. Dara had extended it to more than just holding lands; he owned the souls of men by bonding them with a string of debts. The villagers could not begin to imagine a day when they would be free. From the fields to the timber yard, my grandfather witnessed their misery.

The guilt he felt intensified as he lived with the wealth of his family who profited at the expense of others. Yet he was powerless to change things. He did not know where to start but he knew the workers' conditions begged to be improved. It irked him that he could not voice his disapproval of his father's injustice. His young wife—my grandmother—watched him kick the mother-of-pearl chests out of frustration. His ancestral home, which used to be spacious, was now crowded with luxurious touches, carved ivory tusks, porcelain vases, and statuettes. In their bedroom, her satin shoes and silk garments spilled out of chests. Gold-laced cushions were artfully arranged on a lacquered sprawling bed. Her half-Chinese heritage betrayed a zest for sumptuousness, a penchant for good living which, in his given frame of mind, my grandfather found distasteful. To him, she represented the embodiment of a frivolous world.

The only person in the family to show Kim an unconditional welcome was Dara, who did it with such earnestness that Reama became jealous. Dara displayed his hospitality to a degree resembling devotion. He was aware Kim was foreign, and he fussed a lot more from the moment he heard she was pregnant with his first grandchild. He worried over her loss of appetite, hiring a Vietnamese cook to tempt her palate. He purchased exotic fruits from afar to fatten her up. Most days he sat with her to ensure she finished her food.

Reama seethed with rage. Her fault-finding reeked of a loathing she could not disguise. She reeled off advice in order to sound caring, but no sooner had my grandmother practised what she preached than she countered it with something else. To ease the swelling of her feet, for instance, Reama urged Kim to rest. If she rested, Reama feigned concern about her weight and prescribed exercise. When she went for a walk, her mother-in-law would curse. 'Do you want to die during birth?' Reama scolded her and she went on to say that exercises tightened the birth canal.

Her recommendations, however contradictory, gave Dara the impression that she cared. He chided her for getting too excited when she rattled off one criticism after another, but he chuckled all the same and shook his head in good humour. He told himself not to meddle in women's affairs. Matters revolving around pregnancy, birth and babies should be left to his wife's expert knowledge.

My grandmother recognised in Reama a fearsome matriarch. She could not rebel for she knew it was expected of a young wife to simply yield to her husband's family, to be their possession and servant. Her reward would come, she reminded herself, her difficulties would ease and her stature would change. For that she had to bear sons. One day in the future, the power balance would shift and yesterday's bride would become a mother-in-law. In this way the matriarchal cycle would continue. My grandmother prayed for a son. Inside her womb, she touched the nudging of the baby's limb. Her hands slowly caressed the bulge; according to old wives' tales, a perfect ball foretold a baby girl whereas the oval of an egg indicated a boy.

On an auspicious day for my grandmother, at the end of 1928, the midwife yelled, 'A son!' She corrected herself in a hurry when she saw the frown on Reama's face and said, 'A grandson!'

My father summoned the first boost of energy from his little lungs and uttered a scream. His arrival was like that of a wind that blew away the dark clouds. When he cried, my doting Grandfather clowned, poked out his tongue and pulled funny faces. He was said to strip himself naked and run around the room just to amuse his son. Cherishing the bliss generated by her first-born, my grandmother rested in the belief it would last. She believed she had a knack of foretelling her own future. Because she had been right in predicting a baby boy, she must be equally right in foreseeing a long, happy stability, but life refused to conform to her neat forecast and nature willed my father to change.

From a cute baby he transformed into a temperamental brat, stamping his feet in hysteria, squealing and crying for no reason. In the household of his grandparents, among servants who rushed to his beck and call, it was normal for him to be pampered and spoilt. The pride of having sired a boy slowly lost its novelty for my grandfather, who became increasingly annoyed by his petulance. One day he saw my father spit food on the floor and swipe the spoon brimming with fish porridge from a servant's hand. He picked him up and gave him a spank.

'Surely the boy needs discipline!' he growled and added, 'Other children don't even have enough to fill their bellies.'

He forced my father down on his buttocks, sternly handed him the spoon to hold for himself, placed the bowl of hot porridge in his lap, and bellowed to his two-year-old: 'Eat by yourself!' There and then he forbade the adults to spoon-feed the child. He commenced a program of austerity and a strident education for his son. No more compliance to his demands.

From this time forth, happiness melted like snow for my grand-mother. The first slap on her son's cheeks was the start of a chain of punishments. During her second pregnancy, it was inconsequential to pray for a second son. She gave life to a premature boy who died on the third day. Through this tragedy, Grandfather was distant, Reama was heartless, and the whole household shunned her. Overcome by pity, the wet nurse sneaked into her bedroom to console her, and decided to send word to the patriarch in Tan Chau to come at once.

He arrived promptly unannounced. He was aghast at his grand-daughter's pallor and distress. The cotton sarong Kim wore made her appear messy to him and he reacted. 'Why in heaven's name do you have to put this on?'

He suspected that she was forced to wear Cambodian clothes. In lieu of an answer, Kim heaved and sobbed again. Raised to wear pants, she could not do justice to the Cambodian skirt. If worn properly, it becomes a flattering garment. Neatly tightened around the waist, it normally accentuates the fullness of the hips and many a Cambodian man ogles a woman for this very curve. The more pronounced the curving line, the more they pronounce her voluptuous. My grand-mother failed to master the art of wearing the sarong and the result of her efforts was dismal.

The patriarch sat her down and reproached her for not disclosing her unhappiness earlier. All the while she sniffled in the crook of his arm and used his sleeve to mop her face. His eyebrows bristled in a straight line, his forehead seamed in wrinkles, and a lump constricted his throat. He stood up and marched into the lounge where Dara and Reama were waiting. Not in the habit of mincing his words, he denounced the treatment of his granddaughter as 'savagery'.

'When I gave her to you,' he said, 'she came to your house fresh like a flower and you stepped on her like a doormat. You are people without decency. You made the promise to care for her but failed to honour your words!'

Dara cast his eyes to the floor, at a loss for words, and Reama mumbled a litany of excuses. The patriarch turned on his heel and left the room. He went to console his granddaughter and left in a state of frenzy. He never set foot in Prek Dek again.

When my grandfather came home in the afternoon, Reama intercepted him and told him about the incident and how they had been slighted. He flew into the bedroom, closed the door and started a scene. He accused his wife of duplicity by sending complaints to her grandfather. He challenged her to go back to Tan Chau, and warned that, should she stay in Prek Dek, she will have to put up with him. In a burst of anger, he promised to make her life more miserable. He assured her that life was making her pay for the crimes her race had committed during its occupation of Cambodia, and for the tainted profits from her family's money-lending. She was to expiate the guilt on behalf of her people and especially on behalf of her grandfather in this life, which he swore would be her 'purgatory'. He said, 'she who seeded the winds would reap the tempest.' He slammed the door and disappeared.

Kim was deeply shocked that the Cambodian national hatred was directed against her particularly, that her own husband detested her like a political enemy. She was more than ready to leave, but her son, who had sensed the turmoil, was clinging to her legs. She bent down and hugged him and he heard her say with determination: 'It would be foolish for me to go away!'

That night, Dara sent a bowl of hot chicken soup to her room and begged her to eat. He had expressly ordered Reama to keep away. She realised that his ultimatum was serious and let my grandmother rest in peace.

My grandfather simply vanished. He had apparently left Prek Dek for an undisclosed destination without a word of explanation or farewell. After a month of his absence, my grandmother assumed he meant to desert her. Her presence in the Prek Dek house was increasingly awkward; she explained to Dara that she was 'as good as a divorced woman' and ordered her belongings to be transferred to her grandfather's house.

The Tan Chau family was surprised at her return. The patriarch respected the confidentiality of her marital separation to spare her embarrassment. He publicly explained that she and her little son were waiting for her husband to find himself a job in Phnom Penh and he would eventually send for them once he was suitably established in the city. In jest, the grandfather agreed on a secret pact: he would keep his silence if she stopped taking money from him to give to the poor.

Growing up among a large extended farming family, my father found much to distract and keep him occupied during the day—riding on a buffalo's back to the fields, fishing, attending to the fowls, and watching people work in the compound. The impact of his father's absence hit him at bedtime, which began with questions and ended with tears. He sobbed himself to sleep and it broke his mother's heart; she was unsure herself of what the future would bring. Protected by the patriarch against the rumours that circulated behind her back, she was unpopular with siblings and relatives and his exclusive care over her contributed to her isolation. After good money had been spent on marrying her off, they considered her presence to be a further burden. To her brothers, those old enough to analyse the implications of her return, she posed a real threat. The patriarch's favourite, and on the strength of now having a son who might be regarded as an heir, she may end up scooping the lion's share of the family fortune. Her brother 'Number Three', born immediately after her, in charge of the silk enterprise since she married, was particularly worried. In wanting to be useful and to fill her time, her helping out in the workshop gave him the impression that she was trying to regain her old responsibilities. Their grandfather noticed the bickering and he condemned grandson Number Three for unkindness.

The tension in the family was further complicated by another member of the clan, grandson Number Four, an older brother and the most cherished boy to the Lady in White. He had striking good looks, the bearing of a warlord and a certain charisma that made his mother proud. She exclaimed that he was the image of her Chinese ancestors. Blinded by love, she condoned his faults, the worst being his penchant for women and gambling. A female worker in the silk factory found herself pregnant and was dismissed and given money to keep quiet. A lot more money was spent to pay for his gambling debts. When the grandfather decided to put a stop to this habit and halted payments to his grandson's creditors, it forced the Lady in White, who could not bear the risk of Number Four getting hurt, to sell her jewellery and private valuables. She saw in my grandmother a temporary solution to her financial problems. She went and asked for help but my grandmother inquired about the reason for her mother's mysterious and regular expenditure. She was never told. If a secret should be kept from the patriarch, it should also be kept from her. To the rest of her clan, she was his spy.

On the edge of his ebony bed, the old man could hear and see beyond the vantage spot where he perched. Aware of the goings on around him, he knew that truth should be read between the lines, and men could not conceal their thoughts and their secrets any better than an ostrich could hide. At sixty-five, he had not found a trusted descendant to whom he could delegate his responsibilities. Should the inheritance fall in the lap of his only son, the influence the Lady in White exerted over him would make him channel all the wealth into paying for his grandson's gambling debts. For a while, it looked almost certain that the natural candidate would be Number Three, the eldest grandson who had proven himself by managing the silk business with success. However his forked tongue at the time of my grandmother's return sparked a division in the family, and his behaviour disqualified him from leadership. In his wisdom, the grandfather professed that the head of a group should gather its disparate members into a unity, and everyone should contribute towards the common goal. To induce bickering was to encourage division; a split family meant split wealth, and a split wealth is weak, it would disintegrate in no time. For these very reasons, Number Three must redeem his eligibility.

Nine months passed, when a message came to Tan Chau via Prek Dek. My grandfather summoned his wife and son to come to Phnom Penh with the barest luggage. Caught in her own lie, my grandmother answered his call. Deserted wives or divorced women had no status and their children were social outcasts. Whatever her patched up marriage was worth, her son would benefit from this reconciliation.

Before she departed, her grandfather gave her cash, gold and precious stones. She refused to accept the bulk, but he insisted, 'Where you will be, I cannot reach. I hope you will not need to spend the money I am giving you. Who can tell what will happen in a big city? Anyhow, take it; take it all, I might not be alive for too much longer. The stones are my gifts to the daughters and the granddaughters you will bear.' Choking with pain, she presented a brave face and said farewell to him and her family.

She did not know what lay ahead. The threat my grandfather once uttered in a fit of temper that he would put her through 'purgatory' to pay for her family's sins reverberated in her head, but it did not stop her from going to Phnom Penh. She could not boast that she had courage. Any woman of that era, in that society, would have come to the same decision.

Part Two **FAREWELL TO PREK DEK**

9

City Life

My grandmother Kim arrived at the address in Phnom Penh and found the door of the brick house shut. A curious neighbour on the other side of the fence proffered the information that 'the man who lives there is at work'. She waited to get acquainted but Kim gave her a smile and turned away. More than shyness, her heavy accent when she spoke the Cambodian language made her keep her distance from others. She camped at the entrance and gazed at the grey light of a dying day. Tardy rains were suspended in the sky, wrapped inside a cloak of dark cloud, which muffled the distant roar of oncoming storms.

'I wish for it to rain,' she thought to herself. 'Rains are good omens on the day a person starts a new life.'

Kim could hear the voices of other families welcoming their men home. She stayed seated, too timid to show interest, and reprimanded her son for his mounting restlessness. They eventually slept, my father huddled in her lap, when the towering shadow of my grandfather, Heng, fell over them. They woke up with a jerk. He nodded at them and, with no further ceremony, slotted the key in the lock and opened the front door. My father threw his arms around my grandmother's legs as she got up.

Her fingers raked his messy hair like a comb, 'Try to look present-able to your father.'

She straightened her own creased clothes. Remembering their luggage, she bent down to drag the bags inside—two suitcases, in keeping with his request for the bare minimum. She hesitated over where to put them without daring to show she needed a hand. Heng turned his back on her and walked into the hall. He switched on the light, hung his colonial hat on a peg and proceeded to the back of the house where he parked his bicycle. He returned and beckoned my grandmother, who had been hovering at a distance. He offered to show her the place.

The entrance opened to a long corridor that ran the length of the house. Four rooms were to the left. Outside, at the back, were a kitchen, bathroom and a squat toilet, built around a small courtyard. In the centre of this dirt patch stood a tall coconut palm, its leaves brown and droopy, its trunk marked by the scars of builders' tools. The soil around its base was covered with layers of dried paint and remnants of building waste. How the tree was spared during the construction work was a miracle my grandmother found herself wondering about. She moved closer to see whether it had a chance to live.

'If this palm survives, it should eventually bear sweet fruit,' she said as a way of making conversation. Granddad did not seem to hear and went back inside. Kim was impressed by the availability of electricity and running water. While she was making a second inspection of the house, my grandfather rode off without an explanation.

Kim decided not to panic and busied herself. She cleaned her son and changed him into fresh clothes. Her head shook in quiet exaspera-tion as she occupied herself with further chores, reminding herself to stay calm. She unpacked and cleaned some of the rooms, all the while plagued by uncertainty. Was she going to be abandoned in a place where she knew no one? What plans had he in mind to make her suffer?

Her thoughts were a jumble when the lock clicked and the door swung open. My grandfather appeared, his breath reeking of alcohol. He had gone out to dinner and brought home some food for them. He insisted that my father be woken up for supper. Since there was no dining furniture, the meal was served on the bare floor.

My father was tired and sleepy, and refused to eat. My grandmother sat him up, 'Look,' she said, 'the good food your father has bought!' In a whisper, she begged him to wake up and show his appreciation for the food, but he collapsed into a fetal position. She pulled him up yet again and, leaning his back against her bosom, held him upright with one hand and with the other, started to force-feed him. He uttered a long yawn, wiped his eyes and instead of chewing and swallowing his food, kept it inside his mouth. My grandmother urged him in earnest but he shook his head and half-closed his eyes, sinking helplessly into sleep.

Kim scooped another spoonful of food into his still-bulging mouth. He pushed her hand away, and spilt the food in the process. This scene evoked in my grandfather similar scenes from the past, and brought back memories of Prek Dek, and of grandfather's objection to the spoilt child that my father obviously still was. Hell suddenly broke loose. Heng surged forward to strike a blow at his son, but in stepping close, he kicked the food on the floor. He veered towards the plates and the bowls and sent them flying and smashing against the walls. Shocked out of his sleepiness, my father crawled to a corner where he huddled. When his father withdrew to his bedroom, he sat still, stunned, while his mother, amazingly calm, finished clearing the debris and mopped up the room.

Later she unrolled the straw mat in another bedroom. Her son shook against her. She hummed a nursery rhyme and as her son slept, lay awake well into the night, staring mindlessly at the bareness of the freshly painted ceiling. She felt emptiness and the crumpling of the last vague hope. There could be no happiness in store for her, she concluded.

Outside, the rain was beating down; it pattered and built up to a deafening, torrential beat. She had wished for rain to fall earlier in the day, on the threshold of her life in Phnom Penh. After the rains, however short, she remembered her village glowing with new growth, the promise of a good yield of crops. She gave a sigh of nostalgia; her mind filled with pictures of rural peace in the village of Tan Chau. Her grand-father's face appeared, wizened with age. He who believed he had the ability to do anything he pleased, right now, despite the wealth he had buried and the land he owned, had no effective means of defending his granddaughter from the emotional pain she was suffering.

She dropped her gaze upon my father, reached out to draw him nearer, and her hands clasped his small body as if he were her raft. One day he would grow up, he would provide her salvation. She clung fiercely to this hope. It is a traditional Asian expectation, which rests on the shoulders of the eldest son, heavy like a cross. Meanwhile, she had to have patience.

Kim found a way to survive the storms of her daily life and erected a façade of unusual quietness. She appeared pensive in the face of the worst abuses by casting her eyes toward a distant horizon that only she could see. She used to sit on the floor, her elbow rested on a knee, her back held straight and her head held high. I remember her well for this poise, for her composure while around her Granddad agitated like an angry bull. He picked scathing words to force her to react, but the more he spiced his insults, the more she withdrew into a recess he could not reach. She dealt with his temper by going into a trance that preserved her sanity and hid her heart. She lived next to him but never with him. They slept in separate rooms, and she shared his bed only during his fleeting moments of lust. She fell pregnant easily, and a few months after her arrival in Phnom Penh, despite the hostility and the separate sleeping quarters, she was expecting their next child.

She was told nothing of Heng's employment. She assumed he worked for the government. The largest 'national industry' besides farming, the government employed many people in its administration. The country bureaucracy was massive in relation to its population. A small employee paid by the state was boastful of his position because it implied stability and permanence. There was no doubt in my grand-mother's mind that her husband, given his education, must be an important man.

Heng worked in the office of Douanes et Régies, a body of various services within the Ministry of Finances under the direct control of the French Administration. It looked after imports, exports and the taxes levied on salt and alcohol. His house was part of a new complex for senior government employees and it was considered relatively luxu-rious. A few months after my grandmother arrived, my grandfather downgraded his residence to a less prestigious site. They shifted to a houseboat on the banks of the Tonle Sap River. His decision, driven by reasons he did not feel obliged to share with his wife, deprived them of the comfort of space and amenities such as electricity and tap water. The move, however, put them closer to the Vietnamese community with whom my grandmother started to acquaint herself. The social contact she was able to enjoy outweighed the modern conveniences, which she missed.

Her second pregnancy progressed with difficulty; she doddered to the market daily and attended to all the chores herself. She was glad that their living space had been diminished, since it meant less cleaning in her condition. However, she did not cope well with the monotonous rocking of the waves. She always felt sick and could not tell whether her nausea was the result of living on the boat or her prolonged morning sickness.

My uncle was born two months early and most of his fingers and toes were still joined together by a fine membrane, which made them resemble duck's feet. My grandmother was afraid of infantile death after the previous loss in Prek Dek, but her neighbours trotted out homespun philosophies to console her.

'Babies born at seven months have a good chance of survival. Those born at eight months, well, they die.' Their argument was specious and said with such conviction that Kim felt relieved and finally certain that her premature son would survive. Thanks to their help, she pulled through the first months after his birth. Unlike the native North American squaws who, totally unaided, disappeared from their camps to deliver their own infants, the women of Vietnam have always been allowed to feel weak and vulnerable. They were handled with kid gloves during pregnancy and after the baby's birth, especially after having a boy. My grandmother's neighbours banded together to help her. They cooked and brought food, they minded my father, and they washed and cleaned for her. Most of them, transient peddlers hit by the depression of the 1930s, showed a touching generosity. At the time rice had tripled in price and its production was a third of its previous volume, but still they donated food of which they were themselves in need.

My grandfather nursed my uncle in his arms and baptised him with a short name. Whatever he was called officially, it was the nickname of 'Duck's Feet' that stuck. He remained alive by a miracle, cared for by a combination of Chinese herbal cures and local housewives' formulas. Grandma was suspicious of French medicine and sought advice from her neighbours rather than go to a qualified practitioner. She treated Duck's Feet's sore eyes with drops of freshly squeezed citrus juice, and because the burning sensation made him shriek with pain, she believed the remedy was taking immediate effect.

When Duck's Feet turned two, my grandfather announced that he was being transferred to Battambang and that he would leave a month ahead to find a place to rent. Grandma had been in Phnom Penh for three years but did not know what the capital was like beyond the immediate pocket where she lived. As she prepared to leave her community that had cared for her, she had misgivings about Battambang. Would she find similar good friends there? It would be her second big move to somewhere totally new. She asked Heng where Battambang was and how she was supposed to get there by herself. Illiterate and bashful, she would have nobody to read the signs for her and tell her where she should disembark. She could imagine herself getting lost and knew she would not be brave enough to speak to strangers and seek directions. Instead of reassuring her, Granddad told her to 'Just catch the train and get out at the last terminal'.

Grandma packed and crammed the contents of her household into a few boxes. She loaded them into the first rickshaw while she and her two boys snuggled together into a second. She gave a hesitant order to the two riders to take them 'to the station'. The men stood on the pedals, and as the vehicles lurched forward, the throng of neighbours swarmed closer to grab her hand. The older ones wept openly. They uttered blessings and wishes for her to return one day. 'Come back and see us sometime!'

Grandma held back her tears and waved until they were out of sight. From poor houses in the area where she had lived, the city was now revealing some of its grand residences as she neared the city. Battambang was just under three hundred kilometres away, a long distance for a vulnerable traveller with an infant in her arms and a frightened seven-year-old.

The house in Battambang was a big change from the boat. It was made of timber, tired and rotting. Only the tin roof was new, a good thing too, my grandma thought—it would not leak in the rain and would save her from having to put buckets all over the floor.

She restored order into her life. She scrubbed and mopped away, swished the dirt ground underneath to make room for her boys to play. She spruced up the shabby rented house and turned it into a home. She purchased mattresses and beds, cane chairs and a dining table. Her Chinese heritage from the Lady in White had its influence on her—she avoided taking meals on the floor if she could help it.

Heng was indifferent to the improvements and the addition of furniture, but more importantly, he did not criticise her, neither did he question the provenance of funds, which financed the purchases. She did not bother him for more than a daily sum of money with which to buy food. Since she had been on a spending spree, it looked to him that his regular allowance was more than generous. He did not know she had her private money given to her by her old grandfather before she left Tan Chau.

Out of the blue, Dara came to visit. A total lack of news for five years had left him annoyed and disgruntled. His parental pride was hurt. He whined to Reama about my grandfather's indifference and he promised to disinherit him. The farm would go directly to the grandson. Season after season, as time slowly passed, the prospect of dying in the absence of his only son had become hard to bear. The voice of anger dissipated. The voice of love prevailed, and he started to heed the call of his blood. Early one morning, well before the cocks had begun to crow, he rose, and with only a change of clothes and a hand of bananas, which he threw over one shoulder, he went searching for his son.

He headed for Phnom Penh and began the search that led him to the department of Douanes et Régies. There he ran into a strange silence from the officers. They recoiled at the sound of his son's name and eyed his scruffy hair, smutty clothes and bare feet. The officers saw no reason to show Dara more than an exasperated patience. Defeated, Dara took to the street and squatted at the entrance of the offices, fretful and brooding. With dusk turning into night, the scant traffic and without a soul who seemed to care, it seemed to him that the whole world was deserting him when a clerk, hesitant and apologetic, after checking that he was not being watched, decided to sit by his side. Late that night, after small talk and a simple meal at his place, Nim, who had been my grandfather's secretary, conveyed the bad reputation that surrounded his old boss.

My grandfather had started at the top. People in his position had the chance to stay in a nice house and pay next to nothing for rent. They were chauffeur-driven in expensive cars, their lifestyle plied with unwritten perks. The higher their rank, the more openings they had to line their pocket with extra income. The bureau of Douanes et Régies was a gold mine: it issued orders to stop or approve imports and exports, rules and regulations were circumvented as a matter of course and businessmen paid high bribes to avoid red tape.

In this office steeped in corruption, Granddad showed a staunch disinterest in the financial opportunities his job allowed him to take. His transport was an old bike and his wardrobe was unimpressive. He owned a change of drill shorts, short-sleeved shirts and he wore white socks halfway up his bony shins and a pair of canvas runners. He was without fail the first to show up with the lower ranks and was productive in the morning. After lunch, he told his secretary that things could wait until the next day. He did not like to sign documents under the influence of alcohol. At noon, he rode to a French restaurant where he normally got drunk. Whatever the state he was in, he shut his door in the afternoons. Nim gathered that he must fall asleep on his chair, his head slouched over his desk.

Quite ironically, Granddad was a senior inspector of distilleries, whose proprietors would gladly provide him with alcohol, yet the thought of 'receiving gifts' from them would have insulted him. There was an instance when a box of his favourite drink, Johnnie Walker, came to his office. Apparently he turned up at his regular French restaurant for his midday *pâté de foie* not knowing that it had just changed ownership. The new French mâitre d' was not impressed with Granddad's unassuming attire; neither was he pleased that he should park his unsightly two-wheeler at the front. Granddad was about to step inside when the Frenchman asked a junior waiter to show him the way out.

The case of Johnnie Walker the maître d' sent some days later to Granddad was a peace token, and Nim begrudged having to carry it back. It would have been simpler for Granddad to keep it. The secretary, like most of the other employees, could not see the harm in 'taking'. Corruption in all its forms and sizes was a way of life.

Nim's wage was skimpy and various clients tucked cash inside the forms to entice him to present them to his boss quicker. In Nim's thinking, he was the door that opened to his superior, and those who needed his services were obliged to grease the hinges. The Cambodian bureaucracy was a labyrinth of doors with countless hinges that needed greasing. Who could possibly be hurt by the consequence of such an 'innocent' transaction? In the general understanding, it seemed that my grandfather had tried to make a mountain out of a molehill.

Grandfather Heng's personal view against corruption, instead of earning him a label of honesty, made him a laughing stock at work. According to Nim, he was downright stupid to deny himself the chance to get rich. In a country where people venerate titles, wealth and power, however these are acquired, he applied to the letter his mentor's advice to keep 'his hands as clean and empty as the day he was born'. Because he did not set out to impose his righteous example, his colleagues tolerated his singularity. As long as he was not openly critical of their crooked ways, they put up with his alcoholism. They learned to live with each other's imperfection.

They were doomed to collide. After a colleague took the liberty of using Granddad's personal seal and implicated his good name in a deal of which he did not approve, he summoned the culprit into his room and bashed him up. His eruption was looked on as an infringement on the unspoken pact, and Granddad found himself transferred to Battambang.

During the train trip, Dara reconsidered the aspects of a son he thought he knew but the portrait the clerk had sketched made him realise he was going to meet a stranger. He tracked Heng down at work in Battambang. My grandfather's greeting was tearful—something quite out of character when he was sober—but not so unusual when he was intoxicated. Dara decided to let go a comment on drinking. After inquiring about his mother, his adoptive parents and other generalities, he ordered a car to take them home. Grandfather lived at the end of a cul-de-sac on the fringe of town. My father, the first to spot the car, was excited, he skipped every two steps and scampered upstairs to Grandma and yelled that they were having guests. Before she could absorb the information, Dara had clambered up the stairs into the lounge. Grandmother almost collapsed from shock! Beside her was a screaming toddler. Because of social isolation, Duck's Feet was frightened of strangers; he began to scream louder as Dara swooped down to catch him into his arms.

Dara's steady efforts won Duck's Feet's confidence and over the few weeks of his stay, he proved an inventive companion. He made the boys a billy-cart by fitting two wheels to a crate, and attaching this to a bike with a rope, he towed the grandsons to the local market. He also taught them how to catch sparrows.

Dara did not discuss his intention concerning Prek Dek. My grand-father promised to visit his childhood home in the near future. Dara guessed that his son had made a life in the city and there was no real hope that he would return to the village to stay. Now that his eldest grandson was at school, he figured that education was the means for his descendants to be independent from the farm. His threat to disinherit would have little consequence, and instinct told him not to mention it.

10

Number Four

A second surprise came knocking at my grandmother's door. Number Four, her gambling brother, showed up in Battambang. He did all the right things, arriving with gifts of food for her children and words that touched her heart. He exclaimed he had been tracking her whereabouts for years.

He confined his visits to the hours my grandfather was at work. After the unpleasant incident in Prek Dek when the Tan Chau patriarch stormed in and out of Dara's house, my grandmother believed that renewed contact with her family would not be welcome. This assumption made her secretive about her brother's visits. In her loneliness, she was glad for some adult company.

They chatted about their youth and their village of Tan Chau and from happy memories her brother digressed into his personal problems. He told her she was fortunate to be 'the favourite' whereas he never had the attention from the one person who mattered, their grandfather. Playing on her guilt, he complained that the lack of affection from the patriarch had produced insecurity.

'Our grandfather revered power and wealth and my gambling was an answer to a quick fortune. If I were rich of my own doing, he will change his mind about me and might cease to ignore and call me a good-for-nothing boy. Unfortunately, Big Sister, I was unlucky, and instead of an instant fortune, I was hooked.' He said he had paid dearly for the path he 'was forced to choose'. Out of shame, he confided that he had to leave Tan Chau. Here in Battambang, he was trying to get on his feet but he had no money to start a small business.

My gullible grandmother felt sorry for him. Though she rejected the blame put on her grandfather, she was nevertheless touched by his explanation. She was quick and willing to forgive him for putting their family in awkward predicaments. She poured him hot tea, and after disappearing to her room, came back and presented him with a bag.

'Here', she said, 'consider this as given to you by our grandfather.' His eyes twinkled with a pleasure that she mistook for gratitude. She had advanced him a fortune and was quite convinced that its proper use would change his life's direction.

It did, but far from the way she hoped. Once he got what he wanted, his visits ceased. She concluded that he must be busy establishing his intended business, and only knew of his subsequent activities from the most unlikely source—my grandfather.

Heng came home and confronted her. 'Your brother Number Four came here to see you, did he not?'

She was defensive and gave him an uncertain look.

'Why did you hide his visits?' She remained silent.

'Why was I not told? I want to know everything that goes on inside my house. Allowing a criminal like your brother under my roof!'

To Grandma, it sounded like she had committed a crime for seeing her brother. She chose silence in the face of his condemnations, knowing it futile to say a word. In his state, she would simply add fuel on the fire. She sat on the floor, rolling a piece of betel nut inside a green leaf and started to chew. His insults poured out over her like water over a duck's back.

Unbeknownst to my grandmother, an intensive investigation was being conducted at Grandfather's office. Number Four had been caught red-handed by Battambang customs officers for handling contraband merchandise from Thailand. Once they finished questioning him and established his guilt, Number Four would be transferred to the police headquarters, where he would be charged for illegal gambling. He had participated in cockfights, and although this activity was not illegal, betting on it was. Number Four's arrest for racketeering was a blessing in disguise; police custody protected him from being hurt by a number of gambling creditors.

In jail, he felt that his luck had truly run out. His mother, the Lady in White, had been his saving grace—she could always somehow find means to get him out of trouble—but Battambang was far from the village of Tan Chau, and she could not possibly know of his latest misadventure. Unlikely as it might seem, my grandfather decided to save Number Four. He arranged for Number Four's fines to be paid and requested a pardon from the police chief for the gambling charges. On the grounds that leniency could be granted for a first-time offender, and that Number Four belonged to a decent family, Heng supported these arguments with his personal guarantee. He would himself ensure that Number Four would return to his village where his parents would protect him from bad influences. He appealed to the commissioner's kindness for the release and used the argument that it was good karma to give a man a second chance in life. Number Four never knew of Grandfather's role in his release.

Once free, instead of gratitude—and because he was unaware that any gratitude was due—Number Four openly deplored my grandfather's inaction and joked about his high rank. 'How could he say he is an important man when he was powerless to stop the authorities from throwing me in jail?'

When Granddad advised him to head back to Tan Chau, Number Four hissed, 'What right do you have to chase me out of Battambang?

Are you the governor?' Before he finished laughing, Granddad's fist landed on his mouth.

For a start, Granddad did not want his reputation linked to Number Four's, and he was concerned that by paying his debts once, his gesture might set a precedent. His guarantee to the police was binding, and he was worried he would be held responsible for Number Four's future crimes. Fortunately, Number Four had to abscond. With creditors hot on his heels, he ran out of town faster than my grandfather had wished.

His departure lifted Granddad's stress. In a rare, expansive mood, my grandfather began to tell my grandmother about her brother's wrong-doings. 'Number Four was arrested on terrible charges. They were serious crimes.' This unusual overture was the closest he ever came to an apology to her.

But Grandma was not sensitive to the intention. She retorted: 'Serious crimes? Why then was he freed? The police must lack evidence to convict him. In your opinion, all my relatives are automatically criminals. Number Four did nothing wrong to you personally and nothing wrong towards the law.'

'Your brother is a worthless, insolent scoundrel!'

'Tell me something I have not heard before!'

'He handled stolen merchandise. He dealt in the black market. He double-dealt and swindled money from other criminals. He would sell his own mother if she let him!'

'Why is he not kept in jail?'

'Because I am the fool who paid for his fines! I am the fool who bailed him out! Does that answer your question?' He was so enraged he reached for his bottle. 'Your family are robbers. Villains. All of them! Moneylenders. Terrible crimes against humanity . . . In prison where they belong.'

Grandma was astounded that he had paid Number Four's fines. She would have appreciated his gesture had he chosen to be less abrasive. A strange feeling pinched her chest. She suspected that, behind his surly nature, he was capable of generosity.

Grandfather kept his promise to Dara and during my father's long break from school, he took his family to Prek Dek. The journey was difficult and the road to the village muddy. They were dropped off by the bus stand by the main highway. My grandmother was pregnant again, and recalled the tedious distance to the house. Her feet were swollen but she told herself that each step she made towards Prek Dek was also drawing her closer to her own village of Tan Chau. The hope of seeing her grandfather again revived her sore muscles. The joy of the reunion extended to my grandmother, and made everyone temporarily forget their past differences. Reama was almost sincere in her welcome to my grandmother.

There were occasions during their stay in Prek Dek when my grandmother could make a day trip to Tan Chau while my grandfather was reciprocating social visits on his own, but her advanced pregnancy complicated things. Dara, having avoided mention of the patriarch's name during his last stay in Battambang, had proven that the relationship between the two families was completely severed. The only way Grandmother could obtain first-hand news from her grandfather was to rely on a Vietnamese timber-worker to go to Tan Chau. The messenger returned with news that Number Four was home. Her grandfather commissioned the same man to hand her a parcel of glutinous rice buns. They were uncooked and did not last too well in the hot weather. By the time she received them, they were slightly smelly. 'They must now have a new cook and a slack one too, someone who can't even tie the buns properly,' she remarked to herself.

The buns were loosely wrapped with banana leaves and she decided she was not going to bother cooking them. The rice would surely burst out of the thin layer of leaves and the buns would be too soggy to eat. She left them in her bedroom until they went completely off. And she still could not bring herself to throw them out, bearing a peasant's inherent guilt of waste. As a child, she was pestered to finish every bit of food in her bowl and told she should never forget to thank Mother

Nature. Each grain of rice she did not care to eat would be lent a human voice to speak against her when her soul was about to be reborn. It would convince the deities to send her back to life in the shape of an insect. As an adult, the threat of this punishment remained indelible. Grandma took a knife and slit the first bun in half. With the knife still raised in mid-air, she exclaimed, 'Oh God! Oh God!'

My father rushed closer and asked anxiously, 'What is wrong, Ma?' She broke into sobs.

Each bun was filled with diamonds and gold nuggets. The stones were black, sparkling and rare. She held my father and cried. He had yet to learn about the value of the stones and gold. What was more precious to his mother was the gesture of care from the patriarch. He had somehow found a way to extend his protection to her in spite of the obstacles that separated them. Money and precious stones were the only means for him to provide security.

Shortly after this episode, she received the news in Battambang that her grandfather had died. It was not suggested that she attend his funeral. She lit candles and spoke to his spirit.

When she went to Prek Dek some years later, with four children by her side, she retraced her steps to her native home. Her family's three houses were deserted and partly burned, the family lands vacated and unclaimed. She stood in the middle of the charred ruins and bent down to scoop a handful of ashes. There was nothing but ash and an eerie silence. She put her one-year-old daughter on her hip and with her three older boys walking behind her, she strode towards the centre of the Tan Chau village to inquire about her lost relatives. Nobody was forthcoming but by chance, a woman to whom my grandmother had given money pulled her by the sleeve and invited her into her hut. She whispered that she could find one of her younger brother on a houseboat by the river-bank, some three kilometres from the old family compound.

Number Three, her forked-tongue brother, was now living with his wife and children on the barge, the only possession he could save after the extended family was forced to disperse. He told my grandmother how their grandfather died very suddenly—he was found drowned, lying on his stomach, his face plunged in a shallow pool of fresh rain-water. No-one could tell if he had tripped and fallen face down over the puddle or if he had been murdered. Even if it could be established that his death had been due to foul play, official justice was not far-reaching. The old man had more enemies than they could count.

Before his death, the family had received an increasing number of visits from bandits. Their grandfather refused to sit back and let them rob him without protest. Instead of money, he wrapped dried chicken droppings and pebbles in thick layers of paper, and made many small parcels which he placed in between the ebony slabs of his bed. Sure enough, the thieves came back a month later, and headed straight to his ebony bed where they knew he was in the habit of keeping his cash. Since they could not easily lift open the top slab nor could they waste time removing the nails, they transported the whole bed onto their boat. The bandits were excited at the extra precaution the old man took to protect his possession—to them, it was an indication that a very lucrative fortune was contained between the slabs of timber. As soon as they were out of sight, the grandfather bent in half with a cackling laugh, overjoyed that he finally had his revenge.

The rest of the family shook in fear, although they pretended to join in and mock the thieves. The family was afraid that the thieves would retaliate by hurting them. The grandfather died two weeks later. He did not have time to appoint his successor, hand over his loan records and, more importantly, he did not disclose to anyone the hiding places of the family's wealth. To this day, with wars raging on and off around the area, the direct descendants of Number Three still live in hope near the old compound, sneaking into the family's land to dig at night. In order not to arouse people's curiosity, they refill the holes before dawn. Their searches remain fruitless, but the hope of unearthing the precious stones and metals still persist.

The grandfather's death left the extended family in chaos. A power struggle between them dissolved their frail unity, setting parents against children, brothers against each other. Very little money was left after the constant robberies. The people who owed the old man used the opportunity of his death to defer or forfeit payments.

The family fought over the sale of some of their property assets to facilitate the distribution of inheritance. Two of my grandmother's sisters, then married and living in Phnom Penh, were strongly in favour of getting rid of the land. The males argued that the girls were not entitled to anything since their dowries at the time of their weddings should be considered their fair share. Number Three, although the eldest of the remaining grandchildren, lacked foresight and failed to grab the reins. He neglected the silk manufacture and did not put in more work, only to end up with the same inheritance as the rest of his siblings.

The one person who removed himself from the squabbling was Number Four. Since his return from Battambang, he had changed—on the surface—from chalk to cheese. He married a village girl and lived nearby with her parents, toiling in the fields by day. No-one realised he belonged to a clandestine political movement, a group of dispersed Vietnamese fighters who were trying to oust the French from Vietnam. Coined 'Vietminh' by the French after World War II, they would later be nicknamed 'Vietcong' by the Americans when the US got involved in the conflict. Number Four's political sympathy for the guerrillas was active. He attended secret meetings and was in charge of the insurgents in the village of Tan Chau. The frequency of his escapades increased. His wife suspected he had a second family elsewhere and pressured him to tell the truth. Knowing the truth in this instance was worse for her than not knowing at all. It was an open secret that a commitment to the Vietnamese guerrillas was a commitment for life—desertion brought a death sentence. Those who changed their minds were inevitably found dead. This underground movement sacrificed their ex-members to protect itself.

The French authorities finally woke up to their opposition. They were aware that the base of the insurgents' support lay mostly in the villages. A large number of colonial troops scoured the rural communities and scouted for Vietminh guerrillas. They concentrated on the eastern front, in areas closest to Vietnam where the Vietnamese population was consequently dense. Nomadic troops regularly patrolled the countryside, set up in groups at strategic points, camped long enough to comb the area and moved on.

Number Four's missions aimed at seizing arms and ammunitions from these camps. The Vietminh had a policy of shifting their members' actions far from their native villages. Should they die fighting, their bodies could not be identified. This safety measure acted to protect families and neighbours—the French authorities were said to torture any living relatives to intimidate future recruits into Vietminh forces.

Number Four's target was outside of Chaudoc, a fortified citadel situated on the border of Cambodia and Vietnam to the north of Tan Chau. From Chaudoc, he and his band followed the route the French took and gradually descended southward to his native village. That night was to be his final act of sabotage against the French garrison. His clandestine activities were getting dangerously close to his home.

Pushing the fear out of his mind, Number Four got ready when dusk fell. He put on dark clothes and proceeded towards the enemies' camp. The evening was pitch black and still; from a distance he could see the target. There were a few glittering lights and pacing silhouettes. Closer up, he could hear the faint noise of conversation, someone whistled a tune, and someone laughed. Number Four's men split into two groups. He was among the ones who were to throw hand grenades and the rest were to steal army equipment in the ensuing panic.

Number Four sprang to his feet, a live explosive in one hand, and signalled a go-ahead with the other. The men started toward the camp but Number Four suddenly tripped. In his fall, the grenade rolled away. With his last instinct, he threw himself over it to muffle the explosion, which could kill his men and alert the enemies too soon. Bearing the worst impact of the blast, his body blew to pieces in front of his comrades. The shock crippled them with fear. The mission was a failure.

The next day, before dawn, five bodies were displayed in the centre of Tan Chau. Two prisoners were caught alive. They were tethered back to back, two Vietnamese soldiers stood behind them, pointing rifles at their necks. A few steps back, the French superiors scrutinised the faces of villagers who came to watch. The sun rose high, and it was hot and humid. Flies hovered and swarmed around the cadavers and the blistered lips of the tied men. The news of this macabre exhibit rippled through the village. Number Four's father-in-law went to see for himself the men who had been caught, hoping desperately not to find his son-in-law among them. He tried to maintain an inscrutable expression on his face when he looked at the corpses. When he recognised his son-in-law, his legs began to weaken and his knees began to lock. He plodded away from the ghastly sight slowly, ever so slowly. He could feel his muscles tighten and give up, but he had to plod on. When he arrived at his hut, he barked to his wife and daughter to grab their most essential possessions and leave Tan Chau immediately. He heard people mutter about the fate of the victims' relatives. Some had been already apprehended for questioning. It would not take long before the two prisoners gave in under torture. Before fleeing, Number Four's father-in-law stopped by to inform the Lady in White and recommended that all of Number Four's family should think of escaping.

The clan members sent their youngsters to every corner of their lands to convey the message for everybody to return home at once. In the lounge, they gathered in front of a pot of incense sticks, which had recently been burnt to the spirit of the deceased patriarch.

The Lady in White told them the news. 'Number Four is dead,' she said in a trembling voice. She repeated the necessity for everyone to get away before anyone was arrested. A loud disagreement ensued. The brothers initially objected to the thought, but after a quick moment of reflection, they knew they had no choice.

Somebody said: 'He was the bane of the clan. In life as in death!'

To this untimely remark, the Lady in White retorted, 'How dare you! How dare you! The boy's body has not even had the chance to grow cold!'

One of her sons stood up to her and insisted: 'He brought us only problems. And now this! Contradict me if you will, Ma. But you are blind to his faults and to all the troubles he gave this family! You would have sold us all to pay for his debts. You would have sold your own soul to the devil to keep him happy. In many ways, Mother, you are to blame for this outcome!'

She moaned in his direction but he went on, pressing hard on her pain. 'You remind me of a mother monkey that lives around temples, and on the edge of rivers. She keeps her favourite offspring closest to her bosom, clinging nearest to her heart. This sort of mother monkey always unwittingly drowns her most beloved child when she swims across rivers. Do you know that?'

The Lady in White left the room. She did not turn once to look back but strutted ahead to the centre of the village which was seething with curious spectators. She craned her neck and moved closer. An impassable wall of villagers stood in front of her. Her eyes searched for Number Four. She choked and fought hard to swallow a scream. She was not prepared for the shock that awaited her. Shreds of flesh and organs spilled from her son's chest cage. A head and a torso. Flies filled his lifeless opened eyes and his gaping mouth, his dishevelled hair covered his forehead. She could never forget his torn half-body, and yelled a desperate silent prayer for heaven to bear witness to her most beloved son.

She crept away from his remains, from the crowd and from Tan Chau. On the dirt road that branched toward the main route to Phnom Penh, hiding her face inside the palms of her hands, she could finally vent her sorrow. There were no tears but gut-wrenching dry sobs as she banged her chest with her closed fist. From this day on she drifted from house to house, helpless and impoverished. She stayed with whomever of her many children would have her. She never stopped grieving for the boy she lost.

Whoever lent her an ear heard her talk of his heroism. 'There will be a song sung in his memory. My son fought to free Vietnam!'

Her other children begged her to keep quiet. 'Do you want the police to arrest us?'

When addressing their visitors, they assured them that their mother was losing her mind. 'She is confused between reality and myth. Our brother died young. From an accident. Mother had it mixed up with other stories.'

In her senility, the Lady in White could describe with a frightening clarity the minute details of his corpse lying on the ground. She could not forgive the French for depriving her of the right to bury him properly.

The rest of the clan still resented the memory of Number Four. Through his actions, they had lost their rightful heritage, and worse, they lived with the fear of retribution.

The French finally found out who Number Four was. They came to the family compound and ordered it to be burnt down.

11

Grandfather

From Battambang, my grandfather shifted back to Phnom Penh, which was closer to Prek Dek and more conducive to keeping contact with his parents. In-between visits, news was conveyed through word of mouth. Letter-writing remained an alien form of communication, even to my grandfather, who was literate.

My father was twelve when the relationship with Prek Dek intensified. He was of an age when his mind was capable of storing permanent memories of his grandparents' lifestyle, of a house full of servants, of them instilling in him a sense of importance. The eldest grandson had been told he would inherit the estate. But he was not fooled, even at his age, and realised that his position came with strings attached. He had to be an impeccable role model for his numerous brothers and sisters, born at eighteen-month intervals. He was admonished for the slightest wrong-doing. His results from school had to live up to his father's expectations, and at home, he had to help his mother, do homework, run errands and tutor his siblings. Granddad never proposed that they hire servants, and Grandma never dared suggest the need. It was to stay a taboo subject, even when she had nine surviving children to look after.

My father liked Prek Dek for the servants, the pampering, the blissful pace of rural life and the spaciousness of his ancestral world. He liked it most because his father put on a veneer of calm. The drunkenness and the tempestuous moods were swept behind closed doors. He and Duck's Feet would go fishing most days; they floated on a dinghy, throwing their nets in the pond, which Dara had ordered to be dug for his grandchildren. The lotus flowers would be in bloom, and the children snacked on their crunchy seeds as they competed to catch the most fish. They seldom went home empty-handed; the villagers would offer them their own catch to show off at the end of the day. Dara hinted that the boys could always survive and re-adapt to village life if they were to fail at school. My grandfather laughed politely.

My grandmother kept a low profile and stayed out of sight. Constantly with an infant at her breast, she relied on this excuse to hide in the security of her chamber at a guarded distance from Reama. Fourteen years had passed since she had married, yet her mother-in-law was still eager to flex her muscles. Inside this pugnacious woman, the vicious matriarch would never die.

The old wet nurse kept my grandmother Kim company. Her long service rendered her immune to Reama's unspoken orders against attending to my grandmother. They had been together for three decades but the bond, which came from having been together for so long, was constantly checked by their differences in rank and race. It irked Reama that the nurse and my grandmother were on such good terms. She just had to drop a comment on the subject, even at the risk of being chided by her husband; her tongue had to lash out. 'It is natural, really, for a Vietnamese to befriend another Vietnamese and to forget previous loyalties and obligations', she remarked in passing.

Dara quickly reminded her that she should feel gratified instead of harbouring petty jealousy. The most important blessing for an elderly Asian person is to be surrounded by a large family. He sighed with gratitude and raised his eyes to the sky, with his grandchildren playing a distance away, he said: 'I would have no regret if karma were to take me at this point in my life.' It appeared that his death wish was quickly granted. He suffered from a severe malarial attack and died, surrounded by his son and family.

The Prek Dek household reacted in silence after his death, not quite from mourning but from uncertainty. The servants especially were full of concern that my grandfather, who was and would be an absentee landlord, was likely to retain only a skeleton staff for his mother, and most of them risked losing their jobs. He was not a talkative man and clammed up even more during the bereavement period.

He called a meeting of all the workers and those who owed the dead man money, which concerned, in one way or another, most of the village. Some time after noon, everyone turned up and formed a big circle in front of the house. One of Granddad's adopted brothers from the Mephom's side came to assist and made an introductory speech to pay tribute to Dara. The crowd stayed politely reserved, and listened to the eulogy about a man whom they did not hold in esteem. They really came to hear what my grandfather, their new landlord, had to say, and whether his intentions would impose further hardship on their lives.

Grandfather took centrestage. He summarised the situation his farm was in. It had not been productive for many years and the same could be said about the timber yard. He suggested closing the latter down and converting the land it occupied to farming. After another moment of hesitation, he pointed out that his father, Dara, had depended largely on money-lending, and that many of the villagers were heavily in debt to his father. He qualified what he had said by showing them a wad of loose sheets where Dara had recorded the loans. He squatted, rested the papers on the ground and searched in his pocket. He got out a box of matches, which he carried for the purpose of lighting his pipe, struck a match and set alight the pages in front of him. The flames, burning brightly consumed them. Though featherlight, the papers contained a ton of weight in debt. It was a load of misery for the villagers; it was a yoke of guilt and shame for Granddad.

Heng could not tell exactly when he had conceived the idea of destroying these loan records, but he could put an accurate date to the time he finally saw the peasants' plight. It was the year he was due to study in Phnom Penh. He had idle time before he left Prek Dek, and at his parents' urging, had gone to see his lands.

He had asked his father, 'Where to? Whom should I seek to visit, who could show me the lands?'

His father's eyes glinted with pride. 'Anywhere at all, as far as your feet can walk in a day, you are sure to meet someone who must work for me.'

Thus my grandfather emerged from his cocoon. Out there, anywhere his feet took him, he discovered that his father spoke the truth. He met the men who tended their estate. And they were many. They invited him to sit down to their midday meals and he discovered their truth.

But he could not eat. Slouching on the dirt not far from him was a waif of a child with sunken, cloudy eyes, pecking at a mouldy serve of rice. Grandfather suspected they had no food to go around. For him to eat, somebody else would have to go without. Even in their severe shortage, the peasants were obliged to offer the invitation. They were faithful to an old tradition of hospitality and simply could not let a visitor leave without at least a small bite. Granddad had to do them the honour of receiving their food and he choked when he tried to swallow every grain of rice.

One day after another, he walked through the lands. There were fields upon fields stretching to the horizon. What struck him most were the numerous phantom fields where once corn and rice had grown.

'Why is it that nobody has planted here?' he inquired.

'Not enough seed. We have not been given money to buy the seeds. The caterpillars ate all the crops one bad year and shortage snowballed from there,' the elders replied.

Their greedy landlord—his father—had turned his back on their plight and left them with the permanent pinch of hunger in their belly. They had expenses they could not avoid, religious responsibilities they would not shirk. They had to cover their monks and their own backs with a set of clothes, they had to mend their shacks with new palm leaves, to give their sons suitable ordination ceremonies, to duly marry off their daughters with one piece of silk and dowries . . . and so much more. The yield from the land just kept sinking from bad to worse every year. Finally, they had to dawdle to their landlord's house and, one by one, these poor men grovelled. Dara agreed to lend them money, but the debts accrued, compounded manyfold, perpetuating a debt they could never repay. From that time, my grandfather, although only thirteen, started to query his own destiny and cursed himself for being too young to help. Heng was to remain haunted by the peasants' cruel predicament.

Now as the new landlord, he at last held the reins. He chose to return freedom to his farmers and consigned their debts to oblivion. In front of his eyes, the loan book was reduced to a grey heap of ash. He stood up and in a gesture reminiscent of Pontius Pilate washing his hands after the public judgement of Christ, Granddad rubbed his hands together as if he meant to perform a symbolic act of ablution to cleanse them from the dirt of the papers he had previously held. He raised his voice and declared that all debts had been annulled. They who had been bonded were free. Granddad proposed an indefinite term of free lease. Each farming family would receive a sum of money to buy new seed. Each farmer would be entitled to stay rent free, work and reap the harvest from their block of land until such time as the last of their descendants lost interest in farming and decided to leave of their own free will. He promised on behalf of his own children that no villager would be chased away, nor any inch of the estate they occupied be sold.

He paused and asked for one favour. He needed to entrust his mother's welfare into the hands of the villagers. He looked around for a wise face in the crowd. He picked an old man and tested his memory.

'You were, long ago, considered a part of my extended ancestral family . . .' he started. The old man could recall those good years with Dara's parents, and sighed. My grandfather appealed to him and all the peasants to revive that ancient spirit of unity. Many elderly people drew nearer. One among them, his eyes awash with tears, joined both his hands above his head in a gesture of prayer and he called on the villagers to offer their collective blessing. 'My good son, in return for your kindness, may the Thevodas above reward you with peace and happiness.'

People echoed 'Saathouk', Cambodian for Amen. They promised they would take care of Reama.

My grandfather mingled with the crowd and embraced the elders. He hastened to the temple where he sought audience with his old mentor. He confided that he had given back the land to the people, who had earned the right to be free. The monk nodded his head in approval. He bent forward to lay his hand on his student's shoulder. Fainter than a sough, closing his eyes in profound meditation, he hummed between his lips a long prayer.

The hardest part for Heng was facing Reama. She did not move from the bunk where she had watched in disbelief. In one single afternoon, her son had undone what she and Dara had built in a lifetime. My grandfather could read the awe on her face.

He said, 'I have done the right thing, Mother. I have wiped clean the past and squared with karma. My descendants might regret the decision I made today. They will not inherit this land. I simply hope, in doing what I just did, by abstaining from collecting rent, by wiping off the burden of debts, people can live. I also hope that my deed will stave off the harshest punishments upon my children. They do not have to pay for the sins committed by their forefathers.'

All the while, he was referring to money-lending, which he considered the most shameful of all sins. Time would show that his children deplored his actions, which deprived them of an inheritance. As an adult reflecting on his decision, I viewed it as a legacy of his love and his protection.

Before he returned to Phnom Penh, he offered his mother the choice of continuing to live in Prek Dek or coming to the city with him. She requested time to think. Six months after Dara's death, she agreed to move. The wet nurse was the only employee who begged to come since she had no living relatives.

My grandfather's city house was not equipped to accommodate a large family. It was a small timber house with two bedrooms: one was my grandfather's, and the other was for my grandmother and all the children. Unlike my grandfather's bed, which had a double mattress, the second bedroom had a raised polished bunk, which touched the three sides of the walls. At night, straw mats were laid out to sleep on.

The unexpected arrival of two extra adults called for some rearrangement. Reama took over the lounge where she put her bed. The wet nurse would sleep on the floor. Visitors were received from the back of the house, among the pots and pans, with the view of the shower through the window. The back door, left wide open during the day for ventilation, let in a putrid smell that came from the squat toilet outside. This roof-tiled latrine was a solid rectangular box of masonry, completely at odds beside the brittle shabby house with a thatched roof. There was no door in front of the toilet to give privacy. It was to be the very place of small nightmares for me when I visited my grandparents. Its two platforms were too far apart for my feet to rest comfortably on, and I used to feel panicked by the fear of falling into that deep dark hole in the middle that was the open mouth of a wide pipe above the septic tank. Although flushed with a bucket of water after each use, the unpleasant odour of excrement rose and floated in the atmosphere. Neither strong winds nor stillness of weather could solve this pollution. In this small community where children and adults pulled down their pants to defecate in front of your eyes, it was considered a privilege to have a toilet at all.

Around this house, the dirt ground was bare and hard, and sloped down from the back. Traces of soapy shower water mixed with urine coming from the bathroom trailed in crooked lines to the front yard where my uncles and aunts normally played. Hugged against the small entrance gate, a singular small tree struggled where no weeds could even grow. It was a nothing plant, stunted in mid-growth. In the many years I saw it when I came visiting, I challenged myself to guess what fruit it would bear, if only it were transplanted somewhere less arid. It never managed to sprout more than a few sickly looking leaves all year round. Survive all the odds it did, its roots buried in rock-solid clay through the driest of summer into the wettest of monsoons during which it was almost drowned under water, the tallest of its tips gasping for air. It would stand in my mind as the symbol of how life was in this neighbourhood.

Here the rains stagnated for an average of three months a year, changing the place into a mosquito-infested swamp. The water, still, turbid and unbearably nauseating, had a mixture of human dirt and kitchen garbage floating on the surface. The flood level reached nearly the floor of most huts, and at times when the monsoon was extreme, it went well above.

Poor people were somehow adaptable to the harsh, swift changes dictated by the seasons. They raised their beds; those who otherwise slept on the floor now had to hang up their hammocks. The occasional unwary water snake that strayed and squiggled into their homes ended up in the soup.

Poor children showed an equal propensity to make the best of any weather. With the blustery wind starting to blow before it brought the annual flood, children went collecting pebbles and prepared themselves for being house-bound. They hovered at the edge of the porch, dangling their feet as low down as their legs could stretch. They giggled among themselves and compared with one another how tall they had grown. They played another game in which they threw the stones.

Their most enjoyable entertainment was a sideshow acted out by 'grandfather Heng'. From mid-afternoon, they waited with anticipation. They looked out for him, and there, on the bamboo bridge Granddad would appear. Normally the pitch of his furious voice preceded him. He thundered imprecations at anything except his own drunkenness. While he tried to steady his gait, he damned out loud at the wobbliness of the bridge, and he questioned why someone had chosen such narrow, slippery planks. Hesitant like a tightrope walker, he stopped and steadied himself again. Holding on to the rail, he took in a deep breath and swore passionately.

Out of all the available places in Phnom Penh, I wondered why Granddad insisted on living in this dismal area. Unless a person had no choice, no-one in their right mind would pick this community in which to raise a family. It was undoubtedly this kind of environment that accounted for the high suicide rate among its youths. Adolescents took poison in their meals and were buried hurriedly in crates. Infants and young children died otherwise from undiagnosed tropical diseases, high night fevers that killed them within a day, and a number of them were struck and crippled by poliomyelitis.

Few people in this community lived into old age, the two exceptions being my grandparents' next-door neighbours, two elderly sisters who had lost their children. They were lonely. I used to watch them walk every morning to the front of their hut, and stand under a mulberry tree, their eyes searching for an enormous caterpillar. They gently peeled it from the leaf where it clung and took turns to caress its back and talked to it for hours. I often wondered how they coped when the caterpillar took wings and flew away as a butterfly.

The one modern convenience my grandparents' house did not lack was electricity. The main power station, which serviced the city, was the landmark of this neighbourhood. It was an enormous grey complex, an eyesore with its shapeless form and unpainted cement walls. It blew a constant hot breath and low humming sound into the humid air. I used to run quickly past its high fence to avoid being suffocated. All around the power station, tiny mysterious lanes meandered into dark pockets of dense human agglomerations, and the worst hidden-from-the-world shanty corners where whole families managed to live between four panels of tin.

Other than the poverty, there was an element of restlessness and crime, which did not seem to worry Granddad. Nowhere else would he be safer than among a few misfits, he claimed. The reason being that they never stole from their immediate neighbours and the area where a thief lived was automatically immune from robbery by other thieves.

The majority of the residents tried to make an honest living. They were roving food merchants who carried their wares on shoulder poles along the streets or stopped in a small communal market, leaving their infants unattended at home. The first drops of rain dispersed the crowd of customers and the food could not be sold. In the wet season, these people's daily income dropped dramatically and they would be fortunate to have one meal a day. Here the wet season was accompanied by the groans from the sick and the cries from half-starved and neglected children.

Most of my grandfather's salary went toward buying food in bulk. Rice came twice monthly to his house in vans. Huge fifty-kilogram jute bags were loaded on the coolies' bent backs, full of rice, corn, wheat flour, dried fish and canned food. The wet season rendered food delivery impossible, so Granddad purchased a bigger supply of food to cater for the next three months. His bedroom also became a food warehouse.

Not a speck of this stockpile went to waste: the enormous quantity of food was not meant to provide for only one family. Granddad catered for the whole community's hungry mouths. As a child I remember that dinnertime at his place was a public event. People could get their fill there when their own table was empty. From the moment he burned his father's loan book and refused to collect rent from his estate, Granddad embarked on a private philanthropic mission to clear his social conscience further. While others might choose to hand out clothes to the needy or to the monks, or contribute funds to build a Buddhist shrine, he was inclined to donate food and continue a family tradition. Granddad could not think of a worse suffering than an empty stomach. I equate his belief to the Cambodian worship of the grain of rice.

Heng started to stack up good deeds to counterbalance his bad ones and declared his house an open house. He offered meals at any time, all year round, to all known or nameless faces. As soon as he caught a timid person at his gate, he rushed to the porch and waved them in.

'Come in, come in!' he said quickly. 'Ah, my wife's cooking must smell good from the street! If you can smell the food from my house, I insist that you taste it!' He stretched his neck toward the kitchen and yelled, 'Mother of the children! We have a good visitor!'

The work of feeding these people fell on Grandma. She went shopping daily for vegetables, fresh fish and meat to supplement the dried goods stored at home. By quietly complying she practically lived in the kitchen, bending over her chopping board and her cooking pots.

12

The Next Generation

At twelve years of age my father followed Granddad's footsteps and entered College Sisowath, renamed a 'lycée' after a major refurbishment in 1936, after which it increased its number of students to five hundred. His easy access was due to Heng's old boy status and his official occupation in a government office.

In the thirties a petition was submitted to King Monivong by the students at Lycée Sisowath, complaining about a high Vietnamese intake. No offical action program existed to indicate the school was admitting more Cambodians. However, according to my father, Sisowath was a playground of racial tension and name-calling was commonplace. Students separated into groups, bullying and provoking each other with insults drenched in prejudice. The Vietnamese nick-name for the Cambodians was 'Hang Tho', which referred to a primi-tive tribe of almost naked hunters and gatherers.

Tit for tat, the Cambodians coined the word *youn*, which has a pejo-rative connotation of 'nigger'. Other freshers got sorted out, tagged, adopted or discarded, but my father did not conform easily to a mould. His fair skin could pass for Chinese; in the scale of discrimination, this would put him on a relatively safe ground but he could not speak more than a smattering of Chinese. Because of his bilingual ease in both the Vietnamese and the Cambodian tongues and his fair complexion, it was uniformly deduced that he was a Vietnamese whose family was naturalised Cambodian to gain acceptance. This went against the general trend. Most Vietnamese who settled for many generations in Cambodia remained impervious to the local customs and did not make it a priority to learn the Cambodian language. In their arrogance, they still called the Cambodian provinces, towns and cities by the Vietnamese names assigned under the Vietnamese occupation more than a hundred years before. To the Vietnamese students my father was a product of 'traitors', and to the Cambodians, he was an impostor. Sandwiched in the middle, he had no allies and no safety in numbers, only trouble.

He had a quick response to racial insults; they hit a raw nerve and his pain was instantaneous. He reacted quickly and brutally, and was often sent to the principal's office. Each time, he had to take home a note, which had to be signed by Granddad who administered another dose of punishment in support of the school. In Heng's book, teachers were infallible and impartial in their judgement. My father was put through a long trial by fire.

He spent his savings on boxing lessons. He did not need to look far in his community for some street-wise boys to teach him. He did not just learn technique, but the psychology of gang warfare. Somewhat more confident now, he forced a lid on his temper and held his breath at provocation, waiting for an opportune time to arise away from school grounds.

In his senior years, when older boys were less inclined to use their fists, he found out that their conspiracy of silence was worse than insults and punches. These were boys of the would-be Cambodian elite; they would establish a formal association of old school ties, which they would carry into the workplace. The label of 'impostor' would follow Dad into the future like his own shadow.

From the school ground to the wider society, from the late thirties well into the first half of the next decade, Cambodian nationalism was manifest with the appearance in 1936 of a national newspaper. The *Nagara Vatta* was the first to be written in the Cambodian language, and had a distribution of more than five thousand copies. One of its pet concerns denounced the domination of Vietnamese employees in the Cambodian civil service. Anti-Vietnamese feeling was being revived, and it would peak nearly four decades later under the leadership of Pol Pot, who reigned from 1975 to 1979, and whose Khmer Rouge executed whoever had any Vietnamese blood in them.

The year my father left Lycée Sisowath was the year his brother Duck's Feet started. Less resilient than my father and quicker-tempered still, he came home with bruises and cuts. School entanglements culminated in his dismissal. Grandfather was furious but Grandmother was relieved. She said that going to that school was like going to war and Duck's Feet was better off at home even if it meant that he remained illiterate.

Granddad retorted that she 'could not see beyond her myopic ignorance' and wondered where he should place Duck's Feet. There were a few other institutions. Discounting Buddhist temple schools for younger boys, Chinese schools that catered exclusively for their ethnic community, and a convent school for girls, the list of available schools in Phnom Penh was limited. Lycée Sisowath remained the only decent option for most Cambodians.

To Duck's Feet, his father's long hesitation indicated he had fallen out of grace. He made his own enquiries and a year later enrolled at École Miche, which was founded and run by the Jesuit brotherhood, French at the top and Vietnamese at the base. Its prime mission was to prepare interns for Catholic priesthood but it widened its acceptance to non-Catholics. If people had their pick and the financial means, their children went to Vietnam to board. The ultimate status symbol was sending them to France.

École Miche was popular with the low-income Vietnamese. Granddad categorised it 'a nominal institution which was created for the leftovers and the dropouts' and he thought nothing of Duck's Feet's progress. Little did he know of the Jesuit fathers' long history of education in Europe, neither did he know of their rigorous discipline that did not condone bullying and nonsense. École Miche provided a climate where Duck's Feet progressed in leaps and bounds to the top of his class. A few of his exercise books survived the ravage of time and quite accidentally fell into my possession. (Grandma had lovingly stored them in a box.) They were handwritten in an era when people used feather pens and black ink. His works were immaculate; they were more beautiful and steadier than prints. I browsed through them and discovered his diaries where he recorded events, family incidents, school life and his private world of thoughts, mostly in prose and sometimes in poetry. He wrote down his dreams and his anger. He provided a voice of the generation before me.

I read and reread his letters, which had become faint. Through the faded ink and the sepia pages I relived his life. If society at large was racist, life in his family was a lot more stifling. He found home a sullen place where his parents' loveless marriage plummeted deeper into unhappiness since Reama came to stay. She was an inveterate autocrat and without Dara, there was no-one to curb her sadistic tendency. In a conventional matriarchal cycle, it was high time for any mother-in-law's authority to peter out. Reama was in her sixties and my father was almost a man, but her appetite for domination was insatiable and she encountered no resistance. It certainly did not come from Grandma, who did not exercise the right to fight back. Her courage simply atrophied like an unused muscle. Nor did resistance to Reama come from my grandfather.

Depending on the degree of his drunkenness, Granddad oscillated between a few states. When mildly sloshed, he floated in his own bliss. He cited incantations of some sacred texts in ancient tongues or classical poems in French and shed tears in admiration for the beauty of words and human ability to create literature.

His mother demanded, 'How could such gobbledygook make you cry?' She pounded the bone handle of her feather fan against the timber bench and reeled him into reality. Then she would say, 'By the way, you ought to tell your wife to cut her hair! You dislike finding it in your food.'

My grandmother had hair to her waist and wore it in a bun neatly contained in a fine silk net, in a typical Vietnamese style. She had jet-black swags of it shining with the lustre of eagles' wings; it swayed gracefully behind her slender neck. It was so thick people could not help complimenting her. It was the cause of Reama's jealousy for years and that day she broached it again. Granddad seemed again to let it go. It was a marginal issue in his mind but Reama demanded he should deal with it, insisting, 'The bun—it makes your wife look very Vietnamese!'

He reminded her gingerly, 'Mother, did you or not carefully hand-pick this Vietnamese wife for me?' It was the extent he would go to show his exasperation to his mother. They both brooded, but Reama would always find something else to niggle her.

The matter of my grandmother's hair went unheeded until an unfortunate day when my father bought her a new hairpin. It was encrusted with false diamonds to replace an old ivory comb that had snapped in half. He made the careless error of giving her this present in front of Reama, who exploded. She groped for something to throw. Without looking at the object she picked, she hurled it in my father's direction. It missed and landed in pieces on the timber floor. It was one of the most valuable pipes in Granddad's collection. As soon as he stepped inside the house after work, she rattled on about the hair and the pin and the broken pipe and the silly grandson, 'Squandering money for a diamond pin! For what? For his mother to pin up the horrible long hair!'

She prolonged her rage till dinnertime. Granddad called out for Grandma and said evenly, 'Why don't you cut your hair?'

Reama yelled imperiously for someone to bring scissors and gestured her daughter-in-law to sit in front of her. She pulled loose Grandma's fine silk net, grabbed her hair, and gave cut.

In Duck's Feet's chronicle, the above incident was typical of his home life. It was evenly sad or eventfully tragic. He retreated into his books and coached himself to greater efforts. The Jesuit fathers took him under their wing, and in his second year at school, they agreed to relax their regulations and made him an honorary intern. Duck's Feet boarded for free in the seminary.

Occasionally drawn back to his family by his love for his mother, he would jump the back fence and entered the house. He checked to make sure she was by herself. His younger brothers and sisters would be at school; his father at work and Reama dallying on the porch, observing human traffic in the front lane. He had no desire to bump into her. In the kitchen at the rear of his house, he could find his dear mother, busy as usual with her cooking.

He tiptoed inside, threw his arms around her shoulders and landed a kiss on her ear. She chuckled with delight and whacked him with affection, 'This kind of surprise is too much for my poor old heart.' He combed his fingers through her now short, bristled hair, and put on a smile for her sake. 'I have missed you, Ma!'

She tried not to be sad. 'I miss you too, Duckling!' Then she blurted, 'Come and eat.'

He rubbed his hands in anticipation, 'Ah, my fish casserole! I miss this too!' For this was his favourite. Whenever he dropped in, there was always a plate of it waiting in her pantry. They sat abreast; he shovelled down his food with wooden chopsticks. She could not take her eyes off him. His visits always lasted the length of this small meal and soon she knew he would vanish. Over the back wall, as secretly as he had come in. Each time he left, she stood watching by the back door well after he had scaled the fence, well after his footfalls became fainter than the dropping of a pin. Her mind's eye followed him till the furthest street she knew. She wondered where this school of his was and how he lived, what food the Fathers fed the students and how happy he really was. She turned back to her pots and sighed. She simply adored this boy. As an axiom of nature, many a mother is prone to give her heart more to the one child she fails to keep.

Duck's Feet excelled and skipped two years at school. When he finished the equivalent of middle school, the Jesuit Fathers' connections enabled him to win a scholarship to the famous Chasseloup Laubat School in Saigon (now Ho Chi Minh City). This was an incredible achievement. Only moneyed people could pay its fees and it had the most esteemed academic standard in all the French colonies in Southeast Asia.

Passing the scholarship exams was a lesser test for Duck's Feet than obtaining permission from his father. He was not sure of the reaction he was going to receive and he worried mostly about Reama. She might present arbitrary objections. If she adjudicated against his leaving for Saigon, Granddad had the tendency to agree. He had a way of side-stepping problems in his house and bowed to her demands to be done with her nagging. Duck's Feet had to come one evening, this time by the front door, to duly greet his elders before he proceeded to the kitchen to greet his mother. He realised the importance of appropriate etiquette and timing in his family. Reama had to be shown preferential respect and serious matters such as his studies in Saigon should be better left till after dinner. He tucked the parental consent forms inside his shirt until his mother advised him when he could return to the front room for the signatures.

'Go on out, Duckling, before Mr X leaves, quick!' Mr X was a regular guest who invited himself to dinner everyday. Reama took quite a liking to this man; she enjoyed bragging and he seemed to enjoy listening. Duck's Feet went down on his knees and in an affected fashion prostrated himself in front of her and renewed his greeting. Reama was thoroughly ingratiated in front of her guest and boasted, 'Ah, here is my good grandson! He is a bright student, you know!'

Duck's Feet seized the opportunity. 'Grandma,' he said, 'I would like to seek your permission and your blessing to study further!' She looked delighted, especially after Mr X remarked, 'O you lucky lady, fancy your grandson having to ask if you let him study! I have to beg my kids to go to school!'

In answer to Duck's Feet, she nodded and fanned herself furiously, wearing a broad toothless grin.

He explained, 'I won a scholarship to study in a very good school in Saigon and I need my father to sign some papers.'

Reama got impatient. 'What are you waiting for! Show them and he will sign.'

My grandmother waited at the back, her ears listening to the outcome. Duck's Feet's face glowed and then dimmed slowly at his mother's sadness. She sensed the suddenness of their separation. Neither was capable of saying a word but she managed a feeble smile. To break the spell of her melancholy, he said, 'Ma, before you know it, I will be here, right here next to you.'

She wanted more details: 'And how long will it be, Duckling?'

'Three years, Ma.'

In her mind she was already starting to count down. 'You are not fifteen yet. Going away at your age . . . what happens to you when you get sick? Who will look after you? Where will you stay in Saigon?'

She wanted the answers to more questions so that she could formulate a clear picture of his new life away from her.

'Come,' she beckoned him to her pantry. And there for the last time, she served him fish casserole and rice. 'You are skin and bone. You have to promise me you will eat well.' She pinched his cheeks, a fleeting memory of how chubby they were when he was small. 'Look after yourself, son, and go with God.'

Weeks after he left, my grandmother could not break from the habit of cooking and storing this particular fish dish he loved, knowing too well that he had gone. My aunt Tam remarked that it was a waste. 'Why do you bother to cook this damned food? Nobody in the family likes it.'

My father had a convenient excuse—he was allergic to fish. The other children ran away from it. My aunt Tam was ten, of an age she was expected to stay more in the kitchen to help. She was left with the unpleasant task of eating it herself or discreetly throwing it away. She grumbled at my grandmother's absurdity. One day, she took the dish my grandmother had just finished preparing for my absent uncle and placed it on the altar where Grandma worshipped the spirit of the patriarch. On particular occasions, she gave food and burnt spiritual money in accordance with the Vietnamese ancestral cult. Mimicking this ritual, Tam brought three incense sticks, lit them and kowtowed before the makeshift altar. She accompanied this gesture with an evocation of Duck's Feet's name she invited him to come and consume the 'bloody casserole'.

Grandma was livid; she seized the incense and extinguished it. 'What do you do this for? Why do you make spiritual offerings to a living person? Do you wish your brother were dead?'

She smacked Tam. Undaunted, Tam answered back, 'It's your cooking that is wrong! If I am wrong to put the casserole on the altar for a living brother, how right are you to cook for a living absentee? Duck's Feet cannot sneak in here to this kitchen for the next one thousand days!'

Tam was a bright girl. She was sent to school when she was six. Readiness for school did not relate to the children's age, it was gauged by whether they could withstand the physical separation from their parents without crying miserably once they were dropped in the classroom. Some children did not start their education until they were almost in their teens because of this. Tam did not cry one bit when my father held her by the hand and walked her to the École Providence, a Catholic nuns' school near their house.

My father was instrumental at pushing for his sister to get an education. 'Give her a chance to learn something instead of keeping her home,' he said to Grandma and off his own bat he had the forms prepared for his sister's entry. He was fourteen and already behaved in a caring role as the eldest brother. Tam was eight years younger.

She was mature for her years and displayed a steely determination to do well. Her work was remarkable. Considering her home environment, it was no small effort. She had a lot of distractions. She lived in a house that did not have a proper desk or chair for her to comfortably do her homework. She sat on a foot stool against the edge of the bunk, which was really a collective bed where half her siblings snuggled together to sleep at night. The bunk was high and the stool low, so she had to squat on it to raise herself to a level where her head was above her exercise books. She was interested in her studies and Dad would encourage her with comments that she was 'the first scholar who wears plaits!'

He was Tam's ally and valued the seriousness of her schoolwork. He was himself dedicated and had much the same difficulty in overcoming the bedlam in their family. He defended her against distractions from her three younger siblings. The two boys tugged her sleeves; they hovered around with questions and requests, 'Please teach us to play scissors, paper and stone!' If she ignored them, they seized the nibs of her feather pen and threw them like darts or spilled the ink out of the bottle and smudged her books. Dad would pull their ears and show them the darkness of the evening outside: 'See how black it is? Time to go to bed!'

My father and Tam had chores to do before they could tackle school assignments. The constant traffic of free diners to their house took over their mother's time and mind. It took over a good portion of their time too. Grandma waited on these visitors, she ran back and forth from the kitchen to the front where meals were served as if the home were a restaurant. The wet nurse trailed behind her, offering to help.

Grandma turned around and faced the old lady who had good intentions but crippling arthritis. 'Please sit down, Ma Nui (Vietnamese meaning 'adopted mother'). I have things under control.'

The wet nurse, aware of her disability, mumbled how sorry she was to be more a burden than a contribution. 'Oh God, Oh sky, what would I not give to make these legs and these hands supple again! I could at least clear the dishes for you without the risk of dropping them instead! What a nuisance I am!' She was genuinely heartbroken to leave Grandma short-handed.

'Look, Ma Nui, you did your fair share of work in your life! Thank God for giving you a reason to take it easy now! The children are helping me, so please don't blame yourself.' The wet nurse looked miserable and Grandma had to find something for her to do to make her feel useful: 'I would be grateful if you sit here and look after the stove for me. Just check the food is not burning. Please keep the little kids away too. One of these days they might set the house on fire.' Then she rushed doubly fast to the front, back to the kitchen, washed dishes, served another lot of food to somebody who had just turned up. She was insanely busy in the evening, and Tam and my father had to help out.

At last, when the flow of diners thinned and Grandma could cope on her own, Dad and Tam could concentrate on their schoolwork. When that was done, my father slumped to the floor and slept on a straw mat and a kapok pillow; Tam huddled on the bunk, wherever she found a spare corner to rest her bones. She seldom had a restful sleep for during the night, one of her younger siblings was doomed to kick or stir, and a little baby, whichever was the latest born, would wake up for the night feed. The infant's cries woke up the boys. Tam had the job of putting them back to sleep while Grandma rolled on her side and gave the baby her breast.

If by some misfortune this nocturnal commotion woke up Reama, she was sure to pound her fan on her wall and soon the whole household was awake. She had the talent of turning a baby's colicky tears or some other triviality into a major drama. Like a siren, her voice pitched high and loud, and she tore the middle of the night apart with her abuses. 'After that many children, she [meaning Grandma] still cannot handle them! Nobody can rest in peace in this house!' She worked herself up to a state that kept her awake, then spent the next day complaining about her lack of sleep and how her health was deteriorating. A hypochondriac, she recited a list of imaginary aches and pains, hoping for some sympathy from my grandfather. She sighed, 'Oh I am too weak to move! Will somebody take me to the loo!' She had no strength to flush, and someone had to fetch a bucket of water and flush for her too.

That somebody had to be Tam. This sort of help could not come from a male, nor from the wet nurse who could hardly carry her own frame, nor from Grandma who was with child either in the tummy or on the breast. From the time Tam's head reached Reama's bosom, she was at her beck and call. Tam's hands were roughened by manual work, her eyes chronically red from lighting the stoves. She built a base of rolled papers upon which she put small twigs, and then in order of size she laid the charcoal blocks. Once she had felt pleased when she was allowed to light it for the very first time. 'See? I am a big girl now!' She teased her younger brothers. But since it became a regular chore, the fun had gone out of the exercise.

The number of chores expected of her increased proportionally with her number of years. Now that she was about to turn twelve, and with Dad gone from home on longer study leaves, she bore his load of house duties on top of her own. Ironically before he left on these trips, he urged her to keep up her school studies at all costs. She tried.

In her fourth year at the convent school, she fell asleep in the middle of her lessons. She came to class with half-finished assignments. Her absences became more frequent and stretched longer. Her class teacher questioned the reasons for her bad performance and Tam was quiet about her difficult home life. It took more than this nun's prayer to deliver her from the domestic yoke she had to bear.

Without a word of complaint, Tam stopped school and accepted the fact that she could not study. Dad came back from his field trip and asked, 'Why are you not at school today, little sister?'

Grandma snapped an answer on her behalf and said, 'A girl need not know how to read and write.' In her old-fashioned reasoning, literacy enabled girls to send letters to their lovers.

My father felt sorry that his sister was being landed in a tough domestic situation. This was a normal custom in poor Asian families, where the oldest daughter was expected to understudy the mother in the house. Dad had no immediate solution for Tam but he consoled her with a promise, 'Trust me, I will make sure you will go back to school one day!'

Meanwhile Tam pined for her discontinued education. Half the neighbourhood kept inviting itself to meals, and babies were born at regular intervals. Tam had to fill the role of a full-time servant whom Grandma could not hire. Yet the ridiculous part was that there was no shortage of money to pay for home help had my grandfather allowed it.

In the misery he put my grandmother through, whether he meant to or not, Heng had condemned his own children and jeopardised their future happiness.

13

King and Country

King Sisowath Monivong died in 1941. This date was crucial; it brought a shy unknown prince, Norodom Sihanouk (born in 1922), to the vacant throne. His presence from this time has influenced Cambodian politics until now.

Before his coronation, the royal family was split in two conflicting clans, the Sisowath against the Norodom. Cambodian royalty was adept at squabbling, having nothing better to do. However, this time, there was a concrete cause for dispute. Since 1904, the year King Norodom I died, his natural heirs had lost out. The French residents put his half-brother Sisowath on the throne and Sisowath's son, Monivong, succeeded in 1927. His Majesty King Sisowath Monivong reigned complacently for sixteen years. He was a ceremonial monarch, debauched, surrounded by women and perpetually high on opium. As he lay in state in 1941, royalties and dignitaries were engaged in heated debates over the complexity of determining which line was more legitimate. The Sisowath claimed their legitimacy from this latest reigning king. The Norodom took their argument from two reigns further back, to the time of king Norodom's death when his direct descendants were cheated from the throne.

My brother Vandy was eight, I was four in 1956.
In the background, the Ministry of Information.

Vandy and me in 1956.

My mother and me in 1958.

My young aunt Somalee and me in 1959.

From left to right: Vandy, Vannary, Tha, Vaan, Nee and No. Photo taken in 1963.

My mother and me at Tuol Kok in 1968.

My brother Vandy in 1969.

The total number of contenders between the two combined royal branches exceeded one hundred! The French proposed to resolve this rivalry by finding a candidate who must be a product of the two clans. The choice fell on Sihanouk, whose mother was a Sisowath princess, daughter of the deceased King Monivong. Sihanouk's father was a full-blooded Norodom prince. Both his parents were children to the same father (King Norodom I) but of different mothers. This kind of marital arrangement was common among royalty. Sihanouk himself would enter into matrimony with his own maternal aunt at one stage.

The French disregarded two mature contenders and it was not coincidental that they should pick an eighteen-year-old Sihanouk, bashful and inexperienced, whom they thought would be easy to manipulate. They called him back from Saigon where he was studying at Chasseloup Laubat. He completed the final touches of his interrupted education with a team of French teachers who were appointed to coach him in history and politics. His early reign was docile towards the colonial patronage, and his critics had reason to accuse him of being a puppet of the French. His immediate opponents were the senior editors of the *Nagara Vatta* newspaper, namely Son Ngoc Thanh and the Mohanikai monk Hem Chieu, both of whom were set to free Cambodia from France and the Cambodian monarchy.

In 1941 Europe was deeply involved in World War II. Under the menace of Hitler's Germany, France focused its efforts on defending its homefront and shifted most of the forces back home, leaving only a slim military presence in Cambodia. Japan was doing just the opposite; it sought to expand over Asia. France was lacking military might to oppose these advances. While the Dutch and the British openly declared war against Japan to defend their respective colonies in the Southeast, France resorted to a concession to avoid a costly confrontation with Japan, allowing the latter to keep eight thousand of its troops in Cambodia. The newspaper *Nagara Vatta* detected France's increasing weakness. It began to attack the French and promoted its support for Japan.

On 17 July 1942, the Mohanikai monk Hem Chieu plotted a coup against the French, who arrested and deported him to Poulo Condore, a penal island off the coast of Vietnam. Three days after the arrest, Son Ngoc Thanh organised a rally of over a thousand people and marched toward the office of the French Resident Superior to demand Chieu's release. The demonstrators were photographed, their leaders caught and tried. Thanh escaped to the Thai border and was offered political asylum in Tokyo. The French had blundered in the manner they arrested Hem Chieu, by not allowing him to officially leave the Buddhist Order. This omission to defrock the monk was a grave transgression against local custom, and was seen as an act of arrogance and generally condemned. France had made herself suddenly very unpopular.

Prompted by nothing less than a bad sense of timing, a year after the demonstration over the arrest of the monk, the Resident Superior Georges Gautier decreed the Cambodian language be romanised. This decision reinforced the French unpopularity. Steps were taken to phase out the Cambodian language from official use amidst terrible objections from the Buddhist Church. Everything suddenly came to a halt on 9 March 1945, when the Japanese seized complete control of Cambodia. The day of their full-scale invasion, their planes dropped bombs on the city, their troops disarmed the French and a Japanese moved in to advise Sihanouk. In less than a week, on 12 March, Japan authorised King Sihanouk to proclaim Cambodia independent from France. There was nothing said about Cambodia being also independent from Japan. Son Ngoc Thanh, the protégé of Japan, flew back to Cambodia from Tokyo. King Sihanouk, although fully aware of this man's republican views, was forced to allow him to form a new government in mid-August. Thanh's pro-Japanese Cabinet was short-lived and lasted for only a few weeks, the length of the Japanese occupation. The bombing of Hiroshima on 6 August 1945 and of Nagasaki three days later obliged Japan to capitulate and consequently to give up Cambodia.

Brief though the Japanese control of Cambodia was, its impact was considerable on two accounts. First, on my family: the house in Prek Dek, vacant after Reama's move to Phnom Penh, was confiscated by the Japanese and used as their provincial military headquarters. My grandfather was notified of the fact after the Japanese soldiers had already established themselves comfortably on the premises. The second impact was on the whole country. In the aftermath of the Japanese occupation, which enabled it to declare itself free from the French, Cambodia kept a taste for independence.

In October 1945, when the French authorities moved back to take full possession of Cambodia, they ordered the arrest of the pro-Japanese Prime Minister Son Ngoc Thanh. They caught him in Phnom Penh while he was presiding over the reopening ceremony of the old College Sisowath. By lunchtime, they escorted him to jail in Saigon where they tried him for collaboration with Japan.

France, once back in power, rescinded the independence of Cambodia. The French retained control of the economy but were prepared to loosen their political grip. In the words of Sihanouk, it was a 'fifty per cent independence'. The constitution was amended to give freedom of speech and the formation of political parties. Many factions emerged, but two were the most significant.

The Democrats dreamt of a model of government similar to the French Republic. Some of the dispersed members of the republican group, whose leaders had been Chieu and Thanh, affiliated themselves with the Democrats, and in doing so, brought with them the blessing of the Mohanikai sect. They believed in an independent Cambodia without France or King. In the course of time, they would differ among themselves and a faction of the democrats leaned toward Thailand and the rest toward the Communist Vietminh.

The other party, the Liberals, led by Prince Norodom Norindeth, was conservative. They wished to keep France and King intact. Most of the members were rich landowners who were not eager to revolutionise the existing system and jeopardise their personal wealth. They had the backing of the Chinese business community, quite understandably the backing of the royal family, and of France, which secretly funded their activities.

King Norodom Sihanouk was privately developing another party that in time would become the most important in Cambodia. He secretly wished for an independent Cambodia but one that should be gained peacefully.

After the Japanese left, the French intended to take over the custody of the house in Prek Dek. They showed an ironic civility when they notified my grandfather of the expropriation. Although the end result was the same, my grandfather commended them for their courtesy. They were anxious to play down their position of authority. In their letter, they pointed out that heavier taxes on the lands were due, but an exemption would be granted if my grandfather agreed to the indefinite occupation of the Prek Dek house. The French worded the offer in a way that suggested to my grandfather that they were indeed doing him a special favour. He wrote off the loss of his ancestral house with a philosophical shrug of the shoulders, reasoning that he was not meant to keep it. From this time on, a divorce with Prek Dek ensued; only years later the contact with our native village could be resumed.

The stormy years in the early forties rocked the country and perturbed many lives. The decade was charged with events. It started with the coronation of the new king. The ramifications of World War II followed, bringing Japanese soldiers into Cambodia. There was the aborted coup resulting in the monk's arrest and the big rally; the protest over romanising the Cambodian language; the full fledged Japanese invasion and the bombing of the city; Thanh's pro-Japanese cabinet; the return of the French and finally the relative freedom they accorded to form political parties. Everywhere in Phnom Penh civilians reacted or participated; they got caught up in factions.

Granddad was apathetic to the sweep of political emotions and

activities. His education, his land ownership and his job in the government could well place him with the liberal party, but he simply did not
think that he had personal interests to protect or a contribution to
make. The only stand he made was to refute any link with power and
money, and to align himself with the lower classes. The way he chose to
live was testimony to the deliberate distance he held from the elite.

His unique philosophy was voiced only when he was drunk. His
perception of nobility was linked tangibly to the mud of the rice fields.
He liked to show the callused knuckles on his peasant's hands, which
years of writing with pens could never soften. The lotus flower, he
chanted, though rooted in the mud, symbolised purity upon which
Buddha sat to meditate. Through this poetic analogy, my grandfather
was boasting of his rural heritage.

When I was a child, I was mystified by his theatrical outpourings. I
was his unsuspected spectator and he was a very dramatic actor who
did not set out to perform for an audience. I used to watch him from
somewhere unseen as he rolled out words, which did not at the time
make a lot of sense to me. But I was held captive to the lilt of his
drunken voice which was variously melancholic, excited, irate. I was
strangely riveted by a certain prophetic quality of his speeches. I was
touched by the unmistakable sincerity of his tone. The same enjoyment
I still feel nowadays when I listen to an epic poem or an operatic
performance in another tongue. Granddad had a repertoire of perform-
ances. He repeated them many times over the years, introducing minor
improvisations. When I was older I finally understood what he was
saying. I discovered within him the existence of a tortured soul. To say
Grandfather was a complex man would be an understatement.

To most people, he was the fool who refused the honour of a
promotion to directorship. At the higher level of responsibility, which he
had been offered, he could not combat the widespread corruption even
if he tried. He would gain more enemies without making a difference.
His colleagues were baffled and rationalised his refusal for promotion by

saying, 'He simply cannot count beyond a small sum!' He turned down an invitation to join the liberal party with a diplomatic excuse. In private he had little respect for the 'liberal', 'democratic' or other political parties. The one vital issue, which he wished to see addressed and which was never raised, was about nepotism and bribery in the government. My grandfather predicted that Cambodia would not survive unless it eliminated this malignant disease. Jobs were handed out on the weight of family or political connections to unqualified people. Furthermore work was not carried out unless the employees got 'greased'. This corruption was culturally entrenched in the system; it risked eventually paralysing the whole country. Yet the general attitude, even from those who claimed they cared, was extremely complacent. Granddad was small fry who swam against the current and he knew it would be suicidal to vocalise his disgust more than he already had. The campaign to sweep clean the administration had to come from the top. The king alone had the power to address this problem.

Year after year, Granddad went with other functionaries to the palace to pledge an oath of loyalty to the throne. He was disappointed that nothing was ever said about the need to serve the common good in Cambodia. He would drink to excess after these ceremonies and dragged himself home groaning about the king's blindness, about hypocrisy and greed, calling top names in the cabinet 'sycophants, sons of bitches and eaters of bribes'. He lay on his bed mumbling one thing after another. 'The bloody colonials built many jails. Especially in Cambodia! No schools!'

This roused his anger against the French, about whom he blurted a volley of insults. My grandmother would tell him, 'Father! Do lower your voice! These high-powered men will send the police to handcuff you and drag you off to prison!' He would yell louder in defiance, 'Let them come! Let them if they care!' He expressed his thoughts quite openly when he was in that mood, safe in the knowledge that no authority worried about the antics of an alcoholic. And really, who would listen to this loud-mouthed man anyway?

My father did. Far from being a worthless drunkard, Granddad, seen through the eyes of my father, was an idealist. With minor differences, which included a reactionary avoidance of alcohol, Dad's heart, his work and main ideas in his life were summed up by one factor—he was the eldest son to this singular old man.

At the end of 1945, when Dad left Lycée Sisowath, he enrolled for two years at the School of Administration, which was founded to train its students for public service. He was doing exactly what everybody else in Cambodia would like to do—prepare for a job in the government. My grandfather's prime concern was to steer his eldest son's career away from offices where bribery was the order of the day. The sector with the least opportunity for this form of temptation was the Ministry of Agriculture. Cambodia was agriculturally based and would remain so into the foreseeable future. Knowledge relating to growing crops and fishing was fundamentally beneficial. Granddad had thus pointed my father in the direction he should follow. He obtained a position in the Ministry of Agriculture as he finished his studies at the School of Administration at the age of twenty. He was sent on a study tour of the United States, and upon his return, earned the official rank of 'controller of agriculture', which was a respectable starting level.

He went on field researches to the provinces, but on his return to Phnom Penh, he still lived at home. Young men who had to fend for themselves would not consider his wage sufficient and wages earned by Cambodian public servants were generally low at that time. However, Dad had no real expenses and he had a definite purpose for which he wanted to save money. With due and proper filial intent, he wished to buy the house his parents had been renting. He consulted his father who reacted with a shrug and said, 'Look at my hands, son. I could grab a lot of wealth through stealth and greed. What for, I ask you. Buy this house, you said. What for? To own a deed, a claim on a piece of dirt? I don't worry too much about it!'

Dad did worry, because he wanted to prove that he cared. And he acted according to his personal concept of filial duty. He purchased the house without my grandfather's knowledge and thought naïvely that it would make a happy surprise. But before he officially gave it to him, he harboured second thoughts. He hesitated for weeks, which became months. The rent collector kept coming, taking the rent from Granddad and pocketing his commission. He would then sneak in the back door and give the rest to Grandma. Rumours in this congested community had it that Grandma was having an affair with the agent. My father's well-intended gesture enraged my grandfather. He lost his temper and impetuously slapped his son. 'You schemed with your mother to defraud me in rent. Are you undermining my ability to provide for her?' Dad lay on the floor and wept. He confessed that such was not his intent, 'I wished to give the house to you from the beginning, Father, but I was not sure how to go about it.'

When the tears had dried and the temper abated, my grandfather asked Dad to sit by his bed and to listen. 'Did I tell you not to purchase this house? Is it so important to own it instead of paying rent? Will I be able to take its deed and its title with me when I die? I think not! Listen to me, son. I do not covet possessions and none of you will inherit money or properties from me. What I will leave to you will be invisible. Karma will see to it that you get your share.'

To Grandfather, real wealth was not counted in cash nor was it measured in land.

14

Forbidden Love

My mother, Oanh Liet, was supposed to become a nun. She completed four years of religious education in the Vietnamese language and was confirmed at twelve. Before she joined the convent of the Sacred Heart, she attended a small public school, École Norodom, for three years. She had a boisterous and an irrepressible nature and with her capacity for fun, she was a popular member of a gang. At this secular school where she was allowed a last taste of some worldly freedom, she was the bully who instigated mischief—not a seemly reputation for a future nun.

Her friends guarded the single water tap in the whole school ground, arbitrarily barring access to those girls they did not like, while my mother tried to shove them off with her fists or threatened to pull their hair. The victims protested but ended up scuttling away.

At home she was the favourite daughter, the eldest of nine children from the same mother; she had one older half-brother. She might behave badly behind their backs but her doting parents held her above reproach. Toward them she showed obedience, toward God she had piety.

My mother was an exceptional singer, a soloist in their church choir. Her voice possessed a lot of strength, it could rise confidently high and stirred deep emotions in the congregation. They said, 'To sing like that, she must be close to God!' There were signs that she was. She did church duties, learned her hymns and confessed weekly. Her parents' decision to put her in the nunnery did not depend on the depth of her faith; it related to her father's plighting troth with God before she was conceived.

Her father, Nguen, was a Vietnamese migrant living in Cambodia. He was atheist in practice and vaguely Confucian in thought. A widower, he struggled to raise a small son. And he fussed. Not content with any replacement for his deceased wife, he determined to choose well. He was financially battling, getting on in age and had nothing going for him. The girl he was to marry would be much younger, of his race, well-to-do and Catholic. My grandmother's forefathers allegedly embraced Christ in the eighteenth century when the early missionaries landed in Vietnam, and could trace their ancestry back to Burma and China. When this girl married, the variety of jewellery she wore reflected the truth of her origins. She dripped with rubies from Burma, and was decked in jade, heirlooms from her Sino-Vietnamese forebears who were landowners and herbal doctors back in their villages.

My maternal grandmother, whose maiden name escaped me since it kept changing according to which household she lived in, was an orphan and a ward of an uncle in Phnom Penh. Before there was any hope of a wedding, people agreed that her guardian uncle was of a standard far above the widower Nguen and that the latter would never be able to obtain her hand. Adding to the list of his poor credentials, he was a non-believer. However he refused to be deterred and he paid an eloquent woman to carry his voice and to plead his cause. He humbly admitted that he could not keep the girl in the comfort to which she was accustomed, but he was a hard-working man and he swore that he would spend all the hours of the day earning enough to keep her from want. Among the many promises Nguen solemnly made, the one that worked in his favour, was about religion. Nguen consented to

Catholicism. Before the marriage, he studied his catechism and got baptised. His conversion was not a formality; he became fanatically devout. The children he put in this world were pledged to serve his newly found church. For Thinh, the son from his previous wife, he was bereft of hope. Thinh was unruly. The effort to show him the holy light failed; he rejected this God because ever since his Christian stepmother invaded his house, he seemed to have lost his father.

Nguen was a person of his word. He honoured the assurance he had made to keep his young wife from need and he tried his utmost to rise above financial mediocrity. Straight after their marriage, he entered the household of Monsieur Moncriat, a French Resident who was posted in Battambang. He and his bride offered comprehensive domestic services, from shopping and cooking to sweeping, dusting and polishing the silver, and washing and ironing. They did extra chores to ingratiate themselves to their employers and secure their jobs. They minded the French children and Mrs Nguen, who was adroit in needlework and appliqué, ruined her eyesight in the evening embroidering tablecloths, serviettes and linen. They boarded for free in a small area adjacent to the storeroom and had no food expenses to pay. They accumulated their collective wages and hid them in their pillow.

My mother was born in Battambang, and the birth of two other brothers followed. Montcriat turned a blind eye to the growing size of his maid's family, even though it meant that more children would now raid his fridge for eggs and goodies. Because of this, the Nguen couple was cautious not to request an increase in wages. They dared not even ask for an increase in living space. The one room that was once ample for them and their unruly son had to accommodate three more children. Their family of six crammed into one cubicle and it was not until my mother was nearly seven that she experienced the luxury of living in two rooms. It came about when Monsieur Montcriat transferred to Phnom Penh. At last, a residence of rambling proportions was available, more suited to the importance of Montcriat, who was the head of

Finances in Cambodia. My mother recalled this house and talked of it as if it were a palace. However Madame Montcriat often complained about the lack of basic conveniences, which could not be found in Cambodia. The French lady lived with a nagging nostalgia for France and jumped with joy when her husband's service in the colony came to a close.

Before they repatriated, Monsieur Montcriat rewarded his long-time servants with a golden handshake. This money, added to the savings they had put away, amounted to a stupendous sum in my grandparents' pocket. They set up an eating house in Phnom Penh.

They leased a two-storey building in the bustling street called Rue Paul Luce. Their restaurant was on the ground level and they lived upstairs. The top floor had four rooms and a proper lavatory and shower. They hired three waiters, a cook and a dishwashing hand in their shop; they had a maid for general duties at home and a nanny for the children. The restaurant was thriving and warranted this number of staff. Their clientele counted bachelors living far from relatives who prepaid monthly for their two daily meals. Occasionally, French lieutenants stumbled in to rest their legs and order some iced green tea they did not drink. They came back again the next day, stayed a bit longer but found nothing they liked to eat.

Nguen rushed to their table and greeted them with an exuberant smile, 'Steak on the house, just for you.' The tip they left was more than the price of meat. 'Please come back again, hey, mon général?'

A few more visits, and the Frenchmen were thoroughly at ease. They pulled out a deck of cards, their eyes scouting the place. One got up, tugged Nguen's sleeve and asked for a room where they could play. They paid handsomely for this extra facility and the lucky winner of the regular nightly rounds was invariably generous. Nguen was torn between two forms of fear. He was petrified on the one hand of the police and the church, who both condemned gambling. On the other hand the Frenchmen's uniforms equally intimidated him.

He asked his wife, 'Which authority should I dread most?' She had no answer. Both fell on their knees and prayed for God's mercy.

The coffee shop generated such an attractive income that the landlord boosted his rent. It marked the beginning of a slope in profits, which fell in the early forties when an atmosphere of increasing political unrest was palpable in the city. Customers became scarce. The final straw of bad luck hit the Nguens' business with the sounds of blasting bombs. With the Japanese bombing of Phnom Penh hardly a soul dared to eat out. In the end, the restaurant made hardly enough to meet the high rent. The Nguen couple closed it down and shifted to a cheaper residential place completely out of the central district.

Granddad Nguen left to work on a ferry selling tickets and later on the train that commuted between Phnom Penh and Battambang. He sold food to passengers—anything from peeled jackfruit, oranges, roasted pumpkin or watermelon seeds, iced drinks to banana buns. After one year, he decided to set up shop again. The new restaurant was not in a central location but it brought an income sufficient to support the family.

In 1947, my mother was sixteen and had gone to the convent. Her two younger brothers were interns at a Jesuit seminary. The three were the first group of the Nguen children being groomed for the Catholic church. In those early days, they were allowed occasional visits home, which was in a predominantly Vietnamese community where ramshackle houses were tightly packed together. A small day market catered for the locals, a small church for those Catholic families among them. Vietnamese priests conducted mass on Sundays and there was a cemetery behind the church. People could live, die and get buried in this pocket of the city without ever needing to venture out.

Crooked dirt alleys ran off in confusing directions deep with sludge after the rains or were very dusty in the dry weather. If one knew one's way through the maze of this area, there was a lane, which could be used as a short-cut to the main street. This was the only route that brought in outside traffic.

My father was familiar with this short-cut, which he came to know because of a friend. My father's friend was none other than Thinh, Nguen's first-born, an illiterate drifter who refused to go to school. He did not have a mother's love to bond him to home nor did he feel he had a father who cared for anything but church and work. Thinh went to his father's house only to sleep and eat. He dallied about and picked fights to pass his time. He was the master of thugs and no-one was agile enough to duck from his fists. His enemies retaliated indirectly and victimised his little half-brothers instead. Through no fault of their own, they often scampered home from school crying bitterly. 'Big Thinh's bad friends have just hit me'. Grandma Nguen looked at their bruises, looked to the sky and thrust her hands up and called on God's name. She complained to her husband daily, 'Your no-good son Thinh has done it again!'

Thinh and my father had nothing in common, but Thinh was Dad's boxing teacher. 'Never mind the money, I show you a few kicks and a few tricks for free!' They had a peculiar relationship: Thinh had a patronising affection for Dad, and Dad had a blend of gratitude and awe for Thinh that was probably based on fear.

It was through Thinh that Dad met my mother. The apprentice nun in ordinary clothes was home on a few weeks' break from the convent and the introduction was made very casually. She concealed her instant attraction to Dad's personality and his smile, retiring to her room and berating herself for the sudden beating in her heart. On her knees she pleaded with the Virgin Mary to spare her from Lucifer.

A few days later, she received a letter, confidentially hand-delivered by her younger sister to whom the author had given a bribe, a pack of alphabet cookies. The note contained words of passion to which Mum could not be indifferent. One after another, more letters arrived. She shortened her stay and returned to the holy sisters. She was committed to call on her inner strength to overcome this earthly temptation. She hid the letters under her cot, physically close to remind her of the temptation she had to overcome, the battle of the flesh Mother Superior often talked about. It was now a secret sacrifice she had to make if she were to become an honest nun. She was working through her confusion when chance led a senior nun to her room. The compromising letters were discovered under her cot. She was sent to the Mother Superior who deemed her unfit to become a nun. My mother was asked to leave immediately.

She did not have a cent for transport. As she slowly walked home she thought of the convent's accusation. She shook her head and wondered why her truth was harder for people to accept than a lie. How was she going to explain it all to her parents when she had failed to convince the nuns? Her expulsion would be a blow to her father; she had to try to find a way to break the bad news to them.

It would be late at night when they returned from work. Their fifteen-hour days drew a scanty clientele and yielded a skimpy profit. She knew that they would be drained by fatigue and financial anxiety. But they usually came home with gladness; they kissed their front door and gave thanks to God for at least blessing their children with health and happiness. Despite their happy faces, my mother knew they were in dire straits and she was sad she was going to burden them with an additional problem. As she could hear their voices, she forced herself out of her room to greet them. Her knees felt weak, she swooned before she approached her father. He swooped down to catch her head from knocking on the floor: 'Quick, quick, somebody! Some water! The girl might be dead!' He screamed. At that instant, a spark of an idea came to my mother. She improvised her first serious lie to her parents. She told her father that the sisters had sent her back because she was sick.

The next day, she was in the front porch thinking of Dad, the person who had wrecked her simple life. She wondered whether he was aware that she was going to be a nun. If so, why had he written those wonderful lines? If not, she acquitted him from blame. She was deliberating about my father when he turned up at her gate, smiling. She was quite stunned to see him. He came next to her.

'Why are you unapproachable? Do you dislike me that much?' he asked softly. She nodded yes, she nodded no, and he chuckled.

'Look,' she said. 'I don't think that it is funny! I was destined to become a nun! But your letters were discovered and they created a scandal. I was chased out of the convent and I have not told my parents! The strange thing is I did not want to destroy your letters and I don't even know you.'

He was genuinely astounded, speechless for a while and he replied, 'I'll see what I can do.'

Whether it was his impulsive nature or his point of honour to do the right thing, the fact remained that he persuaded his mother to go to the coffee shop to discuss marriage. The Nguens gave her a flat 'no', which offended his mother terribly. They did not bother to disguise their answer with a polite hesitation. A blunt refusal on the spot was equivalent to them saying, 'you are definitely not good enough to the point we don't even need to think about your request'.

The meeting was brief and my grandmother Kim was belittled. She told my father that she would not go back and beg again. He thought it best for him to go personally and handle the matter. Nguen was taken aback by my father's aplomb. He would have been close to allowing his daughter to give up the convent—he did not know yet about her expulsion—and would have conceded to a marriage if this young man had been willing to join the Catholic Church.

My father remarked audaciously, 'With due respect sir, what I am asking you for is your daughter's hand. It is totally unrelated to the church. I don't agree with forcing on me a religious belief in exchange for a wife.'

Nguen took offence, and the result was disastrous. Secretly Dad was rather relieved. Everything had happened so fast that he had not had time to think things through. When he had written those letters, he had not anticipated the effects they would have. He was willing to atone for the damage that he had created, going as far as putting himself on the line and asking for my mother's hand in marriage. While he had acted honourably his actions were nevertheless dictated by impulse. He was not ready for marriage, neither was his love for my mother serious enough to consider a lifelong commitment. He was pleased to disengage himself with a clear conscience, but felt he owed her the final courtesy of telling her that he had done what he could to redeem himself. He would say to her that it was most unfortunate that her parents decided to refuse him.

He parked his bike and went to see her for the last time. She was slumped on a chair, looking lost. He felt pity and was urged to console her. They were about to part, perhaps for good. Thinh picked this very moment to walk into the lounge and caught them holding hands. It did not look good—she was without a chaperone and the male she was with was his friend. It was obvious to Thinh that they were lovers. He confronted my father, labelling him 'a man without honour' who had abused and betrayed his friendship and his trust. He snarled insults and moved forth to hit him.

Later that night, my mother had to unlock her door and present herself for parental judgment. Thinh had blown the whistle on her. Looking at his stepmother, he shouted, 'Your impeccably good nun turned your respectable house into a brothel!'

He clenched his fists and swiped at his half-sister. She fell on her knees and begged for forgiveness. She wept while he kept kicking. Nguen found no words to defend her and no strength to stop the beating. He slumped heavily on a cane armchair and simply sighed. My mother was inert, too exhausted to pray for mercy, her face down on the floor, her arms around her head. My grandmother, although angry, could not stand the violence. More to the point, she could not accept that the punishment should be put in her stepson's hands.

She screamed for Thinh to stop, but he yelled back. 'Better for her to be dead and buried! If she lives, she will put this family to shame!'

She was furious. 'You are not blameless yourself! Go and take your fight with other thugs in the streets where you belong!'

He spat out insults and twenty years of anger. 'You stole my father from me, you fed him with religious fantasies and you never meant for me to live in the house!'

My grandfather sank deeper inside his chair, speechless, powerless to arbitrate between the two. My mother dragged herself into her room. Had fire swept through the house that night and burned it to ashes, the damage would have been more assessable.

On the surface life went on—it *had* to go on for my grandparents to make a living. The next morning they left for work as early as usual. My mother could not move from her bed. She was bruised and aching all over, her face swollen from the brutal blows Thinh had delivered. Her eyes were bloodshot, she could barely see. My aunt, De Oanh, decided to stay home to look after her and to defend her from Thinh. The maid sent my aunt to the corner street to buy some ice to ease the swelling. De Oanh sprinted out with an aluminium bucket and joined the queue around the mobile stall. De Oanh stamped her feet with impatience, she stretched her neck, stood on her toes and shouted her order loud and clear: 'A big block, please, no need to shave it! No, no, no need to even break it!' With her bucket full, she nudged her way out when somebody pulled her sleeve. My father was snooping around to inquire about my mother. He had feared that she might be subjected to corporal punishment because she had been caught with a male. He had no doubt about Trinh's physical strength if he had beaten her. De Oanh looked at him, burst into tears and simply ran away. He was disconcerted and followed her.

He shuddered when he saw my mother who covered her face and wept. He ordered De Oanh and the maid to fetch her belongings, leaned down and scooped her out of bed and out of a house where she could not be safe. She was bundled into a trishaw, her clothes thrown over her and the rain curtain dropped down to protect her from view. She was now destined to follow my father, who instructed the rider to take her to the other side of the city.

From the moment my mother left the front door of her parents' house and climbed to the third floor of a tenement on the opposite side of the city, she had sealed her own fate. She was worse than dead to her family, and her parents' love could never defend her from the social disapproval of eloping with a man. The brief time she had spent with him and the fact she still remained a virgin were now irrelevant. Her reputation was irrevocably ruined. Within the sanctions of the Asian culture, my father's spontaneous and chivalrous deliverance of my mother was damaging to her. His action put her in a more terrible predicament than the risk of her being beaten to death by Thinh.

It was of no consolation that the bruises on her body had begun to heal when her survival was senseless. Her pious upbringing meant that she would never accept being a clandestine lover and she promised herself that she would plunge to her death from the third floor if my father attempted to seduce her. He was, however, respectful and retired to his own space. He, too, was confused and trying to make sense of their situation. He continued to go to the office and came back with news of the outside world from which my mother was cut off. She stayed imprisoned behind chipboard walls, which subdivided the floor into four cubicles. Next to her lived an extended family: grandparents, parents and children piled in an area no larger than the size of a caravan. In her windowless box, which received fresh air from an open door on to the verandah, she shunned the world out of shame and fear. My father had told her that her stepbrother Thinh seethed with rage and publicly vouched to hunt them down.

At her parents' house, my mother's departure had repercussions. Her father had fallen sick and was refusing to fight for his health. He pushed away the herbal medicine his wife had bought at considerable expense. His mournful sighs assured her he was beyond cure. He was no longer worried about dying and leaving his wife and young dependent children. The concern over their welfare in a country that did not provide social assistance had been the driving force that had kept him fit despite his old age.

In one year, Nguen's dreams had come undone. My mother, his most beloved daughter, was a disappointment. Of the two sons he had placed in the seminary, the eldest was diagnosed with tuberculosis. Uncle Ho, two years younger than my mother, was thought by the Jesuit Fathers to have the makings of an excellent priest. When they discovered his illness, which in those days was often incurable, they acknowledged that the regimented religious life was too demanding on him. They were the first to advise him to renounce his vows and kept him at the seminary to receive proper French medical care. After his convalescence, they proposed to train him to teach in their school.

Xuang, the other son, was struggling to stay an intern. One out of three children dedicated to the service of God was a poor average, and it was a sign to Nguen that he was being rebuked by the Almighty. During his last years, he repented for all sorts of imagined sins he thought he had committed in the past.

He was powerless to resolve the animosity between his wife and Thinh. She deplored her stepson's plan to avenge his honour when his time could be better spent helping her at the shop. Nguen was terrified of being rejected by his rebellious son, and no matter how bad tempered the latter was, Thinh's constant presence at his bedside gave him comfort. During his illness, he gave in to self-pity, complaining about God's rejection and about the loss of my mother. In his weakest moments, he wished to know where she was and what had become of her. Thinh banged his fists on the mattress, furious at the remnants of his father's love for an undeserving daughter. 'She is dead! If she is still alive, I will make sure I will kill her when I lay my hands on her and her lover!'

Across the other side of the city, far from Thinh's malice, my father took matters into his own hands. One morning he invited my mother to dress up and said simply, 'Will you marry me?'

Without further ado, they walked to the registry office. A signature was a far cry from the usual pomp of marriage in their respective families but to my mother, it was a grand gesture of good faith and decency from my father. Without the white veil and the celebration, a marriage on paper was the most honourable move under the circumstances. She allowed herself to accept her destiny. However, she could not help for the love and especially the gratitude she felt for my father to be tainted by guilt.

The symptoms of my mother's pregnancy made them realise that they could not live indefinitely hidden from society. For their own sanity and for the sake of the baby, they had to face the world. My mother had to overcome the embarrassment of being a wife who had not been married with appropriate tradition. She packed and left the cubicle, which had been her first conjugal home. Although it had the appearance of a jail, it had been a shelter. In hindsight, she would look back and remember it as a cosy place where she and my father were at their happiest and most united.

15

The Year of the Rat

My grandfather's acceptance of my parents' unconventional marriage was surprisingly liberal. Furthermore, he suggested my father bring my mother home. Grandma was reserved; she would have liked a proper wedding for her eldest son. She harboured some resentment against the Nguens and had not met my mother to decide whether she liked her or not. She was astonished that my mother was less good-looking than she had somehow imagined. For my father to write love letters, she had visualised a great beauty. My mother's appeal is not skin deep. Her virtues are hidden; they have to be brought out to shine at the appropriate time.

Dad introduced her to a gathering of three generations around a pot of hot tea. Reama represented the eldest, next were my grandparents and down the line were my father's siblings, standing by the kitchen door and giggling at my mother. Granddad's thoughts were lost in the smoky rings he puffed from his pipe. From her bunk, Reama invited my mother to move from the floor and sit next to her. Her request posed a delicate problem. In Asian etiquette, where a person sits reflects the rank of seniority. In answer to Reama's order, my mother risked offending her mother-in-law, who was resting on a lower stool. She had to improvise quickly—instead of hoisting herself onto the bunk, she knelt on the floor and kowtowed to Reama without undermining Grandma. This little incident was the first in an ongoing game of family politics.

She worked hard to win their approval but naturally avoided the chores which she knew could win Grandma. The altar to the Tan Chau patriarch had to be lit regularly and offerings of food had to be placed for his spirit. My mother's Catholic background discouraged the practice of ancestral cult worship, which was considered a direct offence against her God. Grandma, unaware of this taboo, had asked her to ensure that the patriarch was not deprived of attention. It took a lot of time before she performed this task and only God knew of the penitence she privately gave herself to alleviate her conscience from this sin.

She and Dad stole privacy by going out some evenings. They strolled in front of the royal palace and he talked longingly of a brighter future when they could have a proper home of their own. Asian families pride themselves on keeping many generations under the same roof. My father was duty-bound to live with his parents; a time would be right for him to move out later. He made her promises of happiness.

My brother Vandy was born in 1948, in a private hospital in Rue Bouloche. The thirty maternity rooms were owned and run by Dr Duong Diem, the only son of rich Vietnamese landowners who lived on the other side of Prek Dek. They had been acquainted with Dara in the old days. Young Diem and my grandfather were village boys who left their respective villages to study more or less at the same time. Their friendship was formed when Diem came back from France a medical doctor. He and my grandfather regularly met to play cards.

My brother Vandy could not have been in better medical hands. Nineteen forty-eight was the year of the Rat—not a good year to be born into if one believes in the Vietnamese horoscope—worse still if the baby was born at night, since rats have to work to find their food in the dark. It was precisely during the small hours of the morning that my brother decided to arrive. And so it was predicted that Vandy, once grown up, would similarly need to work very hard to make a living.

Vandy seemed to know from the start that the odds were against him, considering the superstitious circumstances of his birth. He screamed his way into life and refused to feed properly. Fortunately he had a number of things going for him. He was a boy, a valued gender, especially as the eldest. He had good looks, and without much subtlety, everyone in my father's family claimed that he took after them. He had the fairest complexion and my mother said that people in the streets sometimes mistook him for being French and her for being his nanny. He suffered every complication that babies do: colic, not sucking properly, jaundice, rashes, poor sleeping habits and chronic diarrhoea. My mother could not remember a time when he enjoyed complete good health. His abdomen was swollen so he resembled a grossly malnourished infant and it seemed that the thin layer of flesh around his navel was transparent—one could almost see through to his internal organs. Had it not been for French medication and the kind guidance of Doctor Diem, Vandy would not have survived.

For support my mother fell back on her religious faith, with regular trips to the church. She sold her gold chain, deposited all the money she possessed in the box in exchange for the candles she would light. The priest who was her family's confessor and had once been hers objected to her presence. She pleaded with him for the right to worship and to be regarded not as an estranged Catholic but a stranger. She was not asking to be absolved for her wrongs, nor was she insulting his congregation by attending mass and mixing with them. She begged to be allowed to pray in front of the statue of the Virgin Mary when nobody was around. The priest swayed his head and walked away. He often found her lonely and crouching with hands clasped, her head bowed to hide her face inside his empty church. She had been excommunicated for failing to marry a man of her faith and for not bringing him into the Catholic flock. She was denied all sacraments, she could not go to confession, and she could not receive communion.

Devastating though it was for her, the Church's rejection forced her to open a direct dialogue with her God. She came out of all this a far stronger believer.

The priest, who usually ignored her, waited one day to talk with her and into her mind leaped the wildest hope. Perhaps he was about to announce a change of heart, which would grant her the privilege of remaining a Catholic. Alas, the priest conveyed a message from her father—she ought to see him soon, before he died. She shivered at the thought of her half-brother Thinh while she longed desperately to comply with her father's last wish.

My father supported her decision; he was keen to mend relations, and was sure that Grandfather Nguen on his deathbed must be in a mood of forgiveness and reconciliation. He insisted on accompanying my mother, but she convinced him that she needed to prepare her father to receive him.

At the back door of her parents' house, her sister De Oanh threw her arms around her waist and cried. Grandma Nguen appeared, her arms outstretched and with tears rolling down her cheeks. She embraced my mother, gulping for breath between sobs and she led her to the kitchen. While the priest was giving my grandfather his last rites, she told her daughter the latest news. She had been evicted from the coffee shop. With my grandfather's bad health, it had been impossible for her to run the business and meet the rent. The landlord had confiscated the furniture and kitchen equipment when payments were overdue. For the time being, she survived on the sale of her jewellery. Piece by piece, her rubies, gold and jade were sacrificed at a third of the market price and at the rate she was losing them, her two younger daughters would have nothing left to wear on their wedding days. Grandma Nguen believed it was mandatory to adorn the bride and avoid loss of face. On a more hopeful note, she declared that Ho, who was cleared from tuberculosis, would finish his studies, earn money and help out with the family. For the moment, she had much to thank her other younger son, Xuang, for his vital contribution.

A year before, Uncle Xuang had left the seminary—yet another disappointment to Grandfather Nguen. None of the children he gave to the Church stayed in the Order; it was beyond doubt that God had refused his best gifts. He understood that in loving Him, he had to pay a tribute of personal sacrifice. Nobody had told Grandfather that since the Crucifixion, God never meant anyone to offer a life for His cause. Uncle Xuang was in his second year at the seminary when he found it hard to conform. He said to me many years later, that he had a natural appetite for the good things in life, which I had spontaneously imagined were unrealistic, but were indeed quite modest. Sleeping long hours and eating regular good meals were to him the utmost luxuries. It was heart-breaking that these simple dreams were seldom realised in his childhood. The Jesuit fraternity was prepared to overlook his difficulties, but they gave up on him when he disclosed his adolescent wet dreams. He was so honest he confessed to every private thought, as he thought this was what was expected of him, and in lieu of praise, his confessor consulted with his superior and the Principal told him he was not meant to become a priest.

Xuang was thrown out in much the same abrupt manner my mother had been sent from her convent. His suitcase was put in a rickshaw and he was packed off home. He found his father sick; his mother unable to make a living and his eldest sister (my mother) already married against the family's will. He was thirteen, and although he expressed the wish to study, he had to get a job. He became a junior assistant in a French pharmacy where he worked overtime to earn more money which he paid the senior salesman to give his father regular injections. In those days, antibiotics were commonly seen as the magic cure for any serious medical conditions, if one could afford them. My grandfather was not properly diagnosed and months of this arbitrary treatment proved futile. Nguen got worse.

The priest had finished 'preparing him to meet God' and my

mother was told to go upstairs. Upon entering his room, he motioned her closer. He could not speak, only his moist eyes spoke of his pain and my mother could hear the wheezing of his chest. She sought his forgiveness, repeating her request without waiting for the answer he was too weak to give. All he could do was press her hand.

In the presence of the priest and Thinh, she explained that she had to go and would return in a few hours to be with him. 'You are not going anywhere,' her half-brother hissed. He claimed that my grandfather had given him the power to execute his will, which was apparently designed to force my mother back into the family. The priest confirmed that her civil marriage was not recognised by the Holy Church, therefore it did not exist, and she did not need a divorce to leave my father. From the religious angle, she had 'committed a sin of the flesh, her excommunication could be revoked if she sinned no more'.

Mum could think only of my sick brother Vandy; she sprang to her feet and ran downstairs. Outside the house, my father was beseeching someone to let him in. He was carrying my brother, who was due for his feed. In the days that followed, my mother, terrified of Thinh, waited at a distance from her parents' house, nursing my brother in her arms. She waited to catch the sight of her father's coffin being carried to his resting place.

One day, the small procession finally made its exit from her old home and slowly disappeared from the opposite end of the lane. From afar, she said goodbye to her father whom she had loved and whom she felt she had betrayed. He had perhaps forgiven her, but my mother found it impossible to forgive herself and it was still hard for her to mention his name without a profound sadness. I remember well All Souls Day every year, come rain or shine, when I used to sit with her at the foot of his tomb. In the light of the myriad candles around us, I watched her withdraw into the past. I cried to see her so far away. I could not guess it then, but I know now that grief, especially that tinted with remorse, can never leave the soul in peace.

16

Around the Dragon

History would remember 1952 to be the year when the Cambodian king made his first hesitant steps toward gaining full independence for his country. It was achieved through diplomatic manoeuvres without the spilling of blood. No-one, including the French, suspected Norodom Sihanouk would possess the political ingenuity to achieve independence. He had earned the reputation of 'playboy' and organised endless parties, indulged in music, produced films in which he starred, and devoted much time to the conquest of women. Besides his legitimate wife, who was his first cousin, he had many other amorous attachments and it was speculated that he had over thirty children. He was forced to take his political role more seriously when his throne was shaken by the steady growth of the left-wing Democrats. Deliberately republican, the Democrats gathered massive support and had just won the majority of votes in the 1951 elections. A month after their victory, they invited the king's number one enemy, Son Ngoc Thanh to make a triumphant return from exile. For Thanh, it was the second time back in power. On 29 October, a long motorcade of three hundred cars made its way through a crowd of half a million people. They lined the streets from the airport to the city to welcome him back. Sihanouk had to react quickly to this man's dangerous popularity.

In September the same year, the Cambodian Communist Party was founded. It called itself the 'Khmer People's Republic Party', abbreviated as KPRP; its members are nowadays better known under the name of 'Khmer Rouge'. The Cambodian Communists, trained at this initial stage by their Vietnamese counterparts, the Vietminh, succeeded in controlling perhaps a sixth of Cambodia. They extracted from the rural population a contribution of funds, which was estimated to exceed the national budget. Despite their growing strength, the immediate worries for Sihanouk lay in the city where the Democrats held important positions in the National Assembly.

In mid-June 1952, the king staged a coup that was aimed to kill two birds with one stone, hurting both Republicans and Communists in one blow. He was able to get rid of the Democrats, dismissing them and their leader Thanh from office and nominated himself Prime Minister and formed a new Cabinet. In response to the students' protests in France and in Cambodia, Sihanouk justified the necessity for his coup d'état by claiming that the nation was under Communist threat. He addressed directly the mass of peasants who represented the broadest base of support for the monarchy. In his speech to them, he promised to deliver independence to Cambodia within the next three years. The royal crusade for independence had just begun.

In February 1953, after entrusting government affairs to his father Suramarit and to Penn Nouth, Sihanouk went to Paris where he sought from the French President, Vincent Auriol, full autonomy to combat the Communist threat. Auriol waved him off and advised him to return home. Instead, Sihanouk proceeded to Montreal in April, then on to Washington where he had a meeting with John Foster Dulles. An interview with the New York Times achieved the desired publicity sympathetic to his mission. The American media embarrassed France for preaching freedom while holding other countries prisoners of colonial rule.

After three weeks in Japan in his quest for independence, Sihanouk went home with no decisive results. As a last resort, he appealed again directly to his people and called them to arms. All the Cambodians, including those who were engaged in the French colonial forces, deserted and responded to the royal command alongside hundreds and thousands of civilians. The response to the king's plea forced the French to take Sihanouk more seriously and to reconsider his request for freedom.

Cambodia officially celebrated its first independence day on 9 November 1953. Both the Communists and the Democrats, who had also promised to fight for independence, and having failed to deliver, were eclipsed. For the rest of the decade, Sihanouk, after abdicating in favour of his parents in order to participate more actively in the running of his government, would rule unopposed.

Nineteen fifty-two was the year of the dragon. Among the twelve animals, which form the twelve-year lunar cycle, the dragon is supposedly the undisputed supreme birth sign. Most married couples time themselves to produce a child, preferably a male, to bear its mark. The infant, they believe, will grow to enjoy a prosperous life. Every twelve cycles, the dragon is endowed with a shining crown, and 1952 was such a year. As if to further manifest its importance, its arrival is normally announced by winds and floods. Coincidentally, 1952 began with torrential rains, gusts of winds blew rooftops away, the season of inundation was prolonged, and it promised to throw off the delicate balance of cultivation in a country that survived on its harvests. The wetness brought disease and it was a year of havoc. Or so said my mother.

When she announced that she was expecting, people who wished her well hoped that she was bearing a baby boy. At the first sign of labour, she packed some clothing, tucked my four-year-old brother Vandy inside his mosquito net, and shifted his mattress against the wall to prevent him from falling off the bunk. She whispered to her mother-in-law that she was due, left him in her care and stepped out of the house, her clothes rolled under her arm. It was nine o'clock at night. My father had been absent for a long time, supposedly touring the villages for his agricultural work. Quiet like a shadow, my mother walked unaccompanied to the main street to catch transport. The rain started to pelt down and sounded like pebbles landing on the road. She hailed a pedicab rider and hopping in his trishaw, told him to take her to the hospital. She did not bargain her fare for she felt sorry for the man who had to work late in such appalling weather. This total stranger who seemed to share the same loneliness she felt touched her strangely. She paid him generously and did not wait for the change; he looked at the money and before he could thank her, she had rushed through the hospital door.

She checked into a small room where a single light cast the shadow of the bed on the tiled floor. It was the same maternity hospital where my brother Vandy had been born. Dr Diem gave her a fatherly greeting, and before he ran to the delivery room to attend to a screaming patient, he shook his head in disapprobation: 'Women! They should try discretion in labour as in love!'

With little fuss to my mother, who restrained from making a sound, especially after she heard the good doctor's comment, I came at five in the morning. To compensate for not being a boy as many had wished me to be, I was healthy and undemanding.

While my mother claimed that my gender did not bother her, I remember her sighing at times, 'If only you were a boy, the Dragon's luck would have its full benefit. What a pity you are a girl instead!' Her first reaction to my gender was clouded by another superstition. Since my sister Virath had died a few weeks before I was supposedly conceived, she was told that another girl born soon after the previous daughter's death could well be the reincarnation of the deceased, in which case I would follow the same fate.

The first opportunity she found herself alone with me, she proceeded to examine me very closely, trying to detect in me any resemblance to my sister. She sighed with relief: Virath was a beautiful baby, fairer and much prettier. I was quite the opposite, with my wrinkled darker skin and bold head. I was not a spring blossom by any definition, and far less a rose—the flower that came to symbolise Virath.

My mother had recurring dreams of an old lady appearing without fail during each of her pregnancies. This woman made her a gift of ginger and according to my mother's interpretation, ginger was my brother Vandy's birth symbol—bitter and hot to the taste but a very necessary condiment.

Vandy's existence has since been explained in terms of this silly ginger root. When he was disobedient, Mum would exclaim, 'What can I expect? He is as bitter as ginger!' Before Virath was born, the same old lady appeared in my mother's dream and gave her a single rose. My sister lived up to her symbol, she was pretty and my uncles and aunts used to fight over the privilege of nursing her.

I was supposed to be a bunch of Chinese chives, dark green stems with a hint of tiny white flowers on each tip. My mother assumed beforehand that I was not going to be a boy because flowers were usually indications of a girl. She knew too that I was not going to be pretty because the chive flowers could never be classed as beautiful. However, my mother was pleased because the herbs she saw in her dream are sweet to eat and she found solace in this single thought. To be doubly sure I was not Virath's reincarnation, she continued to observe my physical development until she was convinced I was a totally different entity.

The next day, Uncle Chea, then in his early teens, was sent to inquire about our welfare and to bring news back home to my grandparents. He gave me a glance and decided that I was not worthy of his esteem. He had been very fond of my sister and had felt responsible for her death. Before she died, he had brought back an owl from a hunting trip to show off. Like the banshee who wails in the Irish folklore, the sounds of a night bird, particularly an owl, cooing around a house or

My young aunt Somalee in 1969. This was the last photo we took together before I left Cambodia.

My friend Rhagsmee and me in 1969.

My school, the Lycée Descartes. Photo taken by a friend in 1996, after the war.

My mother preparing her biscuits in 1968.

My brother Vandy and me in 1968. In the background, the pigeon holes, one of my mother's first enterprises.

My grandmother Kim and my aunt Somalee in 1968, on the veranda of their new apartment.

The group of forty Cambodian scholarship holders about to leave Phnom Penh, 1971. I am second from the right.

the stubborn howling of a dog at night are omens of death in the minds of Asians. A dead owl in one's house is worse. Uncle Chea had brought home a very bad omen. The superstitious adults in the family were haunted by it and were awaiting a major disaster to strike, preferably the near neighbourhood and not the family.

Death did occur, almost overnight. My sister contracted breathing difficulties and three days later she died before my mother could get her to the hospital. Mum claimed that 'swollen lungs' had caused Virath's death. In those days, complications in the chest were either attributed to tuberculosis, which took a long time to destroy a person's health, or it was due to 'swollen lungs', which killed swiftly. It was unfortunate that Uncle Chea should have shot the owl and was made to bear the burden of being the harbinger of bad tidings. In all fairness to him, I suggest that his lack of interest towards me was merely a fear of being accused again, should I decide to die too.

He was our very first visitor. The rest of the relatives arrived, if at all, when we had checked out. Congratulations were few, and even my father did not find time to see me until the third day. He stayed briefly and left. Fatherhood had lost its novelty, and quite besides fathering Vandy, Virath and me into existence, he had an active life elsewhere—a de-facto wife who had given him a son one year older than me, and another baby was on the way when I was born. She was to be my half-sister.

My mother was unaware of his extramarital affair at that stage since he had valid excuses for his long and frequent absences, whether they be field researches to the provinces or overseas scholarships. When his unfaithfulness was a reality she could not deny, my mother concealed the hurt, ignored the gossip and concentrated on bringing us up.

Mum refused to listen to women bringing her indirect news of my father's 'other' life, saying it would be condoning them to let them hurt her more and inviting them to criticise my father. She decided that the knowledge of his affairs did not solve any problems; it complicated matters and distracted her and she would not have been able to fake a happy face for our sake. My mother believed that people like to feed on scandals; they pretend to sympathise but gossiped behind one's back. She reflected on the example of a wife who became distressed by her so-called friends' constant reports on her husband's affair. The woman splashed acid on the mistress's face, was sent to jail, turned insane and her children were as good as orphans. Mum learnt a valuable lesson from this story. Very few appreciated her sagacity. Because she did not lend her ears to gossip, she appeared unapproachable and haughty.

Vandy and I were Mum's reasons for keeping her strength. Metaphorically she posed as 'the boat that should sail us to a safer shore'. We grew up covered by her kisses, a very demonstrative love that was not Asian in character. The umbilical cord was never cut and I was able to feel her pain like my own. Other than Vandy and me, she had nobody to whom she could be close. Grandma Kim had enough on her own plate to take on board my mother's problems as well. Besides not having the time, she was in a delicate position whereby she could not sympathise with her daughter-in-law without risking condemnation of her own son. But she was sensitive to my mother's suffering.

One night as the two women were relaxing after a hectic day and the whole household was asleep, she watched my mother lean her back against the wall and look up ruefully to the stars. That night, like many other nights, she saw my mother hoping in vain for my father to come home. She put her hand out and gently stroked my mother's shoulders, and in a measured voice she said, 'Daughter, there is no happiness in this life for women. We are born to bear most of the sadness. I have not yet come across a happily married woman. Your battle is against mistresses. Mine is against social conscience.'

My mother was deprived of support from her own mother. Grandma Nguen, once a widow, half-forgave my mother. Her resentment against Mum for leaving the church and marrying a non-Catholic lost its passionate edge, but she was never eager to encourage visits.

Mum accepted her mother's treatment, and considered it as part of the punishment she felt she deserved.

Although my father was not much of a partner, she was glad that he still upheld his duties. I guessed by that my father kept sending an allowance for us to buy clothes and food. 'Some husbands when they have mistresses forget about their wives and children completely, they leave them to starve in the streets,' my mother would say. Her gratitude was sincere and she always had a ready excuse. My father used to boast that his marriage to my mother was 'a pot of steel, it cannot break'. During my childhood, I stood witness to the series of tests my father put my mother through to verify that statement and the durability of their marriage.

On the third day after my birth, my father came to the maternity hospital with a gift, a beautiful name, kept just for me. In reality it was a legacy from the head monk in Prek Dek, my grandfather's old teacher. The holy man had thought of three names and insisted that they be given to the 'main' children. By this, he implied the children by the first wife to my grandfather's eldest son. What was quite remarkable was the fact that the three names—Vandy, Virath and Vannary—had been chosen well before my parents met and the monk was in no position to guess that my father would eventually have more than one wife.

In stressing main children, it seemed as if he were enlightened by the kind of vision that could only be accorded to the holy men who lived a spiritual life. It seemed he had been able to see into the future and gave three names for the three children my mother would end up bearing. This monk had intended my name to be full of meaning, and among those I can only remember two. Vannary apparently signifies a golden girl and a girl of high social status. I always feel I owe him a kind of debt, for in the years I was groping for a direction in my life and had lost confidence, the name he gave me was a useful source of inspiration. I was told that he died with a smile on his face for his dearest wish—to witness the independence of Cambodia—had come true.

My mother seized the first glimpse of sunshine that burst between the clouds to bring me home from hospital on my seventh day. She missed my brother Vandy and was worried about him. I was laid next to his sleeping spot and he stood constant guard over me, keeping me safe against my toddling two-year-old aunt Touch, the eighth surviving child of my grandparents who had given her a most unimaginative name. Touch means 'small', and this aunt grew to resent the name she was given. She changed it many times as often as one would change clothes. She was two years older than me, born in the year of the Tiger, a beast that was supposed to have negative implications. People avoid brides who bear this birth sign. Touch could not ignore these superstitions and heard them often enough.

Touch's self-esteem had to endure further blows; she was totally neglected by my grandparents. It was generally true that none of my uncles and aunts was raised in a cocoon, and parental neglect was particularly acute by the time Touch arrived. After a large number of children, my grandmother's pregnancy with Touch had been accidental, and unwanted, almost cursed.

Aunt Touch always tried to reach for my mattress and pull it towards the edge of the divan where she could play with me. She must have thought I was a living doll; she liked to poke at my eyes to see me blink or put her index finger down my throat. I claimed little of my mother's time; I was apparently so easy that I did not even need to be burped after my feeds. I was left in a corner of that thick wooden slab which was a bed for Mum, Vandy and myself until nature urged me to be more adventurous—I started to crawl.

My world during the day was then transferred to the floor, because I ran the risk of falling off the elevated bunk. At the other end of the room, which was, among other things, my play area, the clay stoves resting on the ground attracted my attention. The bright amber flames could have burnt me badly many a time, had my brother not been as protective and vigilant as he was. He would rush to catch me by my little feet and pull me backward when I was about to reach for the hot charcoal. In my crawling position, I would collapse on my chin; it would bump the floor and was often terribly bruised. When this happened, my mother would say that I was better off with a dislocated jaw rather than burning to death.

I could talk before I could stand up and walk, which made me a more stimulating playmate to both my brother and Touch. My hair used to be despairingly scarce and my mother attempted to let it grow long. It seemed that having long hair was the only feature that could distinguish me from a boy, so unattractive was I at the age of two.

My mother used to tie my hair in a thin ponytail and added a ribbon to give it an air of prettiness. One day, to her great shock, she came back from the market to find that my ponytail had been bluntly chopped off. She learnt that my aunt Touch had talked me into agreeing to let her be my hairdresser. She promised to spray me with perfume, an original concoction of longan juice, frangipani flowers and her urine. My mother detected a trace of malice in Touch but contained her fury. I smelt putrid and had to be scrubbed. I had expected my first coiffure to give me great joy in an otherwise monotonous life because 'toys' were an unknown pleasure. Instead of the thrill I had hoped for, I was devastated to see my mother burst into tears and cry louder each time she looked at me. When I had consented to be the subject of a hair trim, I had no idea that hair, especially mine, would take a long time to grow back. I must have been such a pitiful sight that not even fancy ribbons could improve my appearance! My mother had to stick them into place above my ears with homemade rice glue. To this day, my mother refuses to see the humorous side to this incident. Perhaps I should be grateful to my aunt for the healthier, bushier hair that eventually grew back.

17

Vipers in the Nest

We stayed with my grandparents until I was three. My mother, Vandy and I were like a branch grafted to their household, and this arrangement, reserved for official wives and their children, allowed us a sense of privilege and a false security. It mattered that society could not discount the three of us for being less than my father's 'legitimate family'. My mother relied heavily on the importance of this notion of 'legitimacy'; it enabled her to hold on and to forgive my father for the affairs he continued to have.

By force of circumstances, we were complying with the Asian ideal, which gathers many generations under the same roof. It looks good to the outside world. Beyond the appearance of unity, the claustrophobic atmosphere in such a household inevitably breeds frustration, jealousy and resentment. It became more obvious when Duck's Feet returned to Phnom Penh after completing his French Baccalaureate in Saigon. Regarded as being accomplished—first, to have reached this level, and second, to graduate from the prestigious school of Chasseloup Laubat— he nourished the ambition to attend the Sorbonne University in Paris. It was costly and my grandfather passed over his request. To pay for one of

his sons' private studies in France, my grandfather must formally agree
for the Cambodian government to automatically deduct one-third of his
monthly salary and he considered the expense unreasonably high and
unfair to the rest of the family. My father softened the blow for Duck's
Feet and told him the reasons behind the refusal to let him study
abroad.

My uncle did not plead his case. A week later he overdosed with
sleeping tablets. His stomach was pumped at the emergency unit in
hospital where the medical team kept him under observation for three
days. A terrible silence reigned at home; Granddad sulked and Reama
fanned herself and sighed. She awaited a reaction from my grandfather
about the attempted suicide, but he sat and smoked, looking away.
Having checked out of hospital, Duck's Feet returned home on my
father's arm. Grandfather made a slight movement to indicate that he
should sit. He told him to prepare for his immediate trip, rested his
pipe by his bed, turned his back, and went to sleep.

Reama, who had heard his words, banged her fan repeatedly to
wake him up. She smirked and exclaimed out loud. 'Ugh! France! To
study what?'

My grandfather, clearly annoyed, sat up and said, 'If he wanted to
study that badly, and he was prepared to die for it, he might make a
success of his life. It reminded me that I, too, wanted the same thing. To
achieve it, I had to go a world away!'

Within a month, Duck's Feet flew to Paris, taking with him a small
fortune. Grandmother had sold some of her precious stones, my father
his most cherished and newest acquisition, a Canon camera, which he
had saved his last pennies to buy while he was studying in America. My
grandfather had organised for the regular transfer of funds. There were
many expenses: airfare, books, pocket money, winter wardrobe, enrolment and boarding fees at the university. The amount was astronomical
by Cambodian standards, and the figure was kept a secret for fear of
arousing jealousy. Some of the younger brothers and sisters were old

enough to work out that Duck's Feet had just pinched the biggest slice of the cake.

After the first letter, mail from him arrived every six months, once in May and then in December, vague and brief. Invariably, he wrote of irrelevant things, of spring in Paris, of snow in winter and he sent good wishes to us for Christmas and the New Year. With the exception of my father, nobody understood what he was writing about. My grand-mother had never heard of Christ or Christmas, neither did she care to increase her general knowledge. She would have liked more down-to-earth news: her son's health, his performance and when he would finish his studies. The course my uncle was supposedly undertaking was also unclear. News from Paris became more and more infrequent.

Duck's Feet's journey to France was equal to being sent to heaven, and his lack of correspondence was like ingratitude. My father was initially in favour of his brother's trip and volunteered to part with a tenth of his personal salary to go towards his studies. While his generosity was genuine, he also felt it seemed worthwhile paying a small premium for Duck's Feet's sake. One day, the latter would be in a position to earn good money with a good degree. He would help my father and therefore help the family at large. My grandfather was getting old and there were many under-age brothers and sisters who would become my father's direct responsibility in the future.

But my father began to doubt Duck's Feet. As more young Cambodian males now had the opportunity to study abroad through private means or scholarship, few came back with any sound academic achievements. Instead, they proudly paraded down the plane steps with a white European wife. Amorous conquests of that nature were becoming popular and my father prayed that his brother would not marry a foreigner. A French girl would not condone her husband supporting an extended family.

My aunt Tam was particularly bitter over Duck's Feet's luck. She was left to a life in the kitchen while he was able to impose his choice on the family. She did not at first show her grudges outwardly, but her malice and bitterness grew in time.

'Duck's Feet's suicide', she said, 'was a joke and my grandfather fell for it. If he meant to terminate his life, he should have thrown himself in the Mekong River, hung himself in a deserted place or if he preferred poison, the way to surely die was to swallow acid. Sleeping pills? Whoever takes sleeping pills never dies! They always get saved in time! How could Duck's Feet believe that he could sleep to his death in a crowded house like my grandfather's without somebody getting suspicious?' Tam's jealousy poisoned her heart. Secretly, she was pleased that Reama also voiced her thoughts from the time my uncle stopped sending news. My grandmother did not dare to show she missed Duck's Feet.

Leng, another son, had left home when he was hardly sixteen. According to Reama, he was highly strung, fearless and disrespectful, mostly to her. They hated each other. She could abuse him openly because of her position and influence over Grandfather, but Leng, in his place as a grandson, had to control his temper, especially when my grandfather was home. Reama regularly complained to my grandfather, who never seemed to punish Leng. Their clash was doomed to come to a head and it did.

Leng had the chore of taking his youngest brother, Ali, to school. They were sitting down for lunch when Ali wished to be taken to his afternoon classes early so he could play marbles. He ignored Leng's request to finish eating and started to cry, which made Reama interfere. Leng threw down his rice bowl and chopsticks, wiped his mouth with his sleeve and told his brother to hop on the bike. Ten minutes later they both walked back home, Leng carrying his bike on his shoulder, its front wheel bent in half and the brother limped in tow, blood pouring from his nose, sobbing loudly as they entered the door. Leng had gone downhill at full speed aiming at a tree to teach his brother a lesson.

Reama, who saw them come in, shouted frantically. In the midst of the uproar, Leng went to the kitchen and came back to the front room with a knife, which he stabbed on the timber bench, missing Reama by an inch.

'Would you please stop yelling?' he said. 'If you don't, I will be glad to put a hole in your leg!'

Horrified, furious but very frightened, Reama froze. She waited for Grandfather to come home and insisted that Leng be punished. Leng, predicting his father's wrath, packed, hugged his mother and disappeared. He could not have met a more sudden death. His name from that day was not to be mentioned in front of the elders.

With two of her sons gone, my grandmother was distraught to find herself expecting again. Her pregnancy was veiled in prudish concealment—she was in her forties, and embarrassed people should know that she was still sexually active. Contrary to custom, she prayed for a girl. Grandfather, under Reama's influence, believed in the prediction by a respected fortune teller that another boy would bring down the family. The pressure was on to produce a girl. My grandparents already had five sons, and according to superstition, five sons are considered 'five princes' and they are good luck. More than this number, the sons become the source of evil. Granddad reminded me of Henry VIII, who thought that his wives were responsible for the gender of his children. Life was kind for a change, and my aunt was born. My father was afraid that his youngest sister might be given a random name, so he gave her the beautiful name Somalee. She was the apple of my grandfather's eye. Never before had he shown such affection and close attention to any of his children growing up. She brought an immediate change in Grandma's life. My grandfather treated her more kindly for being the mother of a beloved and 'lucky' child.

With Somalee's arrival, my grandfather realised that his house was overcrowded. It was high time my mother moved out. My father took advantage of a small house owned by the Directorate of Agriculture. Less than one kilometre away from the centre of Phnom Penh, it shared a fence with the Ministry of Information and all day long, the daily news was broadcast hourly in two languages—French and Cambodian. In between, chamber music and the monotonous sounds of the Cambodian royal orchestra blared from loudspeakers above our roof.

It was in this house that my small world crumbled when my mother fell ill. She had a miscarriage with serious complications and had to be hospitalised. My brother and I went to visit her just before she was scheduled for surgery. Her room was crowded with people, her limbs were tied and a nurse was forcing a mask over her pale face. Forty years ago, patients had to inhale a dose of ether to knock them unconscious before the operation. Young though I was, I could tell that things were very wrong. To see my mother fastened to a bed and somebody bending over her seemingly to hurt her made me hysterical and I screamed. Vandy begged me not to cry while he was crying himself. That was the only visit we were allowed.

Aunt Tam came to mind us and Dad came to see us often, bringing biscuits and toys. The biscuits he halved, and I nibbled at the crumbs, cautiously rationing them for the days ahead. My brother finished his quickly and conned me into giving him some of my share.

I was also given a big, naked, baby doll with blue eyes that closed when she lay down; my brother had a yellow truck, detailed and solid. Dad paid for my doll but Vandy's toy was a miniature of bigger models he received free from French firms, which manufactured heavy machinery. He had a collection of the samples in his office because his job was to determine which to choose and buy for the Directorate of Agriculture. Vandy's truck was a model of a real one, it was virtually unbreakable, the paint could get scratched, the steel panels could dent with his rough handling, but not much else could happen to it.

I could not say the same for my toy. After a few short days of bliss playing with his truck, Vandy's curiosity turned to my fragile doll. He wanted to discover how her eyes could open and shut. He pulled her head off to see the inside through the neck and he pushed her glass eyes in until they snapped. I found my doll decapitated, her face blinded with two large holes. I held my tears just in time, for I remembered what my aunt Tam had repeatedly told us.

My brother and I cried a lot, especially at night and we kept each other from falling asleep. We consoled each other for it was the time we missed Mum the most. Aunt Tam had run out of sweet words and she made up stories, which hit at the core of our fear. Aiming at me, who was more prone to tears, she said, 'Do you know what happens to children if they stay up when it gets dark outside? Female ghosts, the ones with extremely long tongues and hair down to their feet, appear. They drop their tongues down on little children's heads and lick them bald. The following night, they come back, and when there is no hair to lick, they start eating inside the skull.'

This story scared me into pretending to sleep early and Aunt Tam could then go to sleep herself. To stop us from crying, she added, 'I know that you miss your mother. But if you cry for her while she is still alive, it brings her bad luck. One should only cry for the dead.'

Just in case my brother and I should argue or fight, here was her preventative method: 'When you show that you don't love each other, God will punish you by taking your mother away.'

Aunt Tam could not imagine the impact her stories had on me. When I discovered my decapitated doll, anger tightened my throat but I suffocated my tears. Instead of letting them roll down on my cheeks, I felt them inside my chest and behind my eyes. I shut them, saying urgently to myself, 'I cannot cry, I cannot be upset with my brother.' I was convinced my mother's life depended on my good behaviour. Her coming home was dependent on my being a good girl, and from that time I believed subconsciously that I was responsible for my mother's wellbeing. I was nearly four years old.

Aunt Tam stayed on while Mum convalesced and completely recuperated. There was no indication when she would return to my grandparents. Mum did not urge her because it would seem that she wanted to get rid of her. It was more diplomatic for either my father or my grandmother to suggest it. Grandmother seemed to cope without Tam's help. When Dad did come home, it was never for long enough for the subject of Tam's leaving to be raised. My mother was starting to understand that Dad had waited for an opportune moment to move Tam from his parents' house and that he intended for his sister to now live permanently with us. My mother's sickness had been a convenient way of precipitating the move.

'Tam came to look after you and the two children,' was a statement I often heard from Dad, a reason for the three of us to show her eternal gratitude. Dad would insist to my mother that life owed Tam amendments. 'She has had a raw deal. She was asked to sacrifice herself, and I have to make things right for her.'

Part Three **THE LAST GENERATION**

18

Primary School

When I was four, Mum thought I was ready for school. She had sent my brother at six, and because of the problems he had had adjusting, she was told that she had kept him at home for too long. Mum did not want to make the same mistake with me. French parents sent their children to school before they turned five, but nobody in Cambodia understood why this was so. During World War II in France, men were conscripted and women took their places in the workforce and so their schools admitted children from an earlier age. The necessity imposed by war was the norm in France, and the trend was imported to Cambodia.

Although four years older, Vandy was only two school years ahead of me. He used to wag school by climbing over the school gate and crossing the small lane to go home. The first time it happened, the school was in a sheer panic, and the teacher contacted my father. In those days, Dad's office was in the vicinity of the residential staff quarters and he stormed home and found Vandy playing around Mum. He pulled Vandy away and beat him for causing panic to the teachers and for putting Dad in a situation where he had to apologise to them.

I could not tell exactly how many times my brother had to endure these punishments before he accepted staying at school.

One beating I can clearly recall happened on a Wednesday morning. My father suddenly showed up at home and there Vandy was. Dad jumped to the conclusion that he was skipping classes again, undid his belt and lashed my brother. I was crying, Vandy was pleading that he had a day off, and Mum was arguing Vandy's case, but the belt was whipping the air and cutting into the flesh. The noises from our house triggered one of Dad's colleagues from the office nearby to come to our door.

'Why the hell are you beating your son?' the old man inquired.

My father replied in one word. 'Laziness!'

The stranger went on to ask, 'Lazy for what?'

Letting go of my brother, my father said, 'Too lazy to go to school generally and especially for not going today.'

Our neighbour moved forth, seized the belt from Dad and hissed, 'For your information, today is Wednesday and there is no school as far as I know.'

Vandy made friends who had the same inclination for playing and little time for studying. He used to fill his school bag with hundreds of marbles of all sizes and colours, which he had won during the day, leaving no space in his satchel for his books, pens and pencils.

'Where are they?' Mum would ask.

He would say, with a dash of pride in his eyes, hoping that she could see things his way, 'But nobody steals books! It is safer to keep the marbles in the bag!'

They would retrace his steps back to school, and he had to scale the wall and rummage around the playground, trying to figure out where he had left those books.

Around the table in the lounge, Mum would go over Vandy's daily work with him. He would stare blankly at her, and she knew that he had not registered anything that he was supposed to have learnt. He was always way behind his class. She scolded, she sweet-talked, she cajoled, she cried and sometimes she got carried away and smacked. They both cried; she, despairing that he could be so irresponsible, he, despairing because he never made her happy. I, too, would cry, in empathy with Mum.

Once a month, a report was issued and my father made a point of coming home punctually that day. He would make my brother pay for bringing home bad results and my mother would have to pay for bringing him up the wrong way.

Dad was like a tornado that scooped things up in his path and sent them flying around. After he exhausted himself, he would march into the kitchen where my Aunt Tam would look busy around the stove. He would give her an affectionate pat and remark that there was no decent food for him.

He shot back into the lounge where Mum was still wiping her cheeks, and snapped, 'So you do not expect me to come home any more, you don't cook for me. It seems that Tam does the cooking for you now!' He reminded her that Tam was not a housemaid. If he had any steam left, he would embark on another scene.

Somewhere from a distance I would hide, I would look. Sometimes I ran to my bedroom and scurried under my blankets, burying my head under my pillow. Whether I could hear or see, it made no great differ-ence. My mind could guess what was going on and I took it all in. I was too young to ask why this was happening. But I was at a stage when children are sponges, and absorb all the emotions that surround them. In that house, I soaked up the tears and felt completely battered, as though each blow directed at others had been meant for me. Beyond the hurt, I was terrified.

I had a recurring dream of falling toward an immense tunnel; it sucked me into its endless pitch of darkness. I had to fight against the sensation that I was totally out of control, and screamed in my sleep to bring myself back to consciousness. I would wake up in a bed moist with my own perspiration and, without fail, the mattress wet with urine. I did not shake off this bed-wetting until I was twelve.

My artwork conveyed my fear of the dark pit. The first year I attended prep, the classroom was furbished with tall easels, pots of watercolours, brushes and coloured pencils. Most of the children came from diverse ethnic backgrounds—French, Chinese, Cambodian, Vietnamese and Indian—and after a preliminary lesson to teach us to say a few new French words in the morning, we were left to draw or paint. The teacher casually walked around and peeped over our shoulders, smiling and nodding. I would think hard but invariably centred my white sheet with a black dot, and circled around and around it with more black paint until it was filled with shades of grey and black. My French teacher would scratch her chin at the repetitive theme of my works; she unpinned another child's painting and showed it to me to give me some inspiration. Pointing her finger at the vivid colours, I guessed she indicated that I should produce similar vibrant pictures.

I was trapped in this black hole as if I were in a secret world. I felt different from the other children for I did not learn to laugh, talk, relate or make friends and see the world with normal eyes. I remained aloof in the playground during recess, leaning against a column and ate my bread roll that Mum usually spread with tinned milk. As a treat she would sometimes put in a tiny square of milk chocolate instead.

The boys preyed on me like a wounded bird. They grouped at a distance and charged in my direction, knocking me over. If there was a teacher on playground duty, he or she acted as if it had been an unintentional accident. I would get up, my knees once scraped to the caps, for which I still have the scars. I never cried, but waited for the bell to ring to go back into the sanctuary of the classroom. There, I waited until it finally rang for end of school and Mum would collect me at the gate.

My five years in primary school brought me one friend, Sorith, the second youngest daughter of a very large family. Her father was a general medical practitioner, and she exuded joy and self-confidence.

Now and then she invited me to her house, a large brick mansion with an enormous verandah overshadowed by an old and fertile star apple tree. During its fruiting season, we could tiptoe and reach for its fruit. In her street, every house was beautiful; this area was inhabited by successful professionals and businessmen, politically prominent people and foreign diplomats. I was dropped in front of the grand iron gate by my mother, who was too intimidated to wait with me until the chauffeur came to let me in.

Mum's immediate reaction to the size of the house started to draw my attention to Sorith's and my social differences, 'Look at their garage! It is bigger that an average dwelling!' Normally three of the latest models of some imported European vehicles would be parked side by side. Until then I was unaware of how rich Sorith's family was.

What did occur to me, though, was how happy a family could be. Hers was my first glimpse into a world where life could be cheerful and harmonious. Around her lunch table, her parents sat and chatted, her brothers and sisters talked and sometimes argued. Even when they argued loudly, there was no imminent threat of violence. For no obvious reason to them, I could not stop my eyes from filling with tears during the first meal I shared with them. I quickly tried to mask my embarrassment and explained that I was not feeling well.

Sorith's father touched my forehead and said that perhaps Sorith should not have scared me with those earthworms, which she had laughingly thrown at me when I arrived. She had discovered I had a phobia of anything that wiggled with no legs. The deeper secret of my own dysfunctional family and unhappy home life, I never revealed to them.

My relationship with 'Mom' came at a much later date. She was a quiet and reserved girl, but it took a long time before the two of us sorted out the crowd and recognised our similarities in each other. Mom was one of the purest-blooded Cambodians I had met; her ancestry on her mother's side was impeccable. She came from a long line of governors of some northern province who moved to the capital where they became embroiled in politics. Her father was a handsome man with a European air who headed the Department of Forestry, became a Cabinet Minister and briefly the President of the National Assembly before he was posted to Singapore and other parts of the world.

Mom disclosed that she had a half-brother or half-sister. I mentioned that my father had 'other' children, too, but they were not at our school. I was cautioned to avoid her father's other children—it was a loyalty she expected from me, or perhaps she was merely implying that our society should separate itself into two, those who were legitimate and those who were illegitimate. She did not elaborate further other than show me the faces of her half-relations, and there were many. We did not discuss the details of our families, but underneath the broad picture of our respective fathers' extramarital interests, we put ourselves among those who had been cheated.

Before Sorith and Mom, my life at school had been a desperate attempt to be part of a group. I even tried to buy my way in. Lim Eng, who was a very tall girl and four or five years older than the rest of our grade, was the main ring-leader, dictating to her followers whom they could play with and whom they must shun. I gathered courage and showed my eagerness to be a 'friend'. Lim Eng plainly specified the first condition of membership: I had to bring to her a bag of biscuits everyday for two weeks.

I implored my mother to supply me with those biscuits, which she did, but with much resistance. The biscuits were distributed around without including me and after the two weeks, I was told I was 'disqualified'. Lim Eng spared nothing of my feelings by spelling out the criterion of her rejection: I was Vietnamese.

Lim Eng was Chinese—nothing was wrong with that; she was naturalised Cambodian—still nothing wrong with this. Ironically she affected to be more Cambodian than the Cambodians were. Eng's influence over her gang faded in secondary school. Children whom she used to tower over by a full head caught up in height and gained in maturity. The last I care to remember of her was that she had retained one lonely hanger-on; the two had failed one level together and had to repeat.

I could not resist walking past her once and looking her straight in the eye and saying, 'How are you nowadays, Lim Eng?' But instead of my anticipated satisfaction, I felt like a coward; I had aimed far below the belt. I could not forget her, though. Every time I experience rejection and discrimination, her face is projected in my mind's eye.

I disliked school, perhaps as much as my brother did, but I did not show it because I did not want to be an additional problem to my mother. I had to conform to what was expected of me. Besides, I also had the conviction I could not survive the humiliation if my father ever laid a hand on me. I would die first before I gave him a reason to beat me.

I was not bright. As we climbed up to the next grade where the teacher had the reputation of being nasty and strict, I lost a lot of weight through the fear of failure. He was notorious for hitting the tips of fingers for every mistake in spelling and arithmetic, for slouching and for coughing too much. He used to isolate a poor French boy, François, for punishment. François's attire was always untidy. The teacher described his hand writing as 'a scrawl that looked like the traces of a crab's claws on the sand'. He called him to his desk for various unsatisfactory forms of conduct; he would lift François's small body by the collar of his shirt and hang him on a hook. Sometimes François had the cane waste basket over his head, or he had to stand on one leg in front of the class for the full hour. François was a daily scapegoat, and a frightful warning to any of us that we could run the risk of being in his shoes. I did what I could to please the teacher but could not get all my answers correct. Each error in my work meant a stroke of the square steel ruler on the fingers—mine were permanently blue. However, I passed the year. My marks were borderline, but the comments jotted at the bottom of my early scholastic reports, even from the strict teacher, acknowledged my efforts. My father had to credit me for trying my best.

I generally compensated for my academic mediocrity with the neatness of my presentation. I decorated the capital letters on new paragraphs, ended each lesson with not a mere line across the page, but some ornate geometrical design. I was a slow reader at the start, and when in higher grades in senior school, I struggled with geometry, chemistry and physics. Despite respectable results in algebra, I could not escape the sarcasm of the subject teacher. He was a huge man who had arrived from France and had chosen two years of teaching overseas in lieu of his two years of compulsory military service. The comments he made regarding me were to this effect, 'To you, miss, two and two add up to three!' This would set the whole class laughing at my expense.

My dearest wish was to stay invisible in the chemistry laboratory. By Cambodian standards, our school was the only one that could fund the equipment this subject required. We could conduct experiments to verify a range of formulae and chemical reactions. A trained monkey might have been more capable at making better sense of this discipline than me!

In the beginning of the second semester, in Year Ten, we were handed back the results of some previous test. Our teacher, whose eyes of the palest grey were emotionless, talked of his disappointment how nobody, even the brightest students, had good marks. He rubbed his hands together and made his way towards my table. He looked at me and said, 'Except you'. He invited me to demonstrate on the board to the class how I was the only one who passed the test. He knew I could not possibly have copied the answers from anywhere. He knew too I had 'accidentally' got them right and it seemed to me that he was determined to prove this and in so doing, rob me of any feeling of triumph I might have. Sure enough, I stood like an idiot in front of the class, a piece of chalk in my hand, hesitating to write a single thing on the blackboard. He uttered a brief laugh, finally took over and told me to go and sit down.

Now looking back at all my years at school, I remain grateful to one teacher, Monsieur Michaud, who was extremely encouraging. He was missing his left index finger. I made an imaginary list of incidents and accidents that might have caused him to lose this finger, from frostbite to mountaineering to perhaps a grenade?

I must have been nearly eleven years old, in Grade Five, my last year in primary school when Monsieur Michaud was my teacher. I was still trying to improve my grades. I was fascinated by two students, a boy by the name of Tia Ong To and a girl called Seng Bonga. The two of them competed for first and second places and they excelled across the curriculum. I dreamt of being brilliant like them in my next life.

Meanwhile, in my present life, Monsieur Michaud gave me a lot of encouragement. The day we had to attend the end-of-year prize-giving ceremony, a surprise was in store for me. A crowd of people came— important politicians, and sometimes the king or the Prime Minister was invited to distribute the prizes. That year, His Altesse Royal Prince Sisowath Sirik Matak (Sihanouk's cousin) was the guest of honour. My name was called among the high achievers and I walked in disbelief to the stage where I received from royal hands a small pile of illustrated books. My mother's face beamed with pride. At home, I reread for the thousandth time my results. They were better than my average but in no way good enough to place me third in class, after the two I admired. They had the 'Prix d'Excellence' and I had the 'Prix d'Honneur'.

I met M. Michaud for the last time at a small party, which I had helped to organise before the summer vacation. He invited me to dance the twist to a song by Cliff Richard. As he came to sit next to me, my eyes stared at his hand and his missing finger. I could not help myself from asking 'Why? What sort of accident?' I had to know; it had been nagging me all year.

He said 'Oof! A stupid accident really. I cut myself with an army knife. It developed into gangrene.'

His *adieu*, which marked my leaving junior school, the petit Lycée Descartes, was a fatherly pat on my shoulder and he pronounced a proverb in French, '*Aides-toi et Dieu t'aidera*', help yourself and God will help you. I wished he knew how he had set me on an upward road. A great many things could be attained through perseverance.

19

A Big Extended Family

An attaché of the Australian diplomatic corps in Phnom Penh, Milton Osborne, later turned historian and writer, called my senior school, the Lycée Descartes, a 'school for the elite'. It was impossible for the school to be mistaken for anything less, given its imposing façade and standing uncommonly high at five stories. Situated on a wide street, it was surrounded by other landmarks. Directly opposite was the Hotel Royal, the ultimate Cambodia had to offer wealthy foreign tourists. Diagonally across stood the biggest cathedral in Phnom Penh and in the opposite direction was the small hill, the heart of the city, like the General Post Office in Australian cities, from which point the distance of everything else was calculated.

Lycée Descartes was founded in the early 1950s to cater for the children of French expatriates, diplomats and royalty. It was attached to the centre of Montpellier in France, where important exams such as the Baccalaureate were sent inside sealed envelopes via diplomatic bags to be marked, then sent back to Cambodia. The teachers at the lycée came from France, with the exception of the two who taught the Cambodian language and painting and drawing.

More impressive still was the fleet of Mercedes or Peugeot cars, each with a chauffeur in immaculate uniform and cap, and sometimes a bodyguard waiting to collect the wealthy boys and girls, that stopped at the school. The children were mostly sons and daughters of the high-profile set. One girl changed her jewellery weekly in the five years she was in my class. Such wealth defied my imagination; I could not conceive of it.

Needless to say, my brother and I could not match the social or financial standard of the school's image and it was precisely this image that scared off many parents who wanted to enrol their children. Vandy and I with a few others, whose parents were not easily intimidated by the ostentation, could be classed as the 'circumstantial' mistakes by the school registrar. The year Mum applied for entry for my brother, by a stroke of good luck, there were a few vacancies. However, she left nothing to chance. She compiled a thick mound of documents, and paid for a letter to be suitably worded and typed, and signed by my grandfather with a seal from his office. She had another letter from my father, and a letter of support from his superior who casually mentioned we lived behind the school. Which of the above criteria was most pertinent to our admission, nobody could tell.

My father later used the same enrolment techniques for my two half-brothers and my half-sister, but was unsuccessful, so we were declared extremely fortunate. It seemed an advantage for us to be rubbing shoulders with students who would one day rule Cambodia. My mother was more interested in the solid academic standards the school offered, which was on a par with France. Although a private school, the Lycée Descartes was free, but we had to pay a token fee since the French government covered most of the school expenses.

My mother kept two-thirds of Dad's salary; the remaining third was sliced off to support his second wife and their three children. Dad lived on the money he made from his two other part-time jobs. He was an assistant managing director for a semi-private fishery and canning company, Société de Pêche et de Conserverie, which he helped start and develop, and which was owned by a friend. He designed and supervised the manufacturing of its three ships, each equipped with sophisticated radars to track the schools of fish, huge nets, cool rooms and freezing storage chambers, a large modern kitchen and four luxurious cabins with en suites.

His other part-time job was teaching long-range shooting in a national organisation called Jeunesse Socialiste Royale Khmere. His salary from his main occupation at the Ministry of Agriculture totalled ten thousand riels a month, at that time a considerable amount. The average income for an office worker then was a tenth of his wage. The two-thirds my mother received would have more than sufficed, enabling us to live very comfortably. However, my mother had to care for an unreasonably large family.

It began with our move from the small house behind the Ministry of Information to be next door to Chamcar Mon, the new sumptuous private residence that Prince Sihanouk had built for himself and his last consort, Princess Monique. Our new house belonged to the Ministry of Agriculture. It was located on the west of a fifty-acre block of land. Closest to the entrance gate were the Ministry's main offices and another smaller, charming residential house. To the south of this ministerial property, a row of a dozen townhouses was offered to the families of middle-grade exchange workers from the Philippines. Towards the centre was a workshop and a large depot for heavy agricultural machines. Next to the house meant for us, experimental cocoa trees were planted in neat rows over one acre.

Tucked away like an eyesore was another sort of residential community for the lowest-ranked employees of the Ministry. There was nothing here but sheds of straw, tin sheets, woven palm leaves and rotting timber with no sewerage, running water or electricity. By an extraordinary contrast, the north entrance to the whole ground was guarded at all times. Security was tight because of the expensive machines and more to the point, the Prince was living on the other side of the tall brick fence, reinforced with barbed wire.

Our house had the proportions of a mansion but without grace or luxury. Brick downstairs, timber upstairs, the internal access to the first storey was through a trapdoor. Six generous bedrooms, one lounge the size of a ballroom, a garage for two cars, one bathroom, and an adjacent kitchen were thrown together in a higgledy-piggledy fashion. It was too big for our needs at the beginning, but my father responded by bringing in more people to fill it up. The time had come for him to start showing his traditional duty as the eldest son and the eldest brother.

After Tam, the next member to join our existing family was my cousin Vaan. He was seven or eight when he arrived. I could recall the curiosity Vandy and I felt and our irresistible urge to giggle at his unusual looks. He was a caricature from history. Groomed in the most antiquated Cambodian fashion, Vaan wore a single piece of silk to cover his middle, the rest was bare and powdered with talc. His hair was shaved except for one small spot in the middle at the back, which was allowed to grow long into a curly ponytail. His ankles and wrists were laden with silver amulets and beads and sacred cotton threads. He had long dark lashes, definite black brows arching above a pair of black soulful eyes.

I identified him as the son of Uncle Leng, who laughed when he was angry, the same one who had 'changed into a wild bird and lived in the jungle'. Behind this euphemism, which was often used by my elders to explain his sudden disappearance from family and society, Leng's true story was not magical. When he left my grandparents' house after a serious dispute with Reama, he went into hiding and my father combed the back streets of the capital to herd him into the guardian-ship of a distant relative from Prek Dek who observed orthodox Cambodian customs. In strict traditional propriety, the man imposed a condition, which requested that Leng ordain before he consented to his adoption. In the city, the guardian's respectability depended on this uncompromising adherence to tradition and was enhanced by a golden connection. His eldest sister married Penn Nouth, who, for his loyalty and service to the crown, was ennobled by Sihanouk to the ultimate title of 'Royal Highness', the equivalent of a British knighthood. To a layperson, it was the peak of social acclaim.

Uncle Leng's life took a more complicated turn when he and his guardian's youngest sister fell in love. Their romance was suspected to have transgressed the boundary of acceptance and it became imperative to attenuate the shame of a possible pregnancy. They were hurriedly married. Reama, given her personal aversion to Leng, refused to attend his wedding. My grandfather, out of respect for his mother, was obliged to publicly support her decision. Grandfather's absence during the nuptial ceremonies left my father to assume his role. Although Dad offered a multitude of apologies on behalf of Granddad to explain his absence, it did not minimise the guardian's disappointment.

He highlighted his hurt by saying to Dad, 'It is very irregular and quite unforgivable for your elders, who are neither sick nor deceased, not to come. My most eminent brother-in-law, Penn Nouth himself, believed this humble celebration is worthy of his presence. Doesn't your father think that we are good enough for him to make an effort to come today and bless the newlyweds?'

Dad was at his wits' end. Once a Cambodian accused you of impropriety, there was no known remedy and there was no forgiveness. The after-effects of this slight by Reama and his father against the guardian put Leng in a difficult position. Nothing augured well for him, not even his wedding, which should have been a good day in his life. Leng and his bride were further handicapped by their youth: he was seventeen and she sixteen. His sparse education, his inability to produce an immediate income due to his age reduced him to live with his wife in the guardian's household. With a natural defiance of authority and a combative temperament, Leng had all the ingredients of character and circumstances to doom his marriage. His love for his wife was countered by the stress of financial pressure. After acerbic words said in the heat of anger and some bad feelings, Leng could no longer tolerate the lack of dignity. He packed up and the very month his baby was due, he went away, not to be seen for a very long time. It was likely that he joined the Communist guerrillas or the Khmer Issaraks, both of which were rebels who hid in the forests. The government condemned both groups.

My cousin Vaan grew up in the shadow of an absent father whom he fantasised as a hero, a man with a noble conscience that pushed him to leave wife and child to defend freedom. But within the family, Leng was a skeleton we tried to hide in our closet. Having a political rebel in our midst would pose a stumbling block for my father to build an administrative career.

Leng was an equal embarrassment to his wife's family; they encouraged her to forget the past, get rid of Vaan and start afresh. They beseeched her to give him to our side of the family, and after years of hesitation, she brought him to my father. In an effort to forget that he ever lived, Leng's name was dropped from all our family records and on paper, my cousin Vaan was declared my father's son, and therefore my full-blood brother. In making him officially my mother's offspring, his birth date had to be changed. I was six at the time and Vaan was made younger than me by two years. From the boy of seven he really was, he officially became a four-year-old. His new birth date was changed to the first of April. Of the three hundred and sixty five days in the year, my father had no idea that he had picked April Fool's day. Life had used my father to play its first practical joke on my cousin.

At his real age of eight or his fake age of four, Vaan was accepted at Lycée Descartes. From its preparatory classes—and by being four years older than the other children in his grade—he cruised through junior school.

After Vaan came my Uncle Chea, the owl-shooter and the harbinger of bad news, whose move into our house was approved by my grandparents who were making room for my youngest aunt, Somalee. Chea was pleasant and his stay with us was too short to give us the impression he was intruding. He was seventeen when he came and left a year later to get married. Dad had asked him to hand-deliver a parcel of medicine to a sick old man who was the father-in-law of one of Dad's colleagues. The sick man was a retired governor of the province of Kompong Chnang to the north of Phnom Penh. Under the French Protectorate, his sphere of responsibilities was mainly to sentence people to prison or to the guillotine. He lived out his old age in a three-storey mansion well comforted by the presence of numerous servants. Having lost the use of his legs, he was physically carried everywhere, from his bed to his chair, from his armchair to the car, one of the first Mercedes Benz imported into the country. He was a widower of many years, with two daughters; the elder was married to Dad's colleague and the youngest stayed a spinster by choice until she was twenty-seven. At this age, she saw Chea coming to deliver the medicine and she loved him at first sight. Other than a face faintly scarred by smallpox, Sanee was distinguished looking. Poise, mannerism, speech and grooming suggested that she was a product of money, power and aristocracy. She invited Chea to stay for a meal, and then for the night and another day.

A week later he returned home and announced to my father that he was already engaged. Nothing could be said except to applaud this outstanding match. My grandmother was the only person who ventured a meek objection—the groom was nearly a decade younger than the bride. Had it been reversed, it would have been normal. The difference in wealth was also striking. To my grandmother it looked like Sanee had snatched her baby boy from the cradle, that she purposely chose an immature husband who could not oppose her influence and authority. The three-day nuptial celebrations were so extravagant we were not asked to share the expenses.

From that day, Uncle Chea was unrecognisable. He fell into the ways of the rich, became a spendthrift and, much to my father's disappointment, he stopped going to school. After the honeymoon, his father-in-law planned a tour of the north province where the threesome gadded around the country with Chea at the steering wheel. Their journey diverted west to the Angkorian sites and on the way back into Phnom Penh some months later, Chea's car hit a cyclist on a dirt road. The impact of the speed sent the victim up in the air and he was killed instantly. From the back seat, Chea's father-in-law ordered him to leave the scene when a mob began to rush over. The ex-governor later made a few phone calls to the effect that the hit-and-run accident never officially happened—a man was wiped out of existence as easily as one erased a name written in chalk from a blackboard. My uncle never went to court. He got away with murder because he belonged to the right entourage.

My cousin Vaan and I talked and played a lot together. He agreed to play hopscotch with me, a 'girl's game', he said, but he put aside his boyish 'masculinity' to hop-hop along. I happened to love hopping more often than he was willing to participate and I had to hire him with my pocket money.

'One riel for the whole game!' I proposed.

'No-o-p! Too long.'

I had to bargain, 'Okay. One riel for half a game! That is until I build my first house!'

He adjusted my proposal, 'No! Until one of us builds the first house.'

He was suppler and always won. Halfway through the game, he threw down the stone and said without pity, 'I have accomplished my mission!' And he ran away to play with Vandy.

My eldest brother's activities were of the sort Vaan enjoyed more. I had no option but to join in and the three of us took turns to ride the rusty old bike that had been left by the previous occupants of our house. It was a man's bike, with a horizontal bar across the front. We were too short to sit on the saddle, so our bodies contorted on the side; we rode standing up on its pedals, and with the wind whistling at our ears. We climbed cocoa trees and ravaged their fruits, the very stuff Dad intended to process into chocolate powder for the Ministry of Agriculture. The plan was to duplicate this small plantation into larger ones if the chocolate proved to be of good quality for export. Dad could not collect enough pods to experiment with, not until the three of us were formally banned from the patch. For one whole year, black nets were thrown around the foliage to stop us from picking the fruit.

After Uncle Chea left, his younger brother and two more sisters arrived. The younger brother preferred to go under his chosen pseudonym of Ali, short for Ali Baba. The two sisters were Sao, meaning Saturday, and Touch.

Sao was a passive girl of fifteen who dreamed of romantic love whereas the second had a destructive streak that became more apparent as she grew older. Before Touch stayed with us, she had been a day girl at the convent of the Sacred Heart my mother had attended. From the same nuns, Touch learned religious songs, which she taught me. The lyrics of those hymns stayed in my head before they slowly filtered into my soul. I did not have the maturity to comprehend the abstract concept of religion then.

Aunt Touch and I renewed our friendship from our early childhood. She was ladylike whereas I was still a tomboy, splitting my interests between singing with her and running around our compound with my brothers. Her face was reminiscent of a Japanese geisha—smooth white skin, oval face with perfect small lips and an abundance of jet black hair, which she kept long and loose to her shoulders. She grew tall and slim, too tall for her liking, I guessed, and slouched in an attempt to hide her height. Her school reports from the nuns were full of praise and Dad had no problem getting her into Lycée Descartes. Although two years older than me, we found ourselves in the same school and in the same class. Thanks to my teacher Monsieur Michaud, I was no longer among the average performers. With consistent effort, I managed to rank well in the humanities. Touch generally had better marks than me and she was particularly good in geology. I came first and she second during third term in this subject and she was very upset. The same afternoon, she gathered all her books on the concrete backyard and made a bonfire of the whole pile. She refused to go back to school and stopped talking to me.

For weeks after this, I followed her around the house. I explained to her that my intention was to excel and not to compete. She turned her back while I pleaded. I kept urging for her not to throw away her chance to secure a good education.

'I am not your enemy, Aunt Touch, and you are not mine. I am sorry I had a better mark and you were hurt.'

The glance she returned was full of disbelief and disdain. I was stuck for words. I could not find the right ones, which would bring her back to reason. She began an absurd war against me but one in which I refused to participate.

Dad learnt of Touch's discontinued studies at the beginning of the next academic year. He told her that he could repair the damage and was prepared to obtain a medical certificate for her to retain her place at Lycée Descartes. The prospect of repeating the same level because she had missed the end-of-year exams was not acceptable to her—it would mean that I was going to be a year ahead. Instead, she enrolled at a small private school, one of many that had mushroomed all over the city and gave themselves pretentious names. Like the Lycée Descartes they were called after the other great philosophers of the French Renaissance—Voltaire, Jean-Jacques Rousseau, Montaigne and Montesquieu.

Unfortunately, these schools had doubtful standards and lacked qualified teachers. I know, because I had been given a job to teach in one of them during a long vacation; I was recruited before I had the required experience or knowledge to hold such a position. The director who interviewed me knew I was unqualified but agreed to employ me for two months all the same. The prime objective of these institutions was for financial profit; a large number of students from a large age range was allowed to be lumped into the same classroom. Annual fees were payable in advance, rollcalls and discipline were nonexistent and the dropout rate was alarming. They closed up when parents began to suspect that they were paying dearly for a very poor education.

Aunt Touch was able to enter one of these schools at two levels ahead of where I was at the Lycée Descartes, and was happy to leave me behind. She continued to live with us and share a room with me. Despite our physical proximity, she erected a barrier of silence, which extended to the rest of the household. I could hear her breathing ten steps from my bed at night. I renewed efforts to chat and make up but each time she turned her back and pretended she did not hear. I knew that she wanted to be an air hostess.

My father, whose role was to arbitrate his siblings' ambitions, sneered and put Touch's dream abruptly to rest with an unkind comparison. 'An air hostess', he said, 'is really a waitress on a plane!'

It was around this time that my great-great grandmother Reama suffered a stroke that half-paralysed her. My father insisted my grandfather let Reama stay with us, his most convincing argument being our facility to drive her for her regular medical check-ups. Her speech was slurred but her memories were intact.

She was still as a statue but she could still move her right hand to beat the back handle of her fan against the wall to attract my mother's attention. Mother brought her bedpan, her special food, spoon-fed her and washed her. My brothers and I would assist Mum to lift her upper part to sit her up while she made gestures to chase Vaan away. He was the son of the grandson she despised. She clung to Mum's arm, begging for company. She struggled to talk, to tell my mother the many stories of her youth. Reama lived like that for three long years, encased in a shell of a body that decayed in front of her eyes. The day her body was cremated, not one of her direct descendants shed a tear. My mother did discreetly, not because she was saddened by her death, but because in all her eighty years of life, she said that Reama had wasted precious opportunity to foster happiness. She wielded tremendous power that she had misused or abused. So much love had been lost.

A few months after Reama's death, the wet nurse followed her to the grave. She had not been sick; she simply went to sleep one night and never woke up. A peaceful departure like this was a blessing to a person who had committed no sin.

My grandparents' house was emptying, whereas ours was increasing in number. Somalee, whom they both cherished and who loved them back, remained with them. Granddad still drank heavily but he no longer insulted his wife. He won the lottery on Somalee's sixth birthday in 1960, and collected two millions riels, an enormous windfall. He went back to his village with one million to spend, to give away and to buy more land. He deposited the other half in a bank. He had no idea what to do with it.

20

Portraits

Relatives near and far started to hear of my father's large house and he was widely known for his generosity and reluctance to turn down whomever was in need of shelter. After the influx of brothers and sisters to his home, Dad adopted a cousin from his mother's side. Grandma's sister seemed to have married happily into a Vietnamese family whose matriarch, Mrs Dong, was the proprietor of a prosperous fish sauce factory on the other bank of the Tonle Sap River. Fish sauce factories of various sizes dotted the tip of this river island and hers was the biggest.

To the Vietnamese, fish sauce is what soy sauce is to the Chinese. Next to rice, it is the most basic accompaniment to every dish on the family table. In times when meat and vegetables are scarce and expensive, it is diluted with vinegar and sugar and the mixture is poured over starch to make it a meal. In times of hardship or plenty, it is sure to sell and the manufacturing of it is consistently lucrative.

My grandmother's sister, having married into the company of fish sauce makers, was guaranteed an existence of ease. But illness stole her husband and his death left three generations of women—his mother Mrs Dong, his beautiful widow and his daughter—without male protection. Although they had financial security, to minimise further unpredictability of life, Mrs Dong asked my father to adopt her granddaughter. This decision was painful to her, as it must have been to her daughter-in-law, but the intention was sound and caring. The matriarch was getting old, and in taking stock of the future, predicted the difficulty her granddaughter would face in the case of her sudden death. With the same calculated approach that she normally applied to her business, she foresaw the necessity to take immediate action to protect her family. She believed our house would be ideal for her granddaughter's safe-keeping.

After its independence in 1953, Cambodia was becoming nationalistic and my father was seen to have the means to shield this girl from racism. Since 1955, the government demanded that the Vietnamese carry identification. There were laws that excluded the Vietnamese from important jobs, and a business had to be Cambodian owned before it could be registered.

The Vietnamese who stayed in Cambodia were keen to naturalise if they had the means. For this very reason, Mrs Dong trusted my father to obtain Cambodian citizenship for her fifteen-year-old granddaughter whose name was changed to Sophanee. Too old to be my father's daughter, she was to be my grandfather's illegitimate child, supposedly born out of wedlock by a mistress. To Mrs Dong, being a Cambodian bastard was better than being totally Vietnamese, and Sophanee would live under our roof and learn to speak the Cambodian language. My father promised he would treat this cousin like his own sister. Mrs Dong methodically calculated the expenses of schooling, clothing and boarding, which she insisted on paying. 'Your hospitality for Sophanee should not cost you a cent. I have already paid my granddaughter's school fees in full until the time she leaves. She has a generous wardrobe, but if she wants to buy more clothes, let her come to me. For her food, while she lives with you, I would like to advance to you and your wife whatever you feel appropriate.'

My father promptly refused. He looked in my mother's direction to assure the matriarch that my mother also agreed, 'It will be a pleasure for my wife and me to provide her with food and accommodation. I consider it an insult if you do not accept our gesture.'

Scores of Vietnamese went back to Vietnam after 1953, only to find different discriminations. Saigon, more densely populated than Phnom Penh, more competitive and aggressive, showed little compassion to the newcomers. The Ngo Dinh Diem government suspected the repatriates as sympathetic to the Vietcong guerrillas. Take the example of my grandmother Nguen, who returned to Vietnam after my grandfather's death. My maternal uncle, Xuang, did his national service in the South Vietnamese Air Force where he wished to stay and build a permanent career. He was regularly harassed by the military police, who submitted him to absurd interrogations.

'Why did you come back to Vietnam?' they would ask.

'I am Vietnamese. And Vietnamese people are second-class citizens in Cambodia,' he said.

They had a file that indicated that not everyone in the Nguen family returned to Vietnam. So they shot their questions from another angle.

'You said that the Vietnamese are badly treated in Cambodia. How come your brother Ho and some of your siblings still live there?'

Xuang told them that his brother Ho had a good steady job in Phnom Penh. The police pushed further and hinted at some conspiracy, 'We believe a number of successful Vietnamese residing in Cambodia are funding the Vietcong. How much does your brother earn?' Xuang did not lose his nerve and gave them honest answers, but they kept questioning him in the hope of extracting compromising information they wanted to hear.

In the end, Xuang did make it back to Vietnam, and worked with the Vietnamese Air Force. When it looked certain that he would never rise beyond the desk job where he had been for five years, he moved across to the airline Pan Am. During the period when he was without an income, grandmother Nguen sold spring rolls in the streets.

Sophanee was quite unaccustomed to the complicated politics of a large family. She kept out of them and for the first few months, she used to visit her grandmother and her mother. When her grandmother died, her mother remarried quickly, and her new stepfather was unhesitant in trying to seduce her. According to my mother, few men could resist Sophanee, whose grace resembled that of a swan. She was trapped with us and had nowhere to go, and my mother was obliged to provide for her. She and Aunt Saturday (Sao) formed a quiet pair; they were engrossed in the adolescent preoccupations of polishing their looks, and designing and sewing their clothes. They had rollers in their hair and their faces plastered with egg white—their own remedy to tighten their skin and prevent pimples. They talked of strange things, such as soaking in a bathtub filled with fresh cow's milk to keep the complexion smooth and young. I mocked this wasteful practice but they told me that Madame Ngo Dinh Nhu, the sister-in-law to the President in South Vietnam, indulged in a weekly bath of milk. The Ngo was a budding presidential dynasty, which was despotic, decadent and corrupt. Madame Nhu exemplified the women who held power and in Saigon, people muttered of a *menage à trois* between President Diem and Mr and Madame Nhu. A tribute to her sophistication appeared in a lengthy editorial in *Paris-Match* magazine, which reinforced Sophanee's and Saturday's belief that their idol was the world authority on grooming. Unfortunately, there were very limited means in our house to emulate this woman.

They shared a room in one wing with Heang (Vietnamese for praise), who was of the same age but more down to earth. Heang was bonded to Mum for a pitiful sum after losing her virginity. Over and above the bond money, which tied her down for five years, she earned a small monthly wage from Mum to purchase clothes, shoes and the occasional tube of lipstick.

In Phnom Penh, a handful of rich Chinese wives were known to hunt for virgins to revive their impotent husbands' sexuality. In this manner, they had the control over whom their men slept with and they had a say in chasing the girls away in due course without disrupting their households. Heang's parents sold her to one such woman, and later disposed of like a used rag. Her mother picked her up and dropped her straightaway at our house because she had heard that my mother was desperate for a housekeeper. Heang was more than a servant, she became Mum's companion, her sister.

We had others, neither servants nor relatives, who came in droves into our lives at Chomcar Mon. This last group of people had something in common: they were villagers, attracted by the big city and under the misconception that Phnom Penh was a better place than the rice fields. Cambodia's villages could no longer accommodate or feed a growing rural population. Peasants' debts to unscrupulous moneylenders compelled them to send their children to cities to work and send home their earnings. Young villagers headed in the direction of cities, finding odd jobs along the way. Once there, they sold their strong backs to load bags of corn or one-hundred-kilogram bags of rice onto trucks or ships for export. They were only qualified to do musclework, which paid hardly enough to sustain health. Many contracted tuberculosis or sank into deeper misery than they had experienced in their villages. Phnom Penh and other big towns were flooded with half-employed, half-starved men on the brink of despair who lived on the fringe. They peddled their strength, worked as coolies or pedalled pedicabs for a fare, pedalled their youth away in a country that could not promise them a better future.

Some gave up trying to survive. I remember one story of a villager turned pedicab-rider who could not have been more than thirty-five. He had little energy left in his legs to pedal for a living. An old man before forty, he decided to lend death a helping hand. He rode to a deserted place where he could depart from this world in peace. On a forgotten public patch where big weeping fig trees were left to grow old, he undid his *krama*. This cotton towel had been his sarong when he showered in front of a public water tap; it had been the pillow, which he rolled in a ball to rest his tired head upon at night. It was the only possession he ever had on earth, and he was about to use it to hang himself. He climbed over his trishaw saddle, reached for a strong branch and tied a knot. The other knot he was to make around his neck. But he made a mistake: the knot was tied under his chin—it should have been at the back of his neck. He was left dangling in the air, very much alive, kicking and rotating at the end of his towel.

'Worthless fool', I heard people say, 'he was not even smart enough to kill himself properly!'

My grandfather and my father had a soft spot for people like the trishaw pedaller. They came across many out-of-work and out-of-place villagers when they were on their travels. Dad, especially, had to visit the provinces to prepare for Prince Sihanouk's visits. Sometimes he had to build a hall in a hurry and line it with rugs. The whole ground must be beautified to receive the royal party, which was in the habit of giving little warning. Dad had to hire an instant labour force on location and work frantically through the night. The next day, the Prince and his entourage had to have the impression that wherever it pleased them to set foot in Cambodia, the whole country appeared to be clean and happy. Of those hundreds of coolies who worked temporarily for my father and my grandfather, there were a few they both took pity on and brought them home to Chamcar Mon. Dad gave them permanent positions in the Ministry of Agriculture and put them in a training program. Some of them would learn to repair agricultural machines, trucks and tractors, others to care for plants, or to drive and to go on to work in the private sector as chauffeurs to the rich. Some became security guards in the compound; the rest went into the army reserve where Dad taught the recruits how to shoot rifles.

These villagers boarded with us on and off, sleeping in our back-yard. The understanding was for them to stay with us until they famil-iarised with the city and had saved some wages. In exchange for the free food my mother provided and the free accommodation, they were asked to 'help around the house'. It was left as vague as that, because the chores were so many it was impossible for Mum to specify them. She hoped for the willing eyes to see and for the villagers to volunteer where and when they could contribute. Most chose not to see. Most learned the city ways fast. They learned the gains, the advantages, the dishonesty and the tricks. They travelled back to their villages to get married and they brought their new wives to live with us. My mother congratulated them but found no subtle words to tell them it was time to leave. The villagers and their brides stayed for the free food and paid no rent. They kept their earnings, and the irony of it all was that they lost respect for Mum as the mistress of the house and took her for granted.

One villager stood apart from the rest. I shall always remember his name in affection, one I cannot transcribe into English. The closest to how it should sound is 'E-e-u-n', which I will simplify and call 'E'.

E epitomised the good earth. He was uncorrupted by change and predictable like the seasons of Cambodia. He never acquired the need to cheat or to take advantage. Neither did he acquire the habit to wash! He carried the gruff wholesome smell of the rice fields on his clothes, which he bought on payday and wore continuously for one month, unlaundered until the next new set. By that time, they were not even fit to mop the floor with. He dumped them in the bin, paraded like a proud peacock in his new clothes, his rough unwashed peasants' hands stroking his starched white shirt constantly. He had a smile from ear to ear, and without fail he came looking for my mother in the kitchen. The money he earned for one whole month, minus the expense of his walking wardrobe, he handed to her. He went on his knees to thank her for the food she gave him, and begged her to receive his gratitude.

Calling her 'mother', he said, 'Mother, I wish I had better than paper to pay you for your kind heart!' To this, my mother's eyes filled with tears and she answered, 'Your good feelings are enough repayment. Save that money for your parents in the village and get yourself married one day.'

E was a giant. He grew to that giddy height on rice, fish, sauces and a few vegetables. He could not bring himself to try meat. My mother thought that he needed the largest portion since he had to support the largest frame. The first time he had his meal at our house, she gave him a generous helping of sliced beef, then noticed that he had not touched it. She urged him to eat but he explained he could not.

'Cows and bulls help us plough the earth, Mother. I tried to eat their flesh before but I felt very ill afterwards. I could not help thinking I had eaten the flesh of good friends.'

After four years with us, E went back to his village to be with his parents. He came regularly to visit us at the end of the harvest, each time his arms were loaded with fresh food from his lands. Then came a long gap. He returned to bid farewell to my mother years later, at the time when the elephants started to fight.

21

Two-thirds of a Salary

When Aunt Tam, Father's most beloved sister, moved in with us, the first thing he did was to send her to a two-year secretarial course. After that, he found her a position in a French company, Descourt et Cabot, an import-export business. From the back room where she typed, she was eventually moved to the reception desk.

All Tam's wages went into a wardrobe of tailored suits, high-heeled shoes and matching handbags, cosmetics and lacy underwear, a weekly manicure and a monthly blow wave. Whatever was left over she put towards a dowry. Dad promised he would match her savings a hundred-fold. He was indeed trying to put money aside to buy a house for her and we were waiting for the prospective groom to appear.

Dad thought there must be a queue of men who would want to marry his sister. He was sure she was attractive, and with her financial assets she ought to be able to entice the best. Her future husband must be somebody already important, a graduate from overseas with a good family background. To Dad's prerequisites, Tam added her own conditions. She wanted the man to be handsome and rich. She pouted at the timid approach of a few hopefuls whose looks or dress sense did not meet her requirements. She waited year after year, patiently saving, consciously keeping her manicured fingers from getting dirty or losing their softness by working in the kitchen. Dad insisted that Tam be exempt from housework. In our crowded house where three or more people had to share a room, Tam enjoyed one big area for herself. Dad made sure it was furnished in style. There was an armoire and chest of drawers, a make-up table with a full-length mirror in the middle, a king-sized bed, colour-coordinated satin sheets and a bedspread. Lacy pillow cases and richly hand-embroidered cushions were thrown casually over the thick floor rug. She kept her bedroom locked, and she would only show herself once meals were on the table.

Aunt Tam was elevated to the status of the matriarch in our house. While my father spent his time in the arms of his mistresses, Tam assumed the role of a watchdog with an unmatched fervour. My mother must be kept in line, and her thoughts, actions and whereabouts accounted for in case she stalked Dad's other women or made disgraceful scenes in public, the way some first wives were prone to do.

Aunt Tam showed sympathy to my mother and took on the position of her confidante. My mother succumbed and disclosed her sorrows. 'I am mainly worried about my children. My son Vandy needs a father to guide him with love. His father beats him up instead of trying the gentle way; he wants to change him by force. Like a tree's branch, my son will break under sudden pressure.'

Mum also confided her doubts that Dad could bring up two families by himself and quoted a proverb, 'I ask you, how can one man row two boats at once?'

My mother's words were reported, twisted and used against her in the court of Dad's arbitrary law. He used to consult Tam first when he came home and then confront my mother, 'You told Tam I am a bad father, did you? And what did you mean by your piece of wisdom about rowing more than one boat? What are you trying to say?'

These were excuses for him to throw tantrums to justify his

absence. Mum stopped offering Tam a rope to hang her with but Tam did not run out of accusations. She advanced a very devious hypothesis to explain why my mother was able to remain level-headed in spite of Dad's affairs. 'Your wife must be unfaithful. She must have a man on the side.' Tam substantiated her suspicion with other observations, 'I find it strange that she takes such a long time to come back from the market in the morning.' When I accompanied Mum shopping, she methodically circled the place for bargains. She made five full rounds and waited for the merchants to lower their prices. The goods, which remained unsold after the early rush, were slashed to a level where she could buy more to feed the big crowd in our house.

Crazy and preposterous as it was, Tam's accusations sounded plausible to my father, and he attributed to my mother the same disloyalty he was capable of committing. Mum's dignified calmness was unique and had drawn much praise from good people. While Dad acknowledged their expressions of admiration for Mum, he was secretly wondering why she coped so well. What lay behind her strength? It was facile to think she had a lover and he had no proof. But just the same he called her to the bedroom, turned the lock and punished her. The sobbing and yelling went on and on. Every word rang clear to me, who had camped outside their room.

Mum raised her voice and stood up to defend her dignity. 'I will not allow anybody, not even you, to lower me to that level! Will you be happier if I threw stones or acid at your other women? I refuse to go mad on their account. Will you accept me better if I lose my mind? Like a jealous wife? I am keeping my sanity to raise the children!'

Dad flew out, looked at me with his fiery eyes, his breath short and heavy, and his lips pale. A minute later, he was gone. I always found my mother on the floor, hiding her face from me, and I reached to help her up to the bed. As I grew older, I implored her to take us away, to somewhere else where I would be content with 'a bit of salt and rice, it would be more than what we truly need to live'. I believed there must be a life somewhere else for us—a life where human decency had a place.

There was, but not for us. Mum advanced the following bleak scenario. 'Suppose we get out of here. We can't take Vaan with us. In my situation, I am an unqualified person; I will be a maid in someone else's house. You and your brother will have no status, you would be children of divorced parents—you would not have a leg to stand on in society. You will both be condemned to a future so dim you would not forgive me. Suppose I would marry again. Do you think a stepfather would be any kinder to you both? If your own blood father mistreated Vandy this much, a stepfather would be crueller. Nothing would stop him from molesting you, seducing you, and what could I do to stop it? Believe it, there is a lot to be grateful for, despite how you feel right now. You are both nearly grown ups. Be patient for a few more years and life will be better.'

For the time being, for another few years, we waited. My father's presence at home, however short, was traumatic. I could not tell then or even now how I feel towards him. My mother saw the hatred budding in my heart. She warned me that, no matter what he did, he remained my father and I should not be his judge. She persuaded me to keep my respect for him. In her saintly tolerance and forgiveness for all his evil ways, she knew it would be humanly impossible to ask me to love.

Towards my Aunt Tam, I harboured plenty of bad thoughts. 'Aunt Tam will realise one day what it means to feel our hurt. I hope she will get a very bad husband who will mistreat her. I want her sufferings to be a thousand times bigger than the ones she has given us.'

My mother put her hand over my mouth, 'It is a sin to curse. Let the Tevoda (Cambodian for god) take care of justice. Nothing escapes his attention.' It seemed to me totally irrelevant when she looked at the sky and started to talk mysteriously about the work of nature. 'All rivers flow back to the sea. Every drop of water will eventually return to its source.'

In Asian philosophy, whatever a person says and does will one day reflect back on him or her. A bad word or deed will be paid in full. I insisted that Aunt Tam was a witch and a snake. My mother's words to describe her were, 'She leaves her excrement at the very spot she eats.' Meaning, the person who feeds her, instead of getting due gratitude, has to also clean the mess she makes.

In those days, quite beside his large collection of guns and rifles kept in the room where Mum slept, Dad's newest piece of pride was his Harley-Davidson motorbike with a side-car. His homecoming could be heard from a distance. At times, he came by car, a government vehicle he was entitled to, and in his position he had been assigned a chauffeur. He kept the car but allowed the chauffeur to drive us to and from school.

In the morning Mum used to get a lift to the central market from which point she would catch public transport after shopping. With her two large woven baskets sagging with fresh food, she walked half a mile from the point the rickshaw stopped before she reached home. On our days off from school, we rushed in her direction and my two brothers and I took over the baskets and carried them to the kitchen for her. Mum sat down for a short rest, giving a sigh of pleasure, massaging her short plump fingers to bring circulation back to her white knuckles. I dug into the shopping bags, hoping to discover treats like biscuits or glutinous rice buns for breakfast. There was nothing other than vegetables, vegetables and fish, always fish she could afford to purchase. Meat or poultry was in small quantity for Dad's elusive visits—he was allergic to fish.

Mum would read the disappointment on my face and give me a few coins and send me to the corner hut store to buy three eggs. 'I'll fry them for the three of you.' My two brothers and I used to love this kind of breakfast, and we loved it more since we knew that Mum could not always spare even those little coins for eggs and we had to resign ourselves to leftovers from the previous night's dinner. The most likely food we found was some cold steamed rice, which had gone crunchy. I fried it with chopped spring onions, garlic and a sprinkle of soy sauce.

I was to learn not to venture into the kitchen and to complain of hunger. I learnt especially to help serve Dad's meals, which he would eat by himself, for he came home at unpredictable times and expected something to be ready for him. The small chicken, the pork cutlets or the beef fillet that my mother had to have on reserve were cooked with the greatest care and most of the time were left to go bad if he didn't come home. These were the wonderful foods of which I used to dream, and promised myself I would have one day when I was rich.

Dad would pay extra care not to carve the meat too close to the bone. 'I must leave something for the dogs,' he would say with a smile. Suddenly he looked at me before he fed the hounds, and inquired whether I had eaten.

I had to sound convincing, 'Oh yes, father, I am still very full!' He would remark teasingly, 'Oh? And why are you so skinny?'

Mum quickly bailed me out, 'She has a particular body which we call "a thread", which could never put on weight, no matter what she eats!'

I was slow and picky and I could not compete with the speed of others around our family table. They were skilled at clicking their chopsticks, and scooping large amounts of food into their mouths before I had the chance to start. Vandy, Vaan and I were selective; we carefully discarded the fatty bits and we socialised more than we ate. Vaan in particular came off worst because he imposed on himself an absurd taboo. Ever since he choked on a tiny bone he would not consume fish. After the others had finished and washed their hands, the three of us lingered in front of dishes that were nearly empty. We spooned the sauces onto our rice. It did not worry my mother that the boys were slim whereas she was increasingly obsessed by the concern I was not going to be 'plump enough to find a good husband'.

She suspected I had tapeworms or hookworms. I got dewormed with French medicine and was not allowed to eat or drink for a full day.

'Tapeworms are tough to kill! Try Chinese way.' I swallowed packs of smelly herbs. 'The kind of worms you have in your abdomen must be there for too long. They have grown big heads, sharp claws that dig very deep into your intestine. They extract all the goodness of the food and you are left with the cud, no vitamins to nourish your body.' Mum was a medical authority. Out came another programme of cures—French, Chinese, Indian and the last, the most desperate resort, Vietnamese. She had been warned the medicine could make me very sick. It was a thick sappy mixture from a fruit that the Vietnamese use to dye silk black. The smell alone could have killed me. I closed my eyes, blocked my nose and obediently drank it down. The side-effect was excruciating. For two days, I was coiled up, holding my stomach from cramps; my eyes sunk in their sockets. There was still no sign of the worms. By then, Mum admitted I had none. But she was not giving up.

She put me on a fatty diet. For two long months, at night, she came to my bed with a long glass of lukewarm sweet condensed milk. The cream at the top had scabbed in a wrinkled thick yellow skin; she pinched it and half lifted it with two fingers to show it to me and said 'Yummy!' She would not leave until I drank the last drop. I used to wait with delight for her at night to come and sit on the edge of my bed, to give me a cuddle and smell my hair, her Asian way of kissing me. Condensed milk had now come in between us to spoil the pleasure I felt waiting for her. I pushed the full glass away with horror, 'I hate the milk! I don't mind looking like a toothpick! And I do not want a husband!'

She put to rest her ambition of fattening me. I was sure she was aware of other ways to increase my weight. Although I was a fussy eater, I was capable of the greatest appetite for all the things she could not provide. A glass of canned milk was the cheapest. There were the prawns I adored, chicken, crusty freshly baked bread spread with fresh butter, imported and available from one shop only—a shop that served only foreigners. I loved sponge cake layered in butter cream of pastel colours, decorated with pink roses and soft green leaves intertwining. These,

Mum used to buy on three occasions: Vaan's birthday, which came first, mine in May, and Vandy's in September. She and the three of us stole a lightning celebration to commemorate the events, and carefully cut the two small square cakes into four. They cost a small fortune to buy, and as much as she was slightly embarrassed to exclude the other members of the family, she simply did not have the money.

It was at Chamcar Mon where we met my two half-brothers and half-sister. Dad could not live any more under the pretence that they did not exist. Part of the reason that prompted him to bring them home was that he had split from their mother for yet another woman. His guilt towards them precipitated his decision; he did not want to visit them at their mother's place where he risked her nagging. Our house was more of a neutral ground, and my mother was a lot more accepting. She truly held no resentment towards these children and recommended that we accept them. The manner with which she presented them to us made me in fact thrilled to meet them.

They arrived on a Saturday morning and Dad made the introductions. The eldest boy, Tha, was a year older than me; he was born at exactly the time my sister Virath had died. Dad was obviously so busy with the birth of a son in another household that he did not have time to worry about a sick daughter somewhere else. Next in line was my half-sister, Nee, one year younger than me, and my other half-brother, No. Dad decided that they should call my mother 'Mother Number Two' and that we, children of the first wife, should be considered their elders, irrelevant of our age.

We shifted tables and chairs for a large family lunch that day, the first meal Dad was going to have with us for a long while. Mum made a genuine effort to create an atmosphere of celebration. Out came the best bone chopsticks and the best china porcelain bowls and serving plates, which she normally stored in a sideboard. These were the two sets of dinnerware she had purchased on sale to give to us 'when we got married'.

Nobody knew quite how to behave ceremoniously. When the order came for us to sit down for lunch, everyone grabbed the first seat they could find without giving any consideration to our three guests. They were timid and did not know where they should sit. Mum had made an unfortunate error of calculation; there was one chair short and Tha was left standing uneasily. She sent Vaan to fetch a stool and Vandy an extra setting. The latter had no eye for detail and brought a chipped bowl and a pair of wooden chopsticks, which he put in front of Tha. My father noticed the chip, glanced at the food on the table and invited everyone to begin eating. Then he walked into the kitchen and signalled for my mother to go with him.

The noise of things breaking in the kitchen made me jump off my chair. My father was opening the pantry and throwing food, plates and pots at my mother. I moved forward to stand in-between to protect her, he pulled my arm away and started to hit her in the cheek. I quickly put my hand on her face and his slap, which was aimed at Mum, struck me instead. The blow was hard and I could feel the flesh lift from my bones and my hand swell instantly. My mother took the blows while I was thrown to the floor, my head buried between my knees. I was shutting my eyes and blocking my ears but I felt somebody sitting next to me.

After Dad had left the kitchen, I realised it was Tha. 'I am sorry,' he murmured. 'I am so very sorry that I brought tears in this house.'

I looked up and saw profound distress in his face. 'Don't blame yourself,' I replied, 'I certainly do not blame you.' Tha and I sat together in silence, choked by our tears. Although he said nothing else, I recognised that this half-brother was reaching out to offer me his support. The cruel destiny that had put us in the wombs of different mothers could easily have influenced us to resent one another but our thirst for warmth and affection was so strong that we were drawn to loving each other. From the moment Tha chose to sit by my side to comfort me and we helplessly watched my mother getting abused, we knew that we were equal victims of horrible family circumstances.

Dad accused Mum of letting her stepson eat from a chipped bowl and of purposely cooking the cheapest meal to show that his 'other children' were not welcome. 'All the money I have been giving you!' he said. 'And you cannot present a decent meal!' He refused to sympathise with my mother, whose funds usually ran out mid-month. The most trying test for her was finding the money to run the house until the next handout.

She dreamed up a series of entrepreneurial ideas to solve her regular shortage. She asked my father to buy a petrol station, a pharmacy or a bookstore. He sniggered at her suggestions. 'A woman in your position should not be involved in business, shopkeepers are *petit bourgeois*,' he said. 'If I let you have a shop, it will look to others that I cannot afford to support you.'

She was told to spend less. He would not admit that her monthly allowance was insufficient. He stressed that he gave her two-thirds of his wage and it was a lot of money. His domestic myopia failed to add together ten villagers and an average of ten or more family members who depended on my mother, whereas the other third given to Dad's second wife catered only for her and three small children. It somehow became the norm for my half-brothers and sister to turn up for weekends and school holidays. My mother had to use her own resources to bridge the ten days or two weeks during which her purse was virtually empty.

An account of my childhood would not be complete without mentioning the dogs. They were ten ferocious German Shepherds, trained to hunt. My father went hunting up north with a friend who was a doctor. The doctor kept a small cub which he had captured in a cage on the floor above his surgery in the city. The cub grew into a large tiger and the patients had no idea that an animal was pacing round above them.

My father brought game meat home to my mother until an episode turned him off hunting forever. The last time he aimed his rifle, he shot a mother deer. She collapsed on her hind legs and lifted her head to look for her fawn. Her front legs jerked and she finally fell to the ground with a long shiver, her eyes moist with tears. After this incident, my father promised he would not shoot a living target again. He locked his rifles away in the cabinet. His hunting companion, the doctor, gave up the sport as well and, given his inability to accommodate the dogs in his apartment, they found their way to our house where they roared and fought between themselves out of boredom. They tore each other's ears and finally four of them were killed. Three more died of age and disease, and the remaining three—the youngest, fittest, fiercest and biggest eaters of the lot—survived for the next six years. They had to be leashed in the end. Everyday, Mum had to buy an enormous quantity of meat for them. The pot that she used to cook for the dogs was so big only E was strong enough to lift it above the open fire in the backyard. Mum had been told to fill the dogs' stomach sufficiently, or they might be tempted to kill us for food.

I must also mention the dozens of monkeys we had to babysit for three memorable months. Dad's colleague from the fisheries, Mr Bou, and his wife were going on an extended trip to Paris and my father offered to mind 'his children' during his absence. It was agreed the monkeys would not be allowed to live inside our house and were to temporarily occupy our mango tree in the front. We threw up bananas to feed them while in the backyard the dogs, leashed to the jack trees, were crazy because they could not get to them. I have never been to a zoo which was louder than our garden.

Let it not be thought that I disliked animals. After the mating season in the heat of summer, street dogs gave birth during the next wet season to a spate of half-blind puppies. Very often, a council van circulated slowly around the neighbourhood to catch them. When they spotted a dog, they cast a hook around its neck and pulled it toward the door of the van. Caged behind the wagon bars, the dogs howled from the knowledge that they would be put to death.

After the van made its sinister inspection, I crawled outside our fence. A countless number of pups were calling for their mothers, sprawled on their weak paws among the wet grass. My two brothers and I ran to fetch bags and filled them with as many orphaned dogs as we could carry. Year after year, we had to return them to the gutters; Mum bluntly reminded us she could not take in all the strays. For many nights following our attempt to save them, we could hear them cry. Then a most distressing silence settled on the ditches by the roadsides. I tried not to think that the puppies had starved to death, that the rain had drowned them or that they had been swept into stormwater pipes.

Every way I turned in my childhood, it was impossible for me not to be faced with the helplessness of life. I felt powerless to change not only my own circumstances but the circumstances of everything and everybody around me.

22

The Two Uncles

My uncle Duck's Feet was returning at last from France where he had spent six years. My father assumed that after all that time, Duck's Feet would be a university graduate, an engineer or even a medical doctor. The whole family was enthusiastic about his homecoming. He enthralled us with the hint of a Parisian accent when he spoke Cambodian and Vietnamese. 'It has been so long since I had the chance to speak our languages,' he said. He brought with him a breath of civilisation and sophistication; he was informed, stylish and worldly.

Dad had to shoo us away in order to sit down and hear Duck's Feet's news. 'Tell me all that you did during those years overseas.' An hour into their conversation, we heard my father shouting. He walked out of the house and got in his car, slamming the door. He disappeared into the middle of the night.

It transpired that Duck's Feet did start at the Sorbonne University. After his first year there, he was invited to Saigon by his fiancée's parents. They had heard of his academic brilliance when he was still studying at Chasseloup Laubat and orchestrated a meeting between him and their only daughter, Ying. As he took off to Paris to study further, and it looked to them that he was heading for a promising future. They corresponded and sent him a return ticket to spend his holidays in Vietnam. Before his arrival in Saigon, they took the liberty of planning a full wedding. They sent out invitations, and all he needed to do was to gracefully accept a bride on a silver platter. He was twenty and he was flattered. The girl's family was right in supposing that their offer was too good for any young man to refuse. They possessed the arrogance of wealth and believed that like everything else, love and matrimony could be bought. Ying's parents held the monopoly of Saigon's 'entertainment industry', which included live theatres, cinemas, bars, night clubs, a stable of actresses, dancers, bar girls, musicians, and bouncers. They were also moneylenders. My grandfather, who called a spade a spade, gnashed his teeth in disgust at Duck's Feet's future in-laws. He labelled them 'masters in prostitution, dealers of human flesh and misery', and did not grace the wedding with his presence. Neither did he do a thing to stop it from taking place. He upheld a personal promise. He had been emphatically articulate about not interfering in any of his children's choices in marriage. 'They choose their patterns, I would approve but they must not count on me to go looking on their behalf.' What he did refrain from saying was that his own marriage had been arranged and that his filial obligation had tied him down to a life with a wife he did not want. Grandfather told my father about Duck's Feet's wedding in Saigon. The matter-of-fact way he mentioned it indicated that it was not my father's place to approve or disapprove.

Duck's Feet's bride, Ying, was excited about accompanying him to France where he resumed his second year at the university. After a few months Paris was not what she had imagined. Winter was long and harsh, and although her parents were generous with their regular subsidies, she missed the tropics and the comfort she grew up with. She fell ill in her pregnancy and bought a one-way ticket back to Saigon where she intended to give birth. Ying said to Duck's Feet, 'Finish your degree and I will wait for you in Vietnam.' In leaving him alone, Ying was taking a risk. The world's most romantic city does not leave single men single and lonely for too long.

Ying gave birth to a son. Duck's Feet wrote long letters and implored her to return to his side, to put up with the cold weather and the cheap living for his sake. She stalled, and trotted out one excuse after another. He got tired of waiting and blamed her for preferring material comfort to sharing his bohemian student's life. His love waned and his resentment grew with his loneliness. His interest shifted to a beautiful French girl with enormous brown eyes. She was an artist, who did not bother to probe into his past and ask questions. The brunette fell pregnant and would not have an abortion. Duck's Feet did what he thought was the right thing to do by her—impulsively, he married her and committed bigamy.

The pressure of fatherhood made him give up university. He took up a six-month course of English, went with his French wife to London to brush up on his new foreign language. Back in Paris a few months later, he obtained a job with this English diploma. He had a baby daughter. He found it increasingly hard to make a living and it occurred to him that life would be easier in Cambodia. At least he had a big family back home, brothers and sisters, security in numbers. He departed first for Phnom Penh, with his wife and daughter to follow two weeks later.

My father exploded at Duck's Feet's stupidity. He had come out empty-handed after years of financial sacrifices from Grandfather and Dad, which had gone to fund his supposed education. He had let the family down. Worse than this, he had come home with a huge problem for my father to solve. He had married in Vietnam and married again in France without divorcing the first wife.

'Don't you know that in France bigamy is a criminal offence?' my father shouted. In Cambodia the jurisdiction was ambivalent on this subject. A man could have more than one wife and children from many. To avoid complications, a male had only one official marriage certificate. Duck's Feet had two. In Duck's Feet's situation, he had involved two foreign ladies and not two local girls. His French wife could have him extradited to France where he would be tried under the Code Civil. His Vietnamese wife might choose to sue him as well. For the time being, everybody in the family had to be discreet. The French wife did not know yet that she was the second wife and the first wife did not know yet that the second wife existed.

My father had to act quickly. His brother leant on him and Dad did not forsake his own flesh and blood. Duck's Feet needed somewhere to live in the interim until he found work. The Jesuit fathers at the École Miche did not forget their protégé and employed him as a teacher. My mother had to host Duck's Feet and two weeks later his French wife and their baby daughter. He had the courtesy at least to ask, 'It is important that you approve of my brother's permission to let me stay with you, big sister. I am sorry to impose on you like this.' She was never given the chance to veto any of my father's decisions, but Duck's Feet's politeness pleased her.

Jacqueline, Duck's Feet's wife, was extremely sensitive to Mum's efforts to accommodate her. Her appetite suffered from Mum's clumsy attempts to cook French style. It was always a thin piece of steak, albeit tough, marinated with soy sauce. Mum threw in a few string beans accompanied by steamed rice since potatoes were not within her price range. Jacqueline glanced at the food the rest of us were eating, and she convinced my mother she would rather sample exotic cuisine. Within the first week of her stay, she shot me a remark, '*Votre maman a une vie misérable, n'est-ce pas?*' (Doesn't your mother have a miserable life?) I pretended I did not hear and quickly volunteered to bottle-feed the baby.

As I waited for her to test the temperature of the formula milk, I thought to myself that my mother's life must be very abominable indeed for it to be noticeable to a total stranger within a few days. I found myself liking Jacqueline instantly. I could not begrudge her for being an extra burden; she was understanding and I had no feelings against her.

It was Tam who despised her for attracting a spontaneous popularity and for being Duck's Feet's spouse. She resisted Jacqueline's attempt at friendship first with cold indifference and then with an overt disdain. Jacqueline was startled and annoyed with Tam's attitude; she rose to the challenge and proved to be a capable adversary. Being French and egalitarian, she was neither bound nor handicapped by the Asian cultural respect and fear for any elders. And she detected what motivated Tam's spite. I admit feeling rather satisfied, as if Jacqueline's insults to Tam had come from my own chest. She had an effective teasing method; she played on what hurt Tam most—the Asian complex of being an old spinster. Jacqueline toyed with her and suggested that she was grumpy because she was sexually deprived and frustrated. She would smile and conclude, 'Tam's outbursts of temper should not be taken to heart. One should have pity for the old girl instead of anger.'

Tam literally chased Jacqueline out of our house, wishing her out of Cambodia and back in France where she 'should live among the bohemians and paint in the gutters of Paris'. Tam took her cause to my father in the hope he would side with her. But Dad was neutral and let the two women battle out their differences.

Our house echoed with the noise of their constant snarling. Jacqueline began to confront Duck's Feet and I could hear her yell at him, 'You brought me to Cambodia, to this small spare room in this big and mad family and you think it is better than our life in France?' He refused to deal with her complaints. It seemed to him that Jacqueline had too many of those lately and she was increasingly dissatisfied and critical. A few incidents, relating not to Tam but to Grandma, his beloved mother, influenced Duck's Feet's belief that Jacqueline was naturally difficult to please.

Jacqueline was horrified to set foot in my grandparents' neighbourhood. It was poverty stricken and full of beggars. On a personal note, she disliked my grandmother chewing her betel nut and then kissing the baby with her stained mouth. It appalled her. Jacqueline blurted out to Duck's Feet that these physical contacts were 'unhygienic' for their daughter.

Duck's Feet growled back, 'Don't you dare feel disgusted by my mother.'

The honeymoon was well and truly over. More often than not, Duck's Feet came home after work for a brief moment and then jumped back in his car, leaving Jacqueline crying on my mother's shoulders. Mum gave her the advice that Cambodians always give to any newly married couple, 'Never allow fire to feed on fire.' The wife should stay sweetly calm when her husband is angry. It is a prerequisite for a good marriage in which a woman must take the back seat.

Jacqueline shook her head and disapproved of this wisdom. 'I cannot. I serve no master.' She was of the new generation of western women who were already beginning to lay down the foundation for feminism.

Eighteen months later, she and Duck's Feet rented an apartment in the city. He had resigned from the Jesuit school and went to work at the Bank of Indochina, which paid him more. In their elevation to a better standard of living, he and Jacqueline made a point of showing their gratitude to my mother. Occasionally, they treated her and Dad to a dinner out, 'to give "big sister" a break from cooking'.

A bit of lipstick, a short strand of pearls around her neck, a spray of perfume transformed Mum wonderfully. I buzzed around her, touching her freshly washed hair. I was inebriated by the fragrance she loved to wear on rare occasions, a drop of Jacques Fath perfume. I stepped back to get a complete image of my mother. I would see something noble about the way she held her shoulders, something serene and sad about her eyes and the bittersweet smile on her sensuous lips.

'How old are you, Mum?' I asked one evening.

She bent down and put her arms around me, 'Why do you want to know, Vannary?'

'Because no matter how old you are, you are very beautiful!'

She was in fact only thirty-three. I mentally clicked and stored this portrait of her in my mind. This was how I would like to remember her, not a day older, not crushed or wilted, but as fresh as she could be when she had the chance to dress up and enjoy an evening out.

One evening, over a Chinese banquet for six, which included friends whom Duck's Feet had invited, he was talking generally about banking and about clients. 'By the way', he said, looking from Dad to Mum, 'do you know that your little brother Ho is the youngest multi-millionaire in Phnom Penh?' Mum shook her head, smiled and her eyes sparkled with pleasure but said nothing further to boast about her brother.

It was my father who ventured a comment, 'Your brother might be the youngest multi-millionaire, and I do not have that kind of money. However, I can give you the social status that his money can never buy for his wife.'

Mum just smiled again. She smiled to mask all sorts of feelings my father was not subtle enough to understand. What he had said was embarrassing—it was self-flattering, and it undermined my Uncle Ho. Dad lacked the grace to be happy for somebody else's good fortune, and the guests cringed with discomfort and quickly changed the subject. Ho had done no ill and the irony of the episode was that it was Uncle Ho who had been bailing Mum out every month. The bourgeois shopkeeper had not once stooped to criticise my father for failing to provide for his wife sufficiently.

Learning of Ho's success came as a shock to my father. The last he had heard dated back to the time Ho contracted tuberculosis at the Jesuit seminary. He had left without much of a higher education, but was qualified enough to be employed as a junior accountant in a private firm, which had the exclusive contract to build roads for the government. In five years, Ho had climbed to the head of his department. He had a lucky break; the proprietor was going through a nasty divorce, which involved the splitting of assets totalling millions of riels. The estranged wife tried to bribe Ho, who was the chief accountant of her husband's empire. She apparently strutted into Ho's house with bundles of cash and jewellery and proposed, 'All this is yours if you give me an accurate picture of the company accounts.'

Ho politely declined. His boss, a powerful man, rewarded him amply. For his loyalty, Ho received a large sum of money, which he used to buy children's wear from Vietnam to sell in Phnom Penh. This first venture did not bring an instant profit and he was lucky to break even.

He noticed that Cambodian women were starting to rave about French cosmetics and imported underwear. But they had to be big names—Lou, Rosy lingerie, Jacques Fath and Chanel perfumes, Christian Dior cosmetics and skincare products. Ho did not have enough funds to import these expensive products. But he had an idea. He looked up the addresses of all the most popular labels and wrote to them. He posed as a wealthy entrepreneur who had the means of placing bulk orders and requested they send him as many samples as they could, in an array of sizes and colours of every item of their entire collection. Boxes and boxes of samples arrived and sold faster than hot cakes. Without spending a single cent except for postage, Ho had all of a sudden made enough capital to open a retail outlet in the city. Within a short space of time he had become the youngest multi-millionaire in Phnom Penh. He was not even thirty.

He had a wife, five children, a nanny for each, two chauffeured Mercedes cars and the freehold of a six-storey building in the heart of the city. His shop was downstairs and his residence upstairs was serviced by a private lift. In Phnom Penh, he had two brothers and two sisters. His mother, one brother and one sister had migrated back to Saigon. All of them depended on him for a living.

My mother was his eldest sister. I heard her tease him, 'How can a priest like you be so astute in worldly business?'

His reply was, 'But it is all godly business, big sister. I carry everybody in our family and God has to carry me.'

Then she put forth her hand and exclaimed, 'Carry me now till the next month. I am desperate for a few thousand riels.' He mumbled an objection but he always put his hand in his pocket and took out a pile of notes.

And still Mum was short of cash. Gradually she was too ashamed to depend on him. More than anything, she was concerned that he might start losing respect for her husband. There must be a way for her to make up the shortfall herself.

23

Mum's Enterprises

Before Uncle Ho made his fortune, my mother borrowed from various sources. She was always unable to pay her debts, and had to juggle by getting money from Paul to pay Peter. It was a mad round of financial transactions that indirectly included Aunt Tam, her anonymous creditor. Aunt Tam had secretly invested her savings with a moneylender whom my mother visited regularly. The loans were granted at exorbitant interest, as high as thirty per cent a month.

My Uncle Ho was extremely generous, he paid her debts and subsidised her for years, but Mum wanted to start something of her own to generate an income. She relished success stories of housewives who, from difficult situations, ended up owning good businesses. Mum was not greedy, she prayed for just enough for her to sleep well at night. 'Just two hundred and fifty riels exactly a day for ten days.' She had an advantage—she had a willing partner, our overworked housekeeper, Heang.

The two were keen to sell haberdashery; odd pins and needles, cotton threads and balls of knitting wool, pieces of leftover fabrics, which they made into frilly girls' dresses. They hand-knitted jumpers and cardigans, sold baby's singlets and underwear, and women's cotton bras, hairpins, combs and brushes. The lot was rolled into a neat package, which Heang tied to her bike. Heang squatted in front of the wares, which she displayed on a blanket at the local neighbourhood market close to home. She returned day after day with skimpy takings. Weeks of laborious preparation went to waste. My mother and Heang had been sewing, knitting and embroidering from night until dawn. Mum realised where they had gone wrong. She was dealing with a class of consumers who were not well off and what she had tried to sell to them they could do without. It was the end of haberdashery.

The next venture was aimed at a larger audience—supplying food to restaurants. Mum was on the right track, but it was what she could supply that would determine her success. There was one suggestion from a Chinese chef, which she seriously contemplated. Some restaurants offered pigeons and rabbits on their menus, albeit in smaller quantities but my mother believed the prices were good and she had found the answer.

The backyard changed from the moment she eagerly commissioned rabbit hutches and pigeon holes to be put in place. We rushed in all directions of the compound to gather weeds for the rabbits to eat, which saved her from buying scraps at the market. The pigeons' droppings coated the walls, the car, the clothes hanging in the open air to dry. They landed at times on our heads. When this happened my mother laughed and quoted a superstition. 'It is "good luck" if a bird targets you so accurately!' The rabbits did not breed fast enough for Mum to sell them, some died of disease and half of the pigeons were attracted to the neighbours' roofs to lay their eggs. The few that lived, stayed and multiplied. Vandy grew attached to them and felt sorry for them. He objected to the cruelty of their fate. He disliked the thought they would finish up on a plate in a restaurant, and successfully convinced Mum that she was committing bad karma. Back to square one.

Mum went back to Uncle Ho. His wife was starting to object. Quite rightly, she said that she could not stop Ho from supporting his mother, his unmarried brothers and sisters, but my mother was married to a so-called high official. 'Why on earth should we have to carry her too?' The last thing my mother wanted was to cause an argument between Ho and his wife. Now, more than before, she had to call upon her limited ingenuity.

She dreamed of a heavy-duty Kenwood mixer and a state-of-the-art, temperature-regulated oven. In her opinion these appliances would open up a lucrative home-based enterprise. She would be able to bake sponge cakes, whip Chantilly and butter cream, and sell them to a particular client who promised to buy if she could deliver. Mum built a lot of castles in the air and she was aware of it. The Australian-made Kenwood mixer, the oven and other modern white goods, washing machines, electric or gas stoves were way beyond her reach. In Cambodia, refrigerators were considered luxury items; they normally occupied a central position in the family lounge. Everything in our house relied on human hands—we had not heard that simple things like vacuum cleaners were already available on the market far, far away from where we lived.

Mum designed her own 'oven' and took it to a tradesman to transform it into reality. It was a free-standing aluminium box with two removable trays inside. These were at equal distances from each other, and at equal distance again between the top and the base where pieces of hot charcoal would be scattered evenly to generate heat. Such a device was not suitable to bake sponge cakes but Mum could bake biscuits instead. She had done her homework, researched the demands, the combined cost of flour, sugar, eggs, charcoal and so on, and worked out her personal capacity of daily production. She carefully worked out the risks and the projected profits of those biscuits. She had to make ten kilograms of three popular varieties; fifteen riels profit per kilogram to earn the exact sum of money that would render her life financially problem-free.

The most important hurdle after all her calculations was finding a teacher who would show her how to bake biscuits. In Cambodia and Vietnam, recipes were more jealously kept than heirlooms, and cookbooks were unheard of. Women achieved serious status in being reputed the 'best' in something. Grandmother Nguen, for instance, was extremely talented for producing wonders from fresh fruit. She transformed them into tasteful glacéed fruit that people commissioned for their wedding banquets. The skill, she said, was in preserving the natural colour. Her exquisitely presented persimmons, ginger and citrus slices looked as if they had not been through any cooking process. Grandmother Nguen guarded her recipes with more care than big corporations guarded their industrial secrets. At eighty years of age, she had not yet divulged them to any of her daughters. She would rather give them her jewellery and her fine embroidered linen, than part with the secrets that had given her such fame.

My mother paid a skilled woman handsomely for her three recipes. Ten days later, she practised what she had been taught and soon after that, another home enterprise was about to take place. The first type of biscuit she made was typically Vietnamese, shaped like the thorny stick from the crown Christ wore on the cross. The second was round shortbread, dotted on the top with half a peanut. The third variety was nothing more mysterious than cats' tongues, which Mum had to curl into cigarette shapes. These cats' tongues were the most popular and fetched the best price. They were also the most labour-intensive. Because they were light, it meant that double the time was spent to achieve half the weight of the other two varieties.

Everyday hence, and with no rest on Sunday, my mother sat in front of her new oven after dinner, after everyone had eaten and the dishes were done. She had to produce and deliver ten kilograms of biscuits before the shops closed at midnight. The fastest and most economical public transport was on the three-wheelers; these recent vehicles to crowd Phnom Penh streets in the sixties were the Lambrettas. They stopped running at half-past eleven. Mum avoided taking our family car, the only one of its kind in the whole of Cambodia, a grey Fiat station wagon. Its motor was at the rear; its front was flat like a pancake from the windscreen down to the bumper bar. Its shape was designed in the pre-aerodynamic age; it travelled in the reverse manner to the bullet concept, pointy part behind. I still remember its number plate— PP 2416. It was our reliable but not smart or speedy car that made its mad four-times-a-day run to school and back for ten years. It had been purchased in the spirit of strict economy; it consumed the least petrol and provided the highest number of seats for the money we paid. The day it stalled and stopped dead embarrassingly in the middle of traffic, the most capable of mechanics pronounced it too old and too worthless to revive with costly spare parts. My heart felt a strange pain to see it go to the tip. This car had been a friend. While it was robust and running, my mother complained it still cost too much for her to drive it to deliver her biscuits. I was aware of another reason she would rather catch public transport. She was afraid somebody might recognise who she was by simply recognising our distinct undistinguished car, and my father would not like people to spread the news that his first wife had to sell biscuits at night.

My own routine changed with this new venture and I was glad for it. At long last my mother relaxed. She was overworked but she had eliminated her horrific panic over money. I wasted no time in getting my schoolwork out of the way after dinner and volunteered to help. I sat her down with a glass of sugared iced tea in one hand and a fan in the other, and we took turns to give her a break.

She watched me roll those cats' tongues with a half-broken chopstick and praised me for a good eye for shapes—perfect and even, very 'professional', she said. We laughed heartily and she would look at her watch, 'Time for me to take over,' she said but I refused. After another few trays I got tired and clumsy and started either to burn the biscuits or sizzle the skin on my forearm. Mum pulled my stool from under me,

'This time you rest,' and 'Look at your arm, you cannot afford to be scarred.'

I would assure her it was nothing, but she reminded me, 'No, it is not nothing. You still have to get a husband and no husband wants a wife with bad scars.'

'Let the men marry their Miss Universe,' I said flatly. I was exasperated by her plans for my future, of having to be physically attractive to get a husband. I retorted I had plans for another 'kind of life with no man'.

'Oh? How can it be? You fancy to remain an old spinster, do you?'

'Yes!'

'No grandchildren from you! Too bad! What do you do to survive?'

'I will earn my own keep. I will be a career woman. No man can then stop me from taking care of you in your old age.' I dreamed away of the most luxurious house for us, a trip to France every year, an eternal time to laugh together, no more cooking, no more baking, and no more tears. I added, 'I will buy the right for you to go back to your church, Mum.'

'That, you can not buy.'

'How come they sell candles to light in the church? I will buy all the candles in all the churches of Cambodia for you to light. Then the priests will accept you back in their flock.'

'The priests might. One day. Not because you buy the candles. You must learn once and for all that God is free. Only men have a price.'

'Heaven was for sale once upon a time,' I told my mother. 'The priests were selling it.'

'Priests' doings, not God's,' she clarified.

The last lot of dough had to be cooled and put into the second tin. We quickly combed our hair and carried our goods to the street for a ride to the shop. We rested our packed tins on our laps to protect the contents from breaking. In the city, the Chinese merchant opened the lid to inspect our products, snapped one biscuit in half, tasted it and, looking at my mother, bargained, 'Two riels less per kilogram!'

Mum defended the quality of her biscuits to no avail.

'Please, Tou Che (Chinese for sister),' said the man, 'I have to make a living too, you know.'

Mum had to accept that she was over a barrel. When she held the cash, she was thankful to the man and thankful to her God. I felt anger and a vague humiliation; we had worked ourselves ragged for that cash and God had nothing to do with it.

'Thank yourself more,' I said. 'God had nothing to do with our biscuits. Let's reward ourselves and buy an apple.' It was a Granny Smith, waxed green and preciously wrapped in cellophane paper. We later quartered it at home for my two brothers and ourselves.

Mum put the apple in her bag, a smile lingered on her face and she repeated more thanks to her God as she touched the money she had earned. 'He provided the means and opened the way. A lot to be thankful for.' Her wisdom was too puzzling and complex to understand at that stage. Not until I could glue all the loose pieces together that made up her reactions, thoughts and words did I start to see the big picture. To understand my mother, I had to understand her perception of God. I could not love her without loving Him.

The fruit shop was in the vicinity of Phnom Penh Fruit Market, where the smell of imported apples, the beautiful display of imported grapes, pears or other exotic and expensive Cambodian fruits like durians and mangoes attracted people who were taking a leisurely stroll. Some went directly to the open-air night restaurants behind the fruit stalls for their supper. It was here that Dad liked to dine and we risked seeing him.

The market was lively in the evening around the time we made our delivery. My mother usually tried to grab hold of my empty cake tin, carrying the two herself. She walked fast to avoid the crowd, leaving me ten steps behind. I had to run to keep pace with her, and fought to snatch the tins from her.

'Why don't you want to walk slowly with me, Mum? Why don't you let me carry the stupid tin? It is certainly not heavy now.'

She would rush on further and once in a less crowded lane, she stopped and explained, 'You are very tall, you attract all the eyes of passers-by and I don't want you to be seen anywhere near these tins.'

'Why? Should I feel ashamed because we are selling biscuits? It is the bargaining that is embarrassing. Not the selling. And not you. And I like to walk close to you.'

In the middle of the city, I forced her to forget the crowd. I put one arm around her waist, and she put one arm around mine as we walked in time for the last fare home. On the bumpy three-wheeler, which screamed and swerved and beeped its horn most of the way, I took her left hand into mine. I stroked her hard, thick cracked skin; felt her small platinum wedding band encrusted with the tiniest diamonds. This ring cut deep into the flesh of her finger. It was the proof of her legitimacy. I kissed her palm in profound reverence.

My mother, my dear dearest mother, to me there would be no other like her.

24

Stillness before the Storm

In the period just before his retirement, Grandfather indicated that he would spend most of his remaining days in his village. Whenever my father could get hold of a spare jeep or some other four-wheel drive vehicle from the office, we were squeezed like sardines into the back for a weekend in Prek Dek.

Life in the village had stood still. Despite the fact that half of the village was Vietnamese, the only evident difference between them and the Cambodians was the language they spoke. Regardless of race, every living soul in the fields was somehow assimilated into the colours of the earth, with their varying shades of sun-browned skin. Their eyes were gentle and resigned.

Prek Dek was far from the northern borders, the Vietcong trail and the military turmoil; far from Phnom Penh, which was growing into a modern city. Prek Dek had yet to have a proper road linking it comfortably to the main highway, and its houses were still the same tired huts with no electricity, toilets or bathrooms. People still stored water in pots and dug holes in which to hide their savings. Their existence was rugged, but rural life was not without charm and a certain mystery. At dusk, the horizon was tinted with strokes of iridescent colour, which changed to a luminous gold. From a distance the sound of a flute lamented and broke the silence of the empty fields. Inside our hut, the flame of a candle lit up the room and flickered. We would flock around some old visitors, for there was always somebody who came with many stories to tell.

We children learned to swim in the Mekong. We explored its banks and rowed out to the small river-island. My brother Vandy showed his prowess and with big strokes swam across to the other side. He was an excellent swimmer, at home in the treacherous water like a fish. On the island we found a large hole in the ground, which intrigued us and frightened me particularly. A wild and very big beast must have dug that hole, I thought. However from the thick bush emerged a very skinny grey-haired toothless man. He was the village hermit or the village idiot, and he babbled words we could not understand. Saint or fool, we were not sure. So we took off. He could have been the same man whom we knew had been banished from another village, a man who had been tied to a raft and left to starve and die from exposure. It was the local punishment for the unspeakable crime of incest or rape.

Our ancestral house no longer existed. It was burnt beyond recognition at the time the French converted it into their headquarters. They stored guns and grenades under the roof, which had been a granary. When the fire was anonymously lit, the whole place exploded like a bomb, the pall of smoke billowing high up could be seen far afield. On the same paved ground, the villagers donated their time and labour and constructed a humble house. They had it ready and waiting for the eventual return of my grandfather, their benefactor. To the locals older than my grandfather, he was a lost son who would eventually return to the village that had cradled his childhood.

Prek Dek put on a party to receive us, as lavish as its humble means could allow. Fragrant bananas, pineapples, fish, fresh and salted, and poultry were gathered from each household to fill a big hall. It was like that not only for the first welcome, but for all the number of times we visited. Every time we prepared to return to Phnom Penh, people rushed to our car and beseeched us to accept their gifts. They brought full hands of bananas, sacks of rice, corn, eggs and live fowls with their feet tied together, their wings fluttering. We could not leave unless we were loaded to the hilt with food under the seats, on our laps and on our roof rack. For all we knew, the villagers had given us a vital ration of their food supply. Their generosity had no limit.

On a return trip home to Phnom Penh, my father stopped halfway to give a middle-aged American couple a lift. They hopped in the back next to me. Three hours a week of English at school with a French teacher who put on a British accent could not make me fluent. Between the little French the couple knew and a few words I remembered of my lessons in their language, we had a broken conversation. I was intrigued by their curiosity to explore the authentic Cambodian way of life, to get close to the real heart of the Cambodian race, which was not evident in big cities. They had toured Cambodia in a way few foreigners thought of doing, away from the conventional tourist attractions. From what I could understand, they were impressed. They had stopped in small villages like Prek Dek, been welcomed by the peasants into their poor homes and given the most generous treatment, which they had enjoyed more than a five-star hotel. When we parted, the American lady dug into her bag to find a souvenir for me. She said to my father that I was 'such a lovely girl'. She got out a silver coin, half an American dollar showing the profile of President Kennedy.

In most of the country, Cambodia gave the appearance of being true to its sixties reputation. It was labelled the Switzerland of Southeast Asia, and had managed to stay peaceful and neutral, relatively untouched by the Vietnam war next door. This tantalising impression of peace was carefully nurtured and fed to the population by a tight government control of the media. Local newspapers could only report what the Prince wished to reveal. Foreign journalists who contradicted the commonly held view that Cambodia was anything less than a peaceful paradise were not allowed entry.

I was among those who naïvely believed that the sixties were harmonious years and that Sihanouk was indeed an agile political tightrope walker, balancing relations between the giants of the world. He was friendly towards the United States, the USSR, China and North Vietnam, with which he secretly signed a treaty. It was difficult to keep friends who were at loggerheads with each other. Capitalist America and communist China did not get along; there was a cold war between the Russians and the Americans; China and North Vietnam did not see eye to eye; and America and North Vietnam were fighting.

In the secret treaty between Cambodia and North Vietnam, Sihanouk agreed for Ho Chi Minh's Vietcong forces to enter our northern borders to escape the bombing of the Americans, to rest, recuperate, and to receive a fresh supply of food. In exchange, Ho Chi Minh's government promised that Vietnam would leave Cambodia alone if and when he were to eventually win the war over America. The Americans were aware of this secret pact and knew that the Prince was double-dealing and double-crossing them. They needed to destroy the Vietcong trail, to choke their enemies' supply in the north of Cambodia. They needed Sihanouk to side completely with them. Sihanouk was afraid to take a clear stand. What if the Americans withdrew their presence from the area? Cambodia would be left at the mercy of its hereditary enemies. The Prince claimed that he had to keep walking on that tightrope, pleading sympathy from the world. Now and then he would scream as loud as he could to the world media, accusing the Americans of transgressing on Cambodian territories, of sending their planes to bomb and kill our northern villagers. For America to win the Vietnam War, Cambodians were led to believe by what they heard from the media that it was increasingly imperative for them to get rid of Sihanouk.

The last half of the fifties and the first half of the sixties were for Cambodia a period of peace, albeit a fragile one to those who could see beneath the surface. It was the calm before the storm. Most people could not read the omens, believing that peace was here to stay. We were enthralled by the statesmanship of our Prince, and our country also seemed to have a capable military leader, Colonel Lon Nol, whom Sihanouk had repeatedly praised. It successively hosted visits from important foreign figures. Chou En-lai (Zhou Enlai) came twice from China. President Sukarno flew from Indonesia, Emperor Haile Selassie from Ethiopia. Princess Margaret represented Britain on behalf of Queen Elizabeth II. Marshal Tito visited from Yugoslavia, General de Gaulle from France and the young widow of President Kennedy was invited to Cambodia.

We were busy window-dressing for the world to look on Cambodia with admiration. Fragments of praise written by foreign journalists were translated and filtered into the local media. Most of us were intoxicated by a sense of greatness. We glanced at our old civilisation through the Angkorian temples that our ancestors had built and which the French were helping to preserve as a world heritage. Experts were reclaiming the ruins from the invasion of the forest, from the gigantic walking fig trees, which clawed and swallowed towers of stones under their roots. Each piece of our temples' walls, each bas-relief was patiently restored, sometimes totally reconstructed by archaeologists with the same care that might be given to delicate antique porcelain. We turned to the past for nourishment to take us into our future. We drew an immense pride and strength from the mere fact we were once mighty and could indeed be mighty again. Alas, our future and our hope reposed on the surface of a mirage.

Our lives were then centred round the cult of Prince Sihanouk. We hero-worshipped our Prince. He was our 'father'. In our house, like in the house of every loyal subject, a portrait of him and next to it, a portrait of the Queen Mother, were hung on the main wall of our lounge. People waited for hours on the street kerbs to watch the royal motorcade pass by. We could only see the Prince's hand throwing out of his limousine window many pieces of printed cotton fabrics, which people fought to catch. My own adolescence was imbued with my love for the Prince and my love for my Cambodian heritage. One of my eager wishes was to visit Angkor. Many times, I could almost feel my hands touching the curves of the *apsaras*, smiling heavenly dancers carved in many galleries. I would like to be there, among the blessed pilgrims. I set an imaginary date for this trip; it would be after my graduation from school. I was not to know that fate had other plans. Thirty years later, I am still to visit these temples.

In his own way, my father played a part in the development of Cambodia. At the beginning of 1946, at age eighteen, Dad had entered the School of Administration where he studied for two years. At the end of 1947, he attended the School of Agriculture for another two years while he was employed at the related department. In 1949, before Cambodia's independence, he obtained a French scholarship to the United States and France. He studied the cultivation of maize at different universities, first in Wisconsin, then Minnesota, Louisiana and North Carolina then on to Quebec in Canada. He finished with a stint at Montpellier in France. Upon his return to Cambodia, he supervised the founding of the first agricultural school in Prek Leap, where he taught.

The area was then controlled by a band of insurgents, the Khmer Issaraks, who jeopardised the school construction by menacing and injuring the coolies. One night Dad requested a meeting with the rebel leader. He called him 'brother' and appealed to this man's patriotism to allow the completion of a school, which had nothing to do with politics.

In 1960, Dad finished a thesis on maize and was formally made an agricultural engineer. His qualification was too firm for anybody to dismiss him on the sole suspicion of race.

He participated in a major government project when Phnom Penh was bursting at the seams from overpopulation and desperate to expand its boundaries. On the Pochentong airport highway to the west, which paralleled the railway line going to the province of Battambang, the government proposed to build a long retaining wall of many kilometres. Starting from the Lambert Stadium, close to the eventual site for the French Embassy in the north, this wall would contour towards the west. It aimed at containing the seasonal floods and to connect the newly developed area to modern civilisation. Baptised as Toul Kok (meaning dry hill), it became the most popular and one of the most expensive residential suburbs in Phnom Penh. Its subdivision into half-acre blocks attracted the rich. Here, they could achieve their dreams for a villa or a mansion with ample room left for a proper garden since the central part of the city could not provide the luxury of space.

Dad was asked to allocate suitable machinery to excavate, shift the dirt and build the retaining wall. For his contribution, he was awarded an acre of land, where he eventually designed and erected his own dream home. It was a square-rendered brick box of two stories, painted white with sky-blue windows. We followed its building with excitement, for Mum used to drive us there to show us, 'Look at what your father is doing! A great house!'

After one visit when we saw our father's car at the main gate of the new house, Mum never took us back. She was certain then that the great house was not meant for her after all. My father was living there with the last of his mistresses, a nurse from the Bessieres Clinic.

My father was also responsible for introducing the culture and the appreciation of the avocado in Cambodia. A medical friend had drawn his attention to the nutritional virtue of this fruit, which was grown in the Philippines. Dad developed small plantations and released them for human consumption in Cambodia. He was also instrumental in the cultivation of strawberries in Kirirom, a mountain town whose altitude suited the fruit. These were to supply the tourist hotels.

The biggest project my father was involved in was the construction of a hydraulic dam on Phnom Bokor in Kompong Chnang. According to my mother, my father arrived on-site to supervise a very disorganised team of workers. Hundreds of coolies were recruited and herded from the warm lowlands to work on the mountain; all came unequipped to live in comparatively cold temperatures. Their small wages were sent back to their wives and they did not have the resources to purchase warm clothing and blankets to protect themselves from the weather. The government had overlooked this detail, nor did it allocate funds to build proper shelters to accommodate the workers. The diet was insubstantial and the exposure to the cold severe. Many got sick. The work pace dropped.

My father returned to Phnom Penh to report the situation to his office, which in turn was supposed to report to relevant people in charge. He submitted an urgent request for money to improve the living conditions on the worksite. Bureaucracy took time to deliberate, and lingered longer than my father could wait. He could not let the coolies freeze on the mountain and was compelled to act. He took it upon himself to sign a release of ministerial funds without his superior's backing, and with the funds, bought clothes, blankets, food and building materials.

My father had thus far climbed steadily to the directorship in the Ministry of Agriculture. His was not a station of political power by any means, but the position nevertheless came with some repute and a few people were envious. Dad's most notable enemy was a colleague, Som Ok, who had been busy mapping Dad's progress and waiting for a false step to bring him down. Som Ok knew of our racial mix and his personal agenda was to sweep people like us from the executive echelon of the administration. He wrote an open letter to the national newspaper, the *Neak Cheat Niyum*, which published his concern over the existence of one 'non-Cambodian' official at the Ministry of Agriculture. Although my father's name was not mentioned, people in the office and our family knew at whom the accusation was aimed. Over the years, Som Ok had been listing objections against my father: the borrowing of the ministerial jeep to take us to Prek Dek, the 'arbitrary' placements of villagers by Dad. He noted the people who headed towards our ministerial house wearing Vietnamese dress. My aunt De Oanh and our housekeeper Haeng had to conform after this complaint, and put on the Cambodian skirt and a blouse whenever they entered the compound.

Dad's impulsive move left him wide open to criticism. He had over-stepped the line, bypassed the authorities above him. He had 'thrown the hook over the mountain'. This was the false step Mr Som Ok was waiting for. He called for an 'inquest' which in fact was summarily an accusation. Nobody bothered to verify what my father did with the ministerial money.

The official version accused my father of 'stealing' from the government. The affair was brought before the Prince, who chose to discuss it in the national congress held twice a year beside the royal palace. It was broadcast to the nation. Selected matters of interest were made public. This congress was Sihanouk's way to allow his people—his 'children'—to hear the truth about the country; how it was run, whom we should love, whom we should hate, who was the hero of the day. With my father, the Prince rendered a quick verdict of guilt. Within the calendar month, Dad had to pay back the lump sum he had been accused of embezzling from the ministry, or be subjected to a sentence in jail. It was a staggering amount of money: six hundred thousand riels. Dad lost sleep and his health over the scandal. He was diagnosed with severe diabetes and put on a strict diet. His cheeks were hollowed, his hair turned grey, his waist shrank to half its previous size. He came home a sick impoverished man deserted by his nurse. My mother looked after him, and not once was she skeptical of his honesty. Dad's nightmare was to raise the money he owed the government.

One week before the imposed deadline, he had one option left—to go to my grandfather who had won the lottery in 1960. He literally crawled into the front door of Grandfather's hut, crying for forgiveness and begging for his generosity. My grandfather had been expecting him from the minute he had heard the scandal over the radio. He demanded the truth from his son's mouth.

He was pensive, drawing puffs of smoke and said, 'I cannot be your judge. I have agonised over the shame your action has brought to our name. Society is condemning you. At the end of the day, son, I trust that real justice is in karma's hands. If your account is truthful and the money was indeed spent to attenuate the coolies' lives, it is far from being lost. You will reap the good deeds no matter what happens.'

Dad's payment of the funds did not halt his demotion; he was put down a grade. It took two to four years to climb a step. He had to hand back the ministerial house for which his sunken rank no longer made him eligible. We were asked to leave Chamcar Mon within six months. The shock of my father's drop in rank made me reassess my own identity and my real place in Cambodian society.

From the time of notice for us to vacate Chamcar Mon, my father had a legal battle on his hands against his last mistress. The nurse continued to live in the great house at Toul Kok, proclaiming it her legitimate right as the owner. She alleged that she had contributed to the cost of building it and she had proof she was a resident from the very beginning. She insisted that it be sold and she wanted half of its price. The dispute over this house between her and my father was resolved in court, presided by her uncle. Both my parents were expecting the ruling to be biased. In this event, my father was prepared to challenge the judge, although it would be unwise and an appeal promised to be lengthy. It came as a surprise that the judge deliberated against his own niece. He declared that the house belonged fully to my father and ordered her to vacate the property at once.

In 1964, we moved to Toul Kok, then an already affluent residential area. Because of our new address, from the outside it looked as though we were upgrading ourselves. How we skimmed on the little things that were not publicly obvious! The face our family projected was a vast contrast to the reality inside the house. The same could be said about Cambodia. We put up the façade of peace and prosperity.

25

End of an Era

The Phnom Bokor affair had taken its toll on Granddad. He complained of a chronic sore throat for a few months and started vomiting blood. My mother and I drove him to the general practitioner, who immediately admitted him to the private Calmette Hospital. He threw up clotted blood in the car and while a nurse was admitting him, he splashed her white uniform red. He was X-rayed and pronounced terminally ill with cancer. Smoking and drinking had effectively eroded his oesophagus. He was fed intravenously and doctors were debating how to save his life. Within a week they proposed a complicated procedure: to cut a section of his small intestine and use it to replace the damaged oesophagus. Nobody could guarantee the outcome. Without an operation, my grandfather was condemned to a few short months at the most, during which he would have to be heavily sedated and fed artificially.

He was intellectually capable of making the choice himself and opted for surgery. 'En tout cas, ce sera soit la faim ou la fin,' he said to the doctor in French, playing on words. Translated into English, he meant, in any case, it would be either hunger or death. He had the dark humour to notice how ironical the goddess karma could be. 'She chose to front me with hunger, my greatest dread throughout my life!' And he tapped my father's arm, 'She has not forgiven all the ancestral sins yet, son!'

Within days, they opened him up and experimented with an unprecedented method of organ swapping and grafting. He went into a coma and never regained consciousness. A few of us were standing around his hospital bed when his life-support machine was turned off. It was the first time I had actually seen a man die and I was clocking his last pulse.

Later when his corpse was taken to our home at Toul Kok, each of us had to take turns giving him a symbolic wash. My hand touched his flesh. His trunk was zigzagged with tapes, which concealed long cuts across his stomach, chest and throat. His corpse looked half-mummified and it had a particular smell. The sensation from this physical contact sent a chill up my spine and churned my stomach. I ran and vomited loudly. During the monks' prayer recital, I was rather ashamed of my reaction and decided to atone for my repulsion.

I tried to do what people normally do when they lose a close relative. I tried to show sorrow. I could weep at the sight of crippled or leprous children begging in the streets of my city. I sobbed readily when I read sad books. I was sensitive to the sufferings of fictional characters, the heroine in the novel of La Dame Aux Camélias by Alexander Dumas (the younger), the little street boy Gavroche in Les Misérables by Victor Hugo. I could stay up late devouring literature and my eyes would be swollen the next day. But I found no outpouring of sadness in my heart for my own grandfather. He had been a stranger and had not encouraged attachment. It was as though he had purposely set out to make himself disliked. When alive, he had kept his distance and demanded complete silence in his house. I was terrified to be in his presence; children in our family had to refrain from laughing or talking. His twenty–twenty vision could detect the faintest fluff in his food and he went berserk at Grandma for her negligence. I dreaded the obligatory visits and resented his aloofness and despotism. In my fourteen years of going regularly to his dilapidated hut, he never seemed to notice me.

Twice in my life he directly addressed me by the nickname he had coined for me. It was a distortion of Nary, short for Vannary. 'C-a-a-r-e-e!' he called me one day. 'Show me your feet!' That same afternoon, he called me again, 'C-a-a-r-e-e, show me how the tip of your tongue can reach the tip of your nose.' Each time, I promptly did what I was asked.

He concluded, 'Humph. You are truly a granddaughter of mine. See the high arch of my feet?' And he took off his runners. My grandmother must have disclosed that he and I had these same physical characteristics. About the silly tongue, he did not demonstrate how he could still lick the tip of his nose in the way I could. He simply patted my shoulder and said mysteriously, 'Your tongue is an asset. Just don't show it to people.' He could rest assured that I certainly didn't fancy going around poking my tongue out to others to show it off.

My father fulfilled his last request and we took time off from school to accompany the coffin back to Prek Dek. A long line of mourners dressed in white stood shoulder to shoulder in front of the temple where my grandfather was first educated and where he was now about to be cremated. Flesh to ashes, his body went up in flames in the soaring heat of the Cambodian summer. My mother reflected, 'Such a generous man, really. It was a pity he had a cruel tongue toward your grandmother.'

Granddad was heir to large landholdings and had given away the right to collect rent. He was a high official yet he had skipped the perks of high officialdom and spent half of his monthly wage feeding his neighbours. He had worked in one of the most corrupt offices but never took a cent in a bribe. He had won the biggest pool in the national lottery and continued to live a humble life among the poorest. A father to many children, he was devoted to one, Somalee. He had verbally abused his wife and yet remained a monogamist. The unassuming manner in which he had dressed himself and ridden his worn-out bike to work did not seem compatible with his appreciation for the finest wines and spirits, French delicacies and his collection of exquisite pipes and finely bound books. He was a misplaced peasant in a city, his spirit that of a misplaced monk in a materialistic society.

We had a framed photograph of his unsmiling face, which stared down from the wall. I stared at him many a time and puzzled on the contradictions of his character and his deeds. There was no love lost between him and his colleagues at work, who had not attended his funeral. Instead, they sent one man with a wreath. Yet his village and community declared a week of grieving when he was in hospital and for days after the news of his passing people could not come to terms with their loss.

To me he was neither saint nor villain. He was just a man who had a lot of obvious flaws. Now, thirty years after his death, as my country is dying on its feet and being strangled by corruption, I have to admit that my grandfather was far ahead of his time and had diagnosed the social ills of Cambodia for what they truly were. His irascible exterior masked rare qualities. He had shown a lot of courage in practising what he believed in. He lived and died a very misunderstood and lonely man.

When I was fourteen, he was too abstruse and complex for me to understand. Yet I was intrigued by his startling eccentricities; they provoked me to analyse him more fully. Perhaps the most redeeming judgement of him came from my own grandmother, who in spite of years of putting up with him, said, 'I lived with the richest man in the country.' Then she added, 'A person is not rich by what he keeps and owns. Wealth is gauged by what he gives.' Her words were more eloquent than any expression of love; they explained to me the ultimate reason that had helped her spend four decades in a marriage that appeared to others to have been a mistake.

Granddad's death marked the passing of an era for us. He had been the one who held the extended family together. After his death, the family disintegrated. My father was unable to exert the same sort of central authority.

The sister my father loved most, Aunt Tam, withdrew from him her loyalty when she stopped believing that he could come up with the dowry he promised. She shifted the blame on to him for her unhappy life and in her distorted interpretation said that Dad's efforts to gather his brothers and sisters to live with him were motivated by his intention to control them. The nub of her sudden animosity against him was rooted in money. She could not forgive him for 'taking' my grandfather's winnings to pay his debts; she brainwashed the siblings against Dad and spent weeks trying to persuade my grandmother to sell the lands in Prek Dek and distribute the inheritance. Grandma withdrew the money from the bank, but instead of dividing it, bought a brand new city apartment on Rue Charles de Gaulle, where she installed herself and Somalee. The decision was not quite in line with Tam's advice, but the investment in this apartment was in my grandmother's name. As far as Tam was concerned, at least it was safe now from my father's reach. She pushed for the sale of Prek Dek. Her calculation estimated the ancestral estate to be worth millions of riels. On this issue, Dad refused to budge. He had promised Granddad on his deathbed never to deprive the villagers of the lands. Tam accused him of keeping this estate for himself, wife, mistresses and children. It stirred up an ugly argument, after which Tam shifted from our house in Toul Kok and moved in with my grandmother at Rue Charles de Gaulle. My father called her 'a rat deserting a sinking ship'. Aunt Touch followed suit, then Uncle Ali.

Tam's skill at fuelling discord pitted everybody against each other in my grandmother's apartment. We constantly heard of one brother or one sister falling out with another after some quarrel. Nobody could extinguish the feuds, not even my grandmother whose authority Tam defied. Eventually she ordered Tam to 'either keep to herself or leave the house'. Tam left.

Some time later, she was reported to have been in a public hospital where she aborted a five-and-a-half-month-old fetus. She had fallen pregnant and had been abandoned. Shortly after this she fell into the arms of another man to whom she bore two daughters and a son. Again she was abandoned.

When my mother heard of Tam's condition, she ignored my father's warning and went looking for her. Tam was in a back alley hidden behind the burnished façades of commercial buildings where she was raising her children by begging. My mother cried with overwhelming pity. Tam could not quite stand up; she took my mother's arm, dragging her feet and catching her breath, and whimpered about her abominable suffering. Her daughters' heads were bald, their hair had been shaved to control lice. One of them had a sore eye so badly festering she became half-blind. They limped to our car and we drove home.

My father did not have the ultimate cruelty to refuse his sister a place to live. His first reaction to her miserable appearance was to remark that her pursuit to harm others had backfired on her. I was moved by Tam's severe transformation. It occurred to me that I had wished for this kind of adversity to befall her and perhaps my curses were starting to take effect.

Although Tam returned and clung to us like an old skin we could not shed, a few members began to break away. There were three consecutive marriages. Sophanee found a man to love. Though penniless, he was handsome and young, Jesuit-educated and more importantly he had an honest head on his shoulders. He was a student and protégé of Duck's Feet at École Miche.

After the Bank of Indochina, Duck's Feet went to Esso, where he was a managing director. He took in Sophanee's future husband to work as an accountant for this corporation. The lovebirds got married and called each other chou, which in French means 'cabbage' or 'darling'. They lived amorously ever after.

My Aunt Saturday, a constant companion to Sophanee, was inspired to find a comparable match. She was the only sister who had not deserted Dad. Other than her misplaced idolatry for Imelda Marcos and Madame Nhu, she was stable and immune to Tam's malicious influences.

After Sophanee, she befriended our next-door neighbour, a daughter of a mixed couple, an ex-French Legionnaire married to a Cambodian lady. The Frenchman, having spent three decades in Cambodia, was fluent in the local language and hesitant in his own native tongue. Even his eyes of blue, which must have been sparkling and bright, had faded to an indecisive colour, his complexion was tanned and he was at ease in a sarong and bare chest around the house. His daughter and Aunt Saturday were of an age when bachelors were attracted to them like bees to honey. Among these contenders, mostly army, navy or airforce men, two navigators of the Cambodian Royal Air Force were the keenest. The lieutenant in love with Saturday belonged to a remote Portuguese ancestry—Catholic and very devout.

My father hesitated slightly over Lieutenant Toum's religion, and he was not wrong in assuming that if his sister were to wed, she would have to convert. Dad preferred to concede. His importance as 'brother number one' had been badly undermined and he doubted if he had any real authority left over Saturday even though she had never challenged him. She had no problem about changing religion, after all, she had been through the nuns' school and had full knowledge of the Christian faith.

On a beautiful day, she wore her white bridal gown down the aisle with Dad's blessings. My mother briefly walked back into her church, a member of the bride's party, and watched Saturday proudly walk to the altar. Mum couldn't help wondering if her life would have been better had Dad consented to the Nguens' demand that he convert to Catholicism. For now, she was happy for Saturday. Dad gratified himself that he 'had led' one sister at least to a respectable marriage.

Our housekeeper Heang also married soon after this. A Chinese man who did not care about her lost virginity and her past loved her for who she was. She had decency and a pure devoted heart. He swept her out of housekeeping and wedded her with due ceremony. He was poor and remained poor, and Heang had to more than prove her inexhaustible courage and stamina.

Out of these changes, I finally had a big room all to myself. I had to share it occasionally with my half-sister, Nee, when she visited. I would have liked to love her completely but I sensed she was cautiously reserved. It was the invisible, unbreakable wall between us for having two different mothers, I guess. The eldest of my two half-brothers, Tha, gave no resistance. His wonderful capacity to give of himself had made him straightaway my favourite of the three.

My other favourite brother Vaan had unfortunately dropped out of school. He had done well in junior classes but the abuse from Uncle Ali created irreparable damage. Other factors were eating into my adopted brother's life. The confusion of adolescence; the knowledge he could not help his natural mother, who had made another bad marriage and her drinking. There were the influences of undesirable friends. At fifteen, he was drifting. He struggled at Lycée Descartes in the middle school and was expelled. He became alarmingly worldly, coming home to me and raving about his fights against other gangs, using axes and knives, kicking some French or Chinese boys in the groin 'where it hurt beyond fixing'. He loathed the French who appeared to him to behave as if they still owned Cambodia, and he loathed the Chinese because they behaved as if they owned the economy. He had shocking revelations about what 'happened out there'—the prostitution, the homosexual practices and I was too naïve to know otherwise. I was truly intrigued to discover how it was actually done and asked him to tell me the details, but he was condescending. He winked and walked off, leaving me to my own imagination.

My blood brother Vandy was not an academic achiever either. He stalled as long as he could until he too was expelled from Lycée Descartes. Mum begged him to at least attain the Brevet standard. 1966 was the last year before this formal certificate was erased from the French system. It was indicative of the world's demand for higher education. From then on, the lowest denominator of a person's academic credential would be no less than a Baccalaureate. My mother was pushing Vandy to study that year through private tuition and she forced him to keep it up. She went into seven churches during their deserted hours to light her candles and pray for him. He and I were to sit together for the Brevet. We both passed.

Vandy shelved his books, learned to drive and chauffeured us around. He wasted years doing nothing other than courting girls, or going on long camping trips with friends to the beach. He lived for the moment, grabbing fun and thrills wherever he could find them. He had a short memory for the past, a lot of energy for the present and made no provision for the future. Yet he possessed untapped natural gifts. He could have been a fantastic sportsman. I had seen him swim with no formal training from one bank of a river to another, back and forth, against the strong currents of the fierce young Mekong. Mum had warned him to be careful, she claimed we had a 'history of drowning in the family', referring to the death of the patriarch in a shallow rainpool in Tan Chau.

Vandy was good with mechanical things. He used to observe the mechanics in the workshop at Chamcar Mon where big trucks, tractors and the fleet of ministerial cars were stranded for repair. He would listen to the sound of the vehicles and ventured his opinion on what was wrong and what needed fixing. At first the mechanics were annoyed at the kid who seemed to show off. Often enough they were staggered that he had been right. Vandy could have developed his natural talent into something meaningful. Dad yearned for him to stick to the conventional path of getting the Baccalaureate first, then a diploma in engineering. He insisted that social recognition had only regard for a formal degree and no matter how well one could repair cars, one would always remain a mechanic. Dad chided, sighed and called Vandy 'an idiot', and because he was busy himself in three jobs, Vandy's life drifted without direction.

26

The Turning Point

Out of the four of us who attended Lycée Descartes—Vandy, Vaan, Touch and me—three dropped out. I was the only one left. I had more than proved to my mother that it was worthwhile keeping me there but my schooling became a financial load I could not ignore. Mum was battling, not just against the overwhelming number of mouths to feed, but against the cost of living. Although many of our 'boarders' had gone their separate ways, Phnom Penh was becoming an expensive place and wages were not adjusted in proportion to the escalating expenses.

Mum moaned about the price of food. Fish, bountiful and cheap in the past, was suddenly expensive; at times garlic, which makes any modest food taste more palatable, was not available. Behind the scenes, beyond the comprehension of consumers like my mother, a handful of people in control were playing games and getting rich very quickly.

The economy of Cambodia from the early fifties fell into the hands of the Chinese community. One man in particular, Chou Kong, held the monopoly across the board. He was tightly connected to the policy-makers who told him in advance of the changes in regulations and customs laws. The shortage of some food items was the result of his manoeuvres. Chou Kong bought up all the garlic, created a vacuum to boost the demand, and released it back to the consumers at exorbitant prices. The rice harvest of 1966 was low, and its scarcity was further aggravated by smuggling activities at the Cambodia–Vietnam border, where it was illicitly sold at higher prices to Vietnamese guerrillas. One third of its annual production was regularly and illegally shifted on the black market. Chinese traders paid big bribes, up to one thousand five hundred American dollars for each truck to military chiefs who allowed loaded convoys to reach the Vietcong sanctuary in the north. The public was deprived while army generals and Chinese middlemen made money. Medicines were abominably expensive in shops, since they were more profitable to smuggle.

In answer to the budget deficit resulting from the smuggling, Sihanouk proceeded to nationalise private banks, distilleries and the import–export trade, which directly provoked the collapse of the Bank of Phnom Penh. Its managing director took off to Vietnam after embezzling millions of dollars, most of which were assets accumulated and deposited by the social elite and prominent businessmen. In 1963 Sihanouk founded SONEXIM (the French acronym for 'Société Nationale d'Export et d'Import) and the Magazin D'État (State Store House), the two official bodies that purchased and stockpiled agricultural produce at low prices from the villagers. The government in turn wholesaled them to retailers who were forced to make do with a small ten per cent profit margin. Sihanouk's nationalisation of trade fell flat on its face. To begin with, it was badly run, controlled by a wedge of officials who, other than their loyalty or connections to the Prince, were incapable and corrupt administrators. They became wealthier in the process. The peasants were hostile to nationalisation, preferring to sell their crops directly to the Chinese merchants, who paid them more cash and who gave them fertiliser and seed on credit.

Cambodia relied on foreign aid, mainly from the United States. The withdrawal of France from Southeast Asia in the fifties had given the

Americans the opportunity to enter her old colonies. In the south of Vietnam, the Americans dominated Ngo Dinh Diem's regime, which they financed into existence and paid for its administration. In Cambodia, the United States contributed essential military and economic assistance, which Sihanouk made the big mistake of cancelling in 1962. His decision to swing against America stemmed from self-protection more than national interest after he suspected the CIA arranged the assassinations in 1963 of Diem and his brother Nhu in Vietnam. Despite praise by part of the French media for his courage to stand up to a giant, he was paranoid that the United States may one day choose to eliminate him.

Sihanouk embarked on an open anti-American campaign that led to a cessation of diplomatic relations in 1965. Over the radio, the Prince used the most insulting rhetoric against the Americans. Students were officially permitted to miss school for the day, soldiers wore civilian clothes, and both groups provided a lend-a-crowd to the state-organised demonstration outside the American embassy in March 1964. They waved banners and placards with slogans such as 'US go home'. They threw stones and insults. By 1965, diplomatic relations were marred beyond salvation when an article in Newsweek alleged that Sihanouk's mother collected rent from brothels. Over the years, Sihanouk had set many nasty precedents, especially when he publicly rejoiced over President Kennedy's assassination. Following the shutdown of the embassy, he broadcast a string of scare campaigns. The Americans, we were told, were going to attempt to occupy Cambodia by force; they would use our highways and our broad boulevards as runways for their planes to land in Phnom Penh. The Prince pressed for the urgency of planting trees along the central strips of the capital's wide streets. The population was being influenced to hate the Americans.

The waning and the final withdrawal of American aid brought colossal problems to all sectors of society. The import of luxury items dropped, rentals dropped and the Bank of Phnom Penh closed. The elite were hard hit by Sihanouk's anti-American policy, as was the army. Without American dollars, it could not even renew its uniforms. Its trucks, donated by the United States, fell out of use from lack of spare parts and fuel. Its equipment looked good in parades but was unusable. In spite of a shortage of funds, increasing unrest at the borders called for the necessity to expand the size of the military corps. Twenty thousand more soldiers were recruited among young teenagers.

Rural Cambodia lived under worse conditions. It was crippled by heavier debts to usurers, and terrorised by the threat of landmines planted by the Issaraks. There were random bombs from the Americans who claimed that the border between Cambodia and Vietnam was unclear. The peasants rebelled in various pockets of the countryside. In one such uprising in April 1967, the village of Samlaut was burnt down. General Lon Nol, who had been sent to deal with the upheaval, executed its inhabitants. A great number of them were beheaded. The General was officially a national hero on his return from his bloody mission.

Law and order was handled with increased power given to a Secret Police of which Sihanouk's brother-in-law, Colonel Oum Manorine, was in charge. Dissenting views were punishable by jail or death. I can still see today in my mind as clearly as I saw in 1964 the execution by firing squad of Pheap In. He was a Khmer Issarak whose activities, hostile to the Prince, were funded by Ngo Dinh Diem in Vietnam who in turn was funded by the Americans. Pheap In's captivity and the display of his punishment sent a message to the public—that it was costly to cross the Prince. This man's arrest was turned into a show trial, which Sihanouk used to demonstrate and amplify that the Americans were sponsoring unrest in Cambodia.

I was twelve. For fifteen minutes unedited viewing of In's execution was projected on the screens of cinemas everywhere in the city. The close-up shots recorded the wincing muscles in the man's cheeks. His head suddenly fell on the side, his body, tied to a pole, jerked. The final *coup de grâce* exploded beside the eye where a bullet came to lodge. The spurt of his blood seemed to gush out of the screen onto my lap. I broke into a cold sweat and was seized by an uncontrollable urge to throw up. That day, Mum had insisted on my coming to the movie with her to translate a biblical epic for her.

Two million young people of my generation had better access to education. After a state visit to Indonesia where President Sukarno showed off a few new universities to Sihanouk, our Prince decided to boost education in Cambodia. He allocated twenty per cent of the national budget towards its development. Compared to seven secondary schools, which existed in 1953, the number rose to 139 in 1969. At the tertiary level, nine universities were created quickly. The statistics were impressive. Unfortunately the program was flawed. Little thought was given to directing the courses to areas that could make a contribution to the needs of Cambodia. Diplomas were obtained under doubtful circumstances by those who could pay. Those who were poor and passed on their own merit had dim prospects for employment.

The Prince would not tackle the problem, and accused the graduates of being fussy and unwilling to accept the jobs offered. Added to the disillusionment of holding useless degrees, this new wave of youth was getting conscious that it was imprisoned in a time capsule. Sihanouk, like his Angkorian predecessors, demanded to rule in absolute power. The emerging new generation, which was more educated, could no longer agree. The economic crisis got worse and the scarcity of jobs meant school leavers had to work as labourers in the mines of Battambang or to pedal trishaws in the city.

From the mid-sixties, there were too many new and unresolved problems to be swept under the carpet. Politics were getting more complex and volatile. The Prince was no longer in control. His opponents, who had been secretly murdered, shovelled into prisons or had fled were poised to bite back.

In spite of an ambitious campaign to improve health—the rural population had participated with enthusiasm to build health centres and dispensaries—the increase in the number of hospitals—17 hospitals in 1953 against 60 in 1969—failed to achieve good effects. On average there was one doctor to every 15 000 people. Medicine was wasted or stolen by the medical employees. In the provinces, a so-called free injection in a health centre cost a peasant forty riels in tips to the nurse, a sum equivalent to four days' earnings. People died younger, in their forties, from malnutrition, malaria, venereal diseases, tuberculosis and from the lack of the most basic medication. Leprosy had not been eradicated. The streets were full of deformed beggars in filthy torn rags, squatting outside temples, shops and restaurants.

Amidst the financial strife, the Prince called for restraint. The majority complied because they had no financial means to do otherwise. However, at no other time was it more painfully obvious that the elite was obscenely rich. Some women, instead of normal buttons, had rubies and emeralds sewn on their blouses. Numerous luxurious villas and mansions were being built, with bidets in their bathrooms and marble tiles on the floor. At this same time more and more villagers escaped from the unrest of the countryside and lived in city squalor.

The time was finally auspicious for the communists to come out of the woodwork. People began to listen to them when they pointed out the failings of Sihanouk's policies. In the fifties, not long after independence from France, rural life was peaceful, almost dormant. It was difficult for the communists to proselytise. During this decade of peace, they faded into the background. They fled to the jungle or became schoolteachers. Their jobs enabled them to implant the seeds of their political doctrine. The instability and disillusionment in the sixties provided fertile topsoil for these seeds to germinate at last.

During the election of 1966, money was paid to opponents to bow out, and any other unethical means were used to eliminate rivals. The newly 'elected' parliament was conservative. General Lon Nol became Prime Minister.

The economic situation failed to improve. There was a drought in 1968. The budget deficit was worse. Exports fell. Instead of reducing government expenses, especially the expenses in areas of prestige and luxury, Sihanouk opted to legalise gambling, which brought good annual revenue from the casinos. Gamblers committed suicide after massive losses at the tables; the press was forbidden to report on the social consequences of Sihanouk's policy. The veneer of political stability was cracking and the aura of the Prince was fading.

I would be a liar to claim that I understood the complexity of the politics of that time. My family was among the docile majority. We were affected by difficult changes coming from the outside but we coped with them quietly. By and large I was unexposed to critical views against the government—nothing in the immediate circle where I lived and studied taught me to dispute the information spoonfed by Sihanouk. I was the gullible recipient of his indoctrination. I had no pressing reason to challenge what I heard. As long as I found meals on our table, a roof over our heads, and in spite of having to consume cheaper foods—fish heads instead of whole fish, offal instead of meat—conditions looked bearable. The restlessness I did feel, I attributed to home life. I was more aware of my own crossroads rather than the crossroad Cambodia was facing. In 1966, I was fourteen, and at that age, my view of the world was self-centred. I took it for granted that my country would survive.

As with many fourteen year olds, my personal problems seemed far more formidable. I was aware that being a girl programmed me to be a wife and mother. Culturally I should depend on a throw of a dice, on a man, a complete stranger. I was cynical about the institution of marriage and audaciously I wanted to stand on my own two feet, to be my own master. But I was also tempted to let go, to dream of a man who would love me truly. The awakening from these occasional fantasies came with my conviction that such a male could not exist. Alas, I had only to kiss my mother in the morning, live through the day with her, physically or mentally, or catch her crying by herself late at night to remind myself that my life was not my own.

Had my brother Vandy been more focused and stronger, I might not have felt the need to take on the responsibility of defending Mum in her old age. Because my brother was carefree, I had to step into the role of the eldest son. I realised too that this was the very same role my father must have imposed upon himself. He did not accomplish what he wanted. He was not the champion who stopped his mother's sufferings. He was not the successful brother-shepherd for his flock of brothers and sisters. Finally, he was not the good husband and father for his women and children. His personal career was in tatters. In analysing his failures, I concluded that he had put too much on his plate. I dared to believe I could do better. Unlike him, I had only one person to worry about—my mother, and I had one goal—her happiness.

My mother worried about my plan to stay a spinster because of her. She repeated that I should have a conventional life and refused my sacrifice. 'My reward lies in seeing you properly married.'

She meant what she said. When I turned fifteen, she announced to my father that she knew of a young man's parents who wished to come and ask for my hand in marriage. He had just returned from the United States with an engineering degree and his father was the toast of the country since he had led a delegation to the World Court at The Hague. He had succeeded in winning back a tenth-century temple at Preah Vihear, which the Thais had claimed belonged to them because it was situated at the border of Cambodia and Thailand. The family in question was fishing for a reaction from my parents before they made the official move. My mother asked me first but I laughed it off. I told her I wanted to study, go overseas, come back with a high degree and one day be somebody in my own right. A husband would impede my achieving this. I did not even have the curiosity to know the name of the young man. Mum told me to be less ambitious and sought my father's counsel. He rallied behind me.

When I served him lunch that day, he winked at me and said to my mother the words I would never forget, 'When my daughter decides to get married, let it be at the time she could kill her husband with her pen.' I had thought him terribly chauvinistic and insensitive, but I started to be pleasantly surprised by him. I was grateful he supported the idea that a woman should be better armed against the whims of destiny. Nothing gratified him more than to know of my ambition to be a career woman, and it did not seem unachievable.

In the Cabinet, a few women were already holding top ministerial positions and women had recently been given the right to vote. Slowly, my father and I developed a bond and mutual respect. He followed my progress at school more closely and we exchanged views on politics. I was the unexpected son he wanted my brother to be. In some ways, he made a conscious effort to tame his frustrations towards my brother and started to be a lot more civil to my mother. He opened up his heart and let me in to share his worries and his desires. He had tried to forge my brother from the beginning.

'I cannot forget that our family stands out. We have so many odds against us. For your brother to find decent work, he has to be doubly educated above the rest, otherwise society will dwell on race issues to cut him out.' I could see tears in his eyes. I was respectful not to criticise his method of shaping my brother. Instead of gently coaxing him, he applied the same abrasive treatment he had himself received from Granddad. Now he looked at me as though I was his son, willing to fight for the future of our family.

These were happy years, and I was learning to love my father. But I could still find in him traces of unfairness and an autocratic tendency against which I rebelled. I had never had a direct clash with him until I committed an indiscretion.

A few girls in my class and I were looking for a private math teacher. I boasted I knew of a Frenchman, a penfriend of a girl who taught me to knit and we would pay him to coach us. My brother agreed to drive me to see him but at the last minute, Vandy got shy and told me to go upstairs to his apartment by myself, which I did and which by Cambodian etiquette was very improper. I had at least to be chaperoned during the meeting but I did not take to heart the strict demand of appearances since nobody was to know that I would see this man on my own. The Frenchman was rather full of himself. He bragged about his involvement in writing editorials for Prince Sihanouk and said that he was occupied by important 'state' responsibilities. I learnt two decades later that he was the Prince's private secretary. I patiently listened to his boasting, but at the end of his long speech I could not resist some sarcasm, 'I want to know whether you could give my friends and me some math lessons. If you can't, it takes a simple word "no", not a monologue. There is no need to account to me for your time—I am not interested in how you spend it.'

He was amused by my irritation and a lot more by the fact I was outspoken enough to express it to his face. When he escorted me to the lift, he was a lot less arrogant than he had been earlier. I thought nothing else would derive from this meeting.

A few days later I visited Aunt Saturday, who had just given birth to her second child, a girl. Her husband, Toum, an airforce officer who had recently been made a captain, was talking about the influence of Frenchmen in Sihanouk's inner circle and happened to mention the name of Alain D, none other than the man I had met briefly. Before I could check myself, I told my uncle-in-law that I 'knew' him to be quite arrogant.

My aunt and her husband looked at me with some surprise, 'Oh? You know him?' they asked.

'I met him once,' I said.

Before long, this piece of information was passed on to my father, who straightaway assumed that I was up to no good. He called me to his bedroom and put on a dramatic performance. He did not ask me any questions, and accused me of 'dirtying' our reputation and if I did not stop 'seeing' the Frenchman, he would shoot me. He pointed at the row of rifles. I stared at him, not the least intimidated. I was furious and I had to repress the urge to dare him to shoot me on the spot.

The following day, I looked up Alain D's phone number and rang him. I made the audacious offer to go out with him and told him bluntly not to flatter himself because I wanted to get back at my father. Alain gallantly complied with my invitation. He was amused and fascinated by my rebellious character more than he was really attracted to me physically. We became good friends in the strict sense of the word.

I committed the monstrous mistake of confiding to my mother of my outings and she trembled on my behalf. She was scared of my father. Besides she simply could not believe that a man, especially a Frenchman, would leave me untouched.

'Oy ya ya!' she exclaimed, 'how safe is a silly goat when it chooses to enter the lion's den?' She was expecting me to fall pregnant and make a jolly mess of my life. However hard I tried to explain to her that Alain and I were just friends, she wasn't convinced.

Part Four **THE KILLING FIELDS**

27

The Elephants Start to Fight

In 1969, influenced by the example of a few friends, I was keen to sit for the Cambodian Baccalaureate. Run by the government education system, the Cambodian Baccalaureate was totally ignored by and independent of my French school. In other words, my records at Lycée Descartes would not credit or discredit me whether I passed or failed. This state diploma was not readily recognised outside Cambodia because, unlike a French Baccalaureate from Lycée Descartes, it did not carry enough weight to eventually place me at a university overseas. But I believed it a bonus to have all the same. It would be proof that I was also a product of my country's system, and nobody could accuse me of being only French educated. My decision was again a reflection of my need to affirm that I was Cambodian.

Perhaps more than the bigotry of my country towards Vietnam, more than my own complex of being born half Vietnamese and half Cambodian, Lycée Descartes' method of teaching had a lot to answer for the way I felt. My education had robbed me of the little I had of my Cambodian identity. My first lesson in history related to the beginning of a Gaelic tribe, and we recited by heart the following lines: 'Our ancestors were the Gauls, blond and blue-eyed . . .' They were the fore-bears of the French, not mine. But it was the first prick of the needle, which transfused gradually the blood of French culture into my veins.

The history of my real country was an optional subject, introduced much later in mid-school. A solemn old Frenchman with balding, streaky, long white hair held court for a tedious hour every week in front of our class. Unfortunately by that stage, most of us could not care less about our cultural origin. He mumbled, his eyes fixed on the pages of notes on his desk. He stuttered about the Fou Nan, the Tchen La, the Khmer Empire and names of kings ending with 'Varman', and cities ending with 'pura', alien sounds to our ears.

A Cambodian teacher, who taught us the Cambodian language as a 'foreign' language, treated us with benign leniency. He considered students like us a breed apart, not quite Cambodian and not French either. What the education of Lycée Descartes aimed to achieve with us was ambiguous, but one thing was clear. In its priorities, it considered any discipline relating to Cambodia to be of secondary importance. During recess we were forbidden to speak our mother tongue but we could practise any other foreign language on the curriculum, be it German, Spanish or English. A few Cambodian students were influenced to shun their origin completely, as was the case of General Nhiek Tioulong's daughter. She only befriended the French and snubbed the rest of us, whom she considered an inferior, indigenous bunch. I never heard her utter a single word that sounded remotely native. She was a prime example of a French heart imprisoned in a conspicuously Cambodian body.

Rhagsmee, a close Cambodian friend of mine, was similarly divorced from our culture. In her case, she had been a product of an irregular diplomatic life. Because her father had been an ambassador to London for a very long time, she grew up in Europe and boarded in a Parisian school for eight years. She made awful errors in Cambodian but she had a most talented ease at writing poetry in French. I recall one incident when she was bored by our literature teacher. This man pounded the whole class with dates and facts and his pedagogic method of teaching forced us to learn by heart excerpts of what he considered major works. His voice was dull and very often we doodled to keep from falling asleep. Rhagsmee nudged me with a flick of her elbow, and signalled for me to read a long piece she had written. She used verses faithful to the Alexandrine cadence to satirise a revered playwright of the French classical period, attacking an extract of Corneille from the famous play, *Le Cid*. The plot was inspired by the love between Don Rodrigue and Chimene. They were betrothed but their fathers insulted each other and became enemies. The tragedy began when the Don was pressured by his Spanish knightly duty to kill the girl's father. In a touching tirade, he talked of his heart being torn between love and honour. Rhagsmee transformed it into a comical parody so brilliant that our literature teacher kept it. Instead of sending us to detention, he reread Rhagsmee's work and I heard him admit under his breath, 'Not bad, not bad at all!'

Lycée Descartes shaped us to be French in thought and foreigners in our own country. It refused at one stage to respect the Cambodian public holidays; an act that caused Prince Sihanouk to accuse the school of trying to 'form a state within the state'. Inside our school, the rejection of anything Cambodian contradicted the nationalistic waves outside. Our education confused us, and provoked in me an identity crisis. My school friends and I were broadly conscious that we belonged to an elite. Fifteen years after independence from France, we were still intellectually enslaved and proud to be Francophile—literate Cambodians had not quite weaned themselves from a deep reverence of the old colonial masters and still regarded the French as a superior race. The students from Lycée Descartes, because of their fluency in French and their families' wealth, tended to consider themselves 'exclusive'. Unpopular with the students from the state system, they were nevertheless envied. They did not need to be liked to retain their place among the upper classes.

Although I studied at Lycée Descartes, I did not belong to the ruling class. As in everything else, I was caught on the cusp of situations and of groups. One foot of my family was caught somewhere in the upper middle-class while the other was metaphorically entrenched in the mud, in the lives of the downtrodden. Perhaps like my grandfather, I was emotionally attached to my rural roots, which made me feel I was a genetic part of the lower class and more receptive to their difficulties. I was not unaware of the way they lived, suffered and died.

I remember our new housekeeper who replaced Heang; she worked for us a few hours a day and she came with her sick infant. The baby did not look to be a day older than four months but was nearly three years old. She could not talk or walk. She was motionless, staring with lifeless eyes at nothing, her lips were peeled and blistered by dehydration, and though her mouth opened to cry she could not make a sound. Her mother's malnutrition had caused a shortage of breast milk, which was substituted by diluted sweet condensed milk. This was unsuitable for a baby's diet; she went through a tin a week consuming it regardless of whether it had gone mouldy. Chronic diarrhoea set in, stunted her growth and retarded her other faculties.

When our new housekeeper first knocked at our door looking for a job, my mother was moved to tears. Mum pressured her to take the infant to the hospital at once. The poor woman shook her head and said she had been, but doctors had no advice to give her. Mum understood that medicine had no prescription nor cure for poverty. She rinsed the plastic feeding bottle, soaked it in salt to sterilise it, and boiled rice into a thin broth in her belief that its fluid stabilised loose bowels. Any care Mum could offer was too little too late. The infant withered further, and it was painful to see her, like a tiny bud that would never get the chance to grow and bloom.

Our housekeeper's hut was built on unusually long stilts on one side of the retaining wall, amid the low-lying slum area where the stricken residents perished from snake bites, malaria, influenza and

Arriving in Sydney in 1971.

Mr Chan Sar Serei met my father after I left Phnom Penh, 1972.

Military training after the fall of Prince Norodom Sihanouk, 1970. I am the first on the left.

Aunt Somalee on her wedding day, 31 August 1973.

In Canberra, in 1972, at the residence of the Cambodian Ambassador, Mr Nay Valentin. I was the second from right.

I was sketching classical Cambodian dancers, Sydney, 1972.

The end product was framed and gifted to my supervisor, Mrs M. Bailey.

more commonly drowned during the monsoon. It was during such a flood that her bloated body was fished from the water where she had fallen out of the dinghy to her death, her arms wrapped firmly around the baby on her chest. Her husband was too distraught to live and hanged himself. They were the unmentionable casualties of hideous poverty, the hidden faces nobody wanted to see.

I was saddened but I did not feel guilt. We were not responsible for the inequalities in our society. To a lesser degree I knew what it was like to be poor, to have strappy shoes that fell apart and had to be stapled together to wear to an upper-class school. I made smaller steps, scuffing my feet close to the ground to prevent the sandals from slipping off. Our poverty would not kill us in the way our housekeeper was killed by hers, but it would take only a careless step to slide from where we were to the bottom. There were malicious forces out there prepared to give us a push. The answer to self-preservation lay, I thought, in education.

To sit for the Cambodian Baccalaureate, I had to brush up on the history of Cambodia and its literature to which I had been but fleetingly exposed. I was relatively confident that on the strength of the other subjects in which I was competent, my overall result would be good. On the second day of the week-long test in a state school, I focused my concentration on a literary composition about a Cambodian novel. It was the test I dreaded most. In the classroom was a supervisor who directed his attention to me from the minute he walked into the place. He paced past the desks, stopping longer behind mine, peeping over to read my paper and chuckling. He walked away, only to come back and repeat the performance. I gave him a look that begged him to leave me alone, but instead of respecting my need for concentration, he proceeded to ask me personal questions—which was my school? where was my house? and so forth. I answered in monosyllables. He got annoyed and requested to see my identification. On this card was written in full my parents' names. My mother's maiden name was unmistakably Vietnamese.

The supervisor, in a louder voice, said, 'So you are half *youn* (insulting word for a Vietnamese), I see!' A pause, then he asked, 'What brought you here for a Cambodian test?'

I took in a deep breath. He threw indiscreet racial remarks. I slowly folded my test paper, tore it in half, collected my stationery, got up from my chair and walked out of the exam room. I could not see any point in staying if he was not going to let me write my essay in peace. It was useless to sit for the other tests because my mark in literature would be nought. I did not think of complaining to other officials, I would only draw further attention to the fact that I indeed was half 'youn'. It was not the isolated instance of racial discrimination in my life, there would be more in the future, I was sure of that. I thought I was prepared for the worst, yet when I found myself targeted, I felt disarmingly speechless and wounded.

I told my father about the experience. He ruminated over his meal in silence. Finally he said, 'I hope you have the courage it needs to go where you intend to go. In the Cambodian government, it is going to be rougher than you think. You climb one step, somebody will try to kick you back two steps.'

At the age I was then, I had the faith and the temerity to bounce back. 'Don't worry, Dad, I will help to change a few things.' He gave me a curious, unconvinced look, but he said no more.

Not getting the Cambodian school certificate was an omen I did not take lightly. If I could not work within the government, I had to be able to switch to the private sector. I was keen on languages and hotel management. Naïvely, I trusted that I would become a diplomat, a cabinet minister in tourism, or failing these, an international interpreter or an executive in a holiday resort.

September 1969 was the start of a crucial academic year for me— I was working towards the French Baccalaureate. It was also a critical year for Cambodia, when many political upheavals were setting the country on a road of greater uncertainty.

The conservative parliamentarians 'voted' into the National Assembly in 1966 were more and more convinced of the redundancy of Prince Sihanouk. Under the leadership of the Prime Minister, General Lon Nol, they followed an increasingly independent path of action from the Prince, and favoured the return of American aid into Cambodia. During this cloudy and turbulent phase of his political life, the Prince was making films, which he wrote, produced and acted in. It did not help that his last wife, Princess Monique and her family, were giving the jealous elite and the royal dignitaries ample opportunities for criticism. She was supposedly extracting huge amounts in bribes. The vandalism of the Kep Casino had apparently been the consequence of her demands for a monthly payment of forty thousand American dollars from the Chinese concessionaire who in the end preferred to smash down his own casino rather than keep paying her.

I witnessed a little of the wealth of her family through watching a girl in my class. She was Princess Monique's niece whose father was the head of the Secret Police. Her traditional Cambodian wedding to a French teacher was a glamorous event to which a few of us were invited. I was amazed by the presentation of gifts from all the major embassies delivered to her parents' newly built mansion. The nearby streets were blocked with limousines, policemen redirected traffic, and the curious public flocked in to watch the ostentatious display of money and power. The dowry to the young bride was a figure quoted at around a million American dollars. Or was it two? People who observed the extraordinary speed at which Princess Monique and her family accumulated wealth were not impressed. She would in time become one of the targets for Sihanouk's critics to bring him down. In February 1970 Sihanouk left the country to seek medical attention and at the same time to seek solutions to Cambodia's mounting political problems.

On 18 March 1970 General Lon Nol seized the opportunity of the Prince's absence to oust him. He had the support of the President of the

National Assembly, Cheng Heng, whose son was in my year at school. The third member to back the coup was Sihanouk's own cousin, Prince Sisowath Sirik Matak. Disloyalty and usurpation of power in the extended royal family were common. The most appalling anecdote in Cambodian history involved the slaying of two young princes in the mid-seventeenth century. Chauponhea Chant (known under the name of Botom Reachea II) seized the throne in 1642 after he assassinated his cousin, the previous king. He killed his own uncle, who was father to the king and his nephews, who were the king's small sons. These two young princes were thrown in a dungeon where jail-keepers progressively carved the boys' flesh, cooked it and forced them to eat it until they died a slow death.

The news of Sihanouk's fall stunned the nation. Within a week, portraits of the Prince and the Queen Mother were torn down and taken out to the streets where they were burnt. Old people watched the bonfires and wept, not believing that the sacred monarchy, two thousand years old, could be eliminated so abruptly and ruthlessly. The monarchy had been an integral part of the Cambodian psyche, the source of its culture and pride. Sketches of the Prince's face were crossed out in red paint around the city walls and Lon Nol condemned him as a traitor. Deplorable details of his wife's past—true or made up to suit the spirit of the occasion—gained momentum through the gossip mill. Details of her ex-boyfriends and her origin were part of Lon Nol's smear campaign. The concern of the whole nation was scaled down to the level of trifling gossip over the private life of a woman who was one half of a royal couple.

The denigration of Sihanouk and his wife was in reality a smoke-screen to hide more pertinent matters, which should have attracted closer scrutiny and publicity. For example, Lon Nol's new government had just given carte blanche to American planes to fly into Cambodia and indiscriminately kill suspected Vietcongs and Cambodian peasants alike. Instantly too, the embassy of Communist North Vietnam was ousted from Phnom Penh in the midst of a huge state-organised demonstration of people shouting angrily, 'Vietnam Go Home!' It was followed by the killing spree of Vietnamese fishermen and innocent civilians who lived in houseboats along the Mekong. Axed to death during the night, their mutilated bodies littered the river by sunrise. It was a prelude to worse things to come for the Vietnamese.

My family had reason to be frightened. When Vietnam sent ships to Phnom Penh to reclaim its lost citizens, Uncle Ali joined the repatriated crowd. He had not felt comfortable in Cambodia. We did not hear from him again.

Aunt Touch missed catching a boat when it docked along the Mekong River, and walked to Chaudoc. Over the border the South Vietnamese soldiers mistook her for a disguised Vietcong and arrested her. She was interrogated and tortured until she eventually went insane.

Uncle Chea, whom we thought was happily married to the old retired governor's daughter, suddenly got divorced. His Vietnamese origins became a relevant issue to his Cambodian wife, in spite of a son they had together. Chea drowned his bitterness in alcohol and went to live with my grandmother in her apartment.

Duck's Feet was disgusted by the latest developments and flew to France with Jacqueline and their two children. They were never to return to the land of the 'uncivilised'.

Mum's brother, Uncle Ho, whose business was increasingly jeopardised by racial difficulties, could no longer function. Before the terrible killings on the river, which alerted many Vietnamese to what might await them if they stayed in Cambodia, Ho had been subjected to temporary deportations by the government. Whenever an important visit by foreign dignitaries was scheduled in Cambodia, he was 'invited' to spend an obligatory vacation in a government summerhouse where he was under constant guard by armed secret police officers. Ho thought it wise to cut his losses. He sold his house and converted cash into diamonds, which he smuggled inside powdered milk tins. He filled the boots of two of his cars and went to Saigon. It was the end of a golden era for Ho.

Lon Nol's government received generous handouts from the Americans, and Cambodian officials were now channelling these funds directly into their personal Swiss bank accounts. American bombs dropped over the countryside and blasted deep scars into the landscape. During this period, an estimated six hundred thousand peasants lost their lives. The majority of the rural population now had a more urgent need to take refuge in big cities. They were unemployed and living in squalor. Within less than a decade, the population in Phnom Penh jumped to over two million.

For safety, my father sold our house at Toul Kok, which was too close to a military base, and shunted us to another place. The building was two stories high. Downstairs was divided into three separate self-contained apartments. The whole complex reached the limit of the fence on three sides, and the first floor overhung the roofs of smaller houses around us. We could see through their low windows how our neighbours lived by day or night. In times of fear, when the sounds of guns echoed through the city, it was strangely comforting to feel the proximity of other humans outside our own family. Dad invited his ex-de-facto wife and her children to come and live with us. They set themselves up in one of the apartments. In the second apartment my Aunt Tam lived with her three children. The third one was given to a Prek Dek relative, the Mephom's granddaughter and her family. Having to bring my father's 'other woman' under the same roof did not please my mother. But under the special circumstances of war she was too considerate and kind to object. Her stepchildren were entitled to all the measures of safety my father could provide.

Phnom Penh was now in the state of emergency. All the students, including Lycée Descartes' Cambodian students, were called to perform national duties. We had military training in the afternoons, where we learned about grenades, how to handle and shoot guns and rifles, and moving with a weapon in both hands. We also did a lot of marching, standing eight abreast in neat lines with proper uniforms. I was one of the tallest, so I was at the front from which point the rest of my row had to keep in step with me. Nobody could. One, two, one, two, I failed to hear the beat and fell out of step constantly. Not until somebody else took my place as a leader did we begin to march harmoniously in time.

We were playing soldiers and most of us did not realise that the undertone was far more serious than we suspected. If we had stopped and thought about it, we would have realised that we were being trained to kill. I had difficulty identifying who our enemies were. It was only yesterday that Sihanouk had told us to hate the Americans and to trust China. Now Lon Nol told us the Americans were our friends and our benefactors.

The fires of war from Vietnam were finally spilling into Cambodia. My mother explained to me that they kept burning because the people in the south of Vietnam liked a capitalistic way of life and the people in the north believed in Communism. During the negotiation of their independence in Geneva, the southerners feared they would have to comply with a Communist rule. In my mother's words, it was a disagreement between two brothers, the one from the north and the other from the south—a family argument. And they should have been given the chance to sort out their differences and solve their problems within their family. According to her, the American President had hopped in and had taken sides. He helped the South fight against the North. He had been motivated by his deep-seated fear of Communism spreading in the world.

Who were my enemies? I simply did not know. Many close relatives of mine adhered to different loyalties. In this absurd war, there was a dark possibility that one member of the same family could find his own flesh and blood standing in the firing line. Uncle Leng, who was perhaps a Vietcong or a Cambodian Communist, could well shoot my half-brother one day, because Tha enlisted in Lon Nol's airforce. Uncle

Leng could kill his own brother, Uncle Ali, should the latter be a soldier in the South Vietnamese force.

Despite the compulsory military drilling, helping my mother bake biscuits at night and studying in-between, I graduated at the end of 1970. It was a turbulent year, beginning with Sihanouk's overthrow, which shook many people.

Up to that point in their history, most Cambodians still felt they owed much to Sihanouk. He could be accused of having made dreadful mistakes. He had turned a blind eye to the corruption of those around him, had ignored the escalating youth unemployment in the sixties, had ignored the social consequences of legalising the casinos, had nationalised trade, which had led to total disaster. He had ordered the revolt of Samlaut to be quashed by Lon Nol and had not cared how his general proposed to deal with it. Lon Nol in turn ordered his troops to slay almost the entire village; villagers' heads were piled onto trucks for Phnom Penh to prove that his mission was a success.

For twenty-nine years since his ascent to the throne in 1941, Sihanouk had ruled and encouraged his people to get educated but had not allowed a pluralist government and punished any criticism as a direct affront to his royal person. This period represented the only time the Cambodians were truly ready to bring about a democracy had they been given freedom by Sihanouk. To me, it was a missed opportunity. The most unforgivable act by Sihanouk was his escapism. When the situation in Cambodia got very volatile in the late sixties, he chose to make films instead, and at the beginning of 1970, he chose to go overseas and left Cambodia to miraculously sort itself out.

In spite of what he had done, I was among those who secretly cried at the news of his overthrow. I felt a personal loss as if a close member of my own family had died, and was left for the rest of the year with a sense of desertion and confusion. Sihanouk had been the only leader I ever knew and loved. Deep in my heart I trusted that he was a leader, and had the coup d'état not taken place, the only person who could continue to steer us from being caught in the Vietnam War. After all, Cambodia was his to own—he had a personal interest to ensure our survival.

Lon Nol's new government ousted Sihanouk and invited the Americans back into our country to solve Cambodia's problems. However, in the face of the assurance of now having a big power on our side and all the funds it could offer, I could not be convinced that a foreign ally and all the Cambodian men in the new regime would care for anything more than their personal interest.

When I finished school in 1970, my future rested more on uncertainty and my adulthood commenced against a backdrop of doom and gloom.

28

White Freedom

The Baccalaureate was but the first rung of the ladder I had to climb to get the education I craved. The logical destination to further my studies was France, at the Sorbonne University in Paris. I immediately filled in enrolment forms from the French Embassy and wrote to the dean of the hall of residence for foreign students to secure my place.

My father was quiet about how I proposed to study in France. He did not offer to support me and I knew he did not have the financial resources to do so. I could not humiliate him by asking the impossible. I had nourished the grand dream of going abroad which he encouraged in principle, but it was up to me to find the means. I was hoping that the French government would provide assistance. Previously, a good result in the Baccalaureate from my school warranted an endorsement to study in France, with the air fare paid for by the French government. The exit visa for the scholarship holder was a simple formality.

But things had changed since Lon Nol came to power. His right-wing government stopped condoning the attitudes of the left-wing Cambodian students in France, and put on hold exit visas as further arrivals would augment their numbers and fuel their political activities.

The French cultural attaché, M. Carpentier, told me that scholarships were still available, but with a major difference. He said I had to find my own way, pay my own fare to France, and once there, I could lodge my application.

His only help consisted of a letter of recommendation, to be presented to a relevant office in Paris. Given my academic standard, he had no doubt I would be offered a scholarship. Other than not having the funds to buy my ticket, I was faced with the difficulty of getting an exit visa from the Cambodian Passport Bureau. Without contacts in the right places, I heard it would cost sixty thousand riels in bribes or four months of my father's salary. The roundabout way to obtain a visa to Paris was to arrange a *marriage blanc*—an unconsummated marriage— with a French citizen. My parents would certainly not be pleased at this, and I did not know any Frenchman who would consent to this mad scheme.

By a long shot, my good friend Alain D might. Unfortunately, he had gone back to Paris before the coup d'état. He told me it had been for a short holiday, but with the changes that ousted the prince to whom he was connected, it was unlikely that he would come back.

While I was sorting out my plans to study overseas, I enrolled at the Law Faculty at the University of Phnom Penh, where a blonde Swiss woman lectured us on International Law. I found the course very interesting but had no intention of working in the legal fraternity. In Cambodia, the practice of law was not a good occupation; it was not given the prestige it deserved. After my lectures, I continued to go back to the French Embassy to keep an eye on any change that may occur in the system. M. Carpentier was tired of being subtle and sympathetic, and told me to go looking elsewhere.

My heart was set on France and I had given it my best shot. I made an alphabetical list of embassies in Phnom Penh and visited them everyday. It was a courageous thing for me to do because even in peacetime, there were three places a well-brought-up single girl should not frequent. Unless she was connected to a male foreigner—a connection that implied she was a prostitute or a very loose girl—she should avoid being seen in tourist hotels, nightclubs and embassies. Dancing was permitted on special occasions during the Cambodian New Year and even then, elderly people closed in around the floor and monitored the general behaviour. The boys stayed two respectful steps away from their partners. The Cambodian popular dances had seen to it that no traditional beat involved physical touching between the two sexes.

I was brought up to be extremely prudish and to regard western liberties as being indecent. I was asked to turn my face away when we drove in front of bars. They glittered with fairy lights and I could hear the sounds of western music behind our wound-up car windows. I could imagine what must be going on inside the clubs. Bodies of men and women tangling closely together to some slow tune while the voice of some adult in my family would condemn those bar patrons. The strictness of our society was brought home to me when the French actor Alain Delon came to Cambodia to make a film and stayed at the Hotel Royal in front of our school. He was our idol—the model of good looks and we were all secretly and passionately in love with him. We had to go to tedious lengths to organise a group expedition across the road to get his autograph. Somebody's chauffeur, her bodyguard and her brother had to accompany us to meet the famous movie star so our daring move would look relatively innocent.

To be seen inside an embassy invited a different disapproval, and could lead to more than a smear on one's reputation. If the government of the day was pro-capitalist, and a Cambodian civilian was seen entering the embassy of a socialist or communist country, it was sufficient cause for the secret police to put the individual's name on record. It gave the government ample ground to suspect that he or she was conducting counter-government activities. Whether the secret police were keeping track of my whereabouts or not, I could not be sure. I had a youthful disregard for public opinion, especially when my future was

at stake. I walked into the embassies of Britain, Canada, Japan, the United States and to others that traditionally were never known to give away study grants. Those that did, gave them to students who were to do courses in engineering.

A few receptionists raised their eyebrows at my bravado and I was out in the street, usually within five minutes. One by one, through a process of elimination, I had worked through my list of embassies. My dreams were cut short. I faced a bleak future in Cambodia, which was itself hopelessly without a clear future. I cried for days, not out of self-pity, but out of frustration and powerlessness.

It suddenly occurred to me that I had not given a thought to the Australian embassy, an omission that had a lot to do with the huge gap in my general knowledge. The little of Australia I had learned was condensed to a few brief paragraphs in my geography book. It was a new nation, and I knew of its main cities—Sydney, Melbourne and its capital, Canberra—and its mining capacities. That was all.

I went in and explained my dilemma to the first man I saw, in the best English sentence I could compose. I asked if 'you have a scholarship for me'. The answer came back, 'As a matter of fact, yes, we do.'

Had I not controlled myself, I would have jumped into the arms of this man and kissed him. He was cautious not to give me too much hope. I did not strike him as being fluent in English and besides, he explained that the grants were directed to forty Cambodian public servants. They were called 'Colombo Plan Fellowships', which offered a nine-month course of English in Sydney. Since I was not a public servant I did not qualify. After my initial excitement, I sank to such a low that the man felt sorry for me.

The 'Colombo Plan' came in two categories: 'fellowships' for post-graduates and 'scholarships' for undergraduates. It was part of the parcel of foreign aid Australia provided to the Third World and it favoured English-speaking countries. No longer available nowadays, it was an excellent scheme that aimed at establishing good relationships and a cultural bond between Australia and the recipient countries by means of education. The scholarship or fellowship holders were bound to return to their homeland once they finished their studies in Australia. To my knowledge, because Cambodia was French-speaking, it was not a regular beneficiary of this aid, and it was sheer good luck that forty scholarships were made available in 1971.

'Please come back in a week,' the man at the Australian embassy said. 'The Cambodian government might not be able to spare as many as forty of its public servants to go abroad. In which case, Australia is willing to compromise and offer these fellowships to young students like you. I would do some revision in English if I were you.'

I never prayed so hard, and so unceasingly. I revised and expanded on my English grammar, the irregular verb conjugation and the vocabulary from a dictionary. I started systematically from the first letter of the alphabet, making sure this time I was not missing the one with 'A' as in 'Australia'. I remembered I had read the translated French version of Charles Dickens' novel *Great Expectations*. He was the secret benefactor of the central character in the book. Australia—it could be a Promised Land!

In my state of mind, a week took a long time to pass. I returned to the embassy and to the good news that indeed, forty students would go to Australia instead of forty public servants. There would be a series of tests supervised and corrected by the Australian diplomatic mission but the Cambodian Ministry of Education would have the final say.

I was up against a class of Cambodian students from a particular state school that was unique. Unlike the main stream of other state schools, it was a 'Khmero-English' institution where its students had the benefit of English as a medium in most subjects. I was comforted that my knowledge in French would in some ways help me out because English and French languages, although known to be false cousins in many aspects and in many words, were based on the same ancient origins of Latin and Greek. I might not speak English with ease, but

I had a good passive understanding of the language and in any written test, which allowed more time to think, I was confident I could do well.

The results from these tests were pinned up on the board of the Cambodian Education Office. The names of successful candidates were laid out in order of their marks and ranks. Mine came seventh and next to it was handwritten in red ink an immediate convocation for me to see the Director of the Ministry of Education. It was irregular that I should be the only person he requested to meet. The secretary showed me into his office and a small man answered to the name of Chan Sar Serei. Its beautiful meaning impressed me; the past two generations of parents had finally turned their backs on superstitions and now selected names that bore the mark of glory, bravery or beauty. This director's given names were Sar Serei, the first indicating the colour white, which also symbolises purity, and the second word means free or freedom, hence 'pure freedom'.

He was slow in his manner and his face glowed with kindness. Before he invited me to sit down, he confirmed whether I was the girl he wanted to talk to. He asked, 'You are Vannary?'

I said, 'Yes.'

He went to the point. 'You are half Vietnamese!' He looked at me for some time. His smile was too genuine to belong to a prejudiced person, I thought. Then again, the nicest people could be racist.

I waited and prayed in my heart, 'Please, God, not again.'

He assured me that I was going to Australia, whereupon I breathed more easily and could concentrate on what he had to say. He wanted to let me in on a few facts. He had had to fight for me against three other men who sat on the same panel with him who had rejected me on racial grounds. They would have preferred to allow a pure Cambodian to benefit from the scholarship. Chan Sar Serei countered them with argument of a different sort. He could not deny I was part Vietnamese, but he was impressed that despite being French-educated, I did do well in an English test against students who were English-educated. It indicated to him that I was rather 'intelligent' and he was sure I would do Cambodia proud if his three colleagues let me go abroad. They discussed my case and weighed the pros and cons. Chan Sar Serei was my vehement advocate, he gave them his personal guarantee and they conceded.

He looked at me again for a long time and asked me not to forget that I had a responsibility to prove him right. 'I strongly believe that you will live up to my expectation. You will live up to your country's expectation.'

Emotions choked me and I could not speak. He did not wait for me to. Our meeting ended quite abruptly. It spared me from making a display of patriotic feelings, which could have sounded trite. I have never forgotten this man, his words and his innate sense of fairness. He alone redeemed all the insults I had received from others. If ever there was a hand God had lent to save me, it was to this man who signed my passage to freedom. I called it my 'white freedom' which, in a miraculous and coincidental way, meshed with the meaning and the sound of my benefactor's name.

I heard later that Sar Serei made a point of meeting my father. My mother, who was deeply moved by his gesture, sent me a photograph of Sar Serei sitting close to Dad. Twenty-six years on, as I am writing these lines, I wish my words could somehow reach him. Wherever he is, I would like to affirm that I bear lasting gratitude for his faith in me. Whether I have proved him right is not easy for me to say.

I left Cambodia at the end of 1971. In my small vinyl suitcase were packed a few blouses and traditional Cambodian long silk skirts we called *sampot*, a hand-knitted garish pink cotton cardigan my mother had given to keep me warm in the 'cold Australian winter'. I wore a tiny pair of gold earrings, an inexpensive but sentimental legacy from childhood; my mother had had my ears pierced when I was one month old.

The twenty diamonds of various sizes, some black, some white, which my grandmother handed to me when I announced to her my overseas trip, I left with my mother. These precious stones did buy her rice and food during the hard times that followed. My visit to bid my grandmother goodbye proved to be the last time I saw her alive. She disclosed to me a reading of my destiny by an astrologer. I was, she said, 'a leaf, which would be blown by the wind far from the trunk of the tree that bore me life'. To her, my departure for Australia marked the beginning of a course towards that destiny. 'You will never be returned to us . . . Exactly like your Uncle Duck's Feet.' She whimpered with nostalgia for her son.

Grandma was an inveterate believer in her bible, two thick volumes in which were held predictions for one whole century on the lives of individuals according to the exact hour, day, month and year of their births. On the destiny of Cambodia, she claimed: 'It is written in The Book. In Phnom Penh, human blood will spill and flood the foot of its central hill . . .' The prophecy gave me goosepimples I tried to dismiss it as mere superstition.

In my purse I had a lucky silver coin, the American half-dollar given to me by an American tourist couple, and fifty American dollars from my father. For days before my departure my mother sobbed with joy and with sadness. She was happy I was going to fulfil my dream, and sad because to fulfil my dream had to take me so far away from home. She was somehow certain I would never come back.

I told her as I wiped her cheeks, 'I will be back for you, Mum', but she only said 'che sera sera'. She was familiar with this expression from a popular song sung by the French singer Dalida. Mum pronounced these foreign words with such a funny accent I found myself laughing in spite of the tears in my eyes. She did not go to the airport to see me off, in case her emotions would overpower her.

With thirty-nine other students, I caught an Air Cambodge flight to Singapore where we would link with a Qantas flight to arrive in Sydney a day later.

From my window seat on the plane, I could see my city shrinking below as we lifted higher towards the white clouds. At that height, it occurred to me that I was given the chance to glimpse the earth from God's perspective, where divine vision reduced our earthly ambitions into microscopic and insignificant dimensions. I wondered how much must a man own, in property and power, to look big in God's eye. Suddenly I thought of Grandfather. When he was alive, he must have posed the same question. The message of his philosophy, which had been incomprehensible to me, was beginning to make sense. Four years after we had cremated his body, I suddenly found myself crying for him on the plane.

We landed in Singapore late at night. For the enterprising Chinese, no hour, however late or early, was a bad hour to do business and make money, even from a group of students from a poor country such as Cambodia. We were put in buses courtesy of a department store downtown and no sooner than the doors opened automatically, than we clustered around the goods and spent in frenzy. I had never seen such abundance and variety. I bought my first watch and a pair of patent black court shoes I had always wanted. I believed I looked smart enough to take the world by storm.

29

The Land of Great Expectations

A Qantas jet flew us over a seemingly never-ending mass of ocean and across a never-ending mass of land toward Sydney. We landed on a warm Friday afternoon. The Australian Department of Education sent its people to meet us, a driver for each Commonwealth car and a supervisor for each group of five or six. We were taken to our allocated boarding houses. Mine was on the North Shore, in Green Street, Cremorne. The place was a mansion partitioned into tenements, grand and old like other homes next to it. In the front, a narrow paved path curved romantically along the edge of the cliff. Way below the steep drop, countless wooden steps descended to the ferry stop where the waves came lapping in on the rocks.

Because it was the weekend, we were each given five dollars to spend. On Monday, Mrs Bailey, the guardian of welfare for my group of five girls, promised she would call on us again. I was worried by the small sum she had given us. I had no idea what the money could buy. In Cambodia, five riels bought nothing much, certainly not to live on for two full days. I thought that five Australian dollars would not be any different. I did not realise that where we were placed, meals were part of the package. I was to learn that it took a lot of spending before I saw the end of this money.

I walked to a quaint little store they called a 'milk bar' and ordered a kilogram of silverside slices.

The store owner corrected me, 'You mean a pound?' (Australia had not gone metric yet.)

I showed her my five-dollar note and asked if I had enough to pay.

'Yep,' she said, and I got a lot of change. For seventy cents I had just bought a lot of sliced, cooked red meat. I kept eating and eating, and ever since then I cannot bear to look at silverside.

The meals at the boarding house were strange to my palate. I could not come to grips with one slice of ham, a bed of two lettuce leaves, a few slices of cucumbers, and some tomato wedges as a satisfactory meal.

I made a mistake on the very first night. I failed to understand the kitchen maid, who was a lovely countrywoman with the broadest nasal Australian accent. She rang her bell along the corridors and invited the guests of the house to 'tea time'. I was neither hungry nor thirsty and decided to skip a cup of tea. An hour later, then two, I started to wonder when they would serve dinner. Hunger pushed me to overcome my shyness and I went into the kitchen to ask. I learnt that in Australia, 'tea' also meant dinner and I had missed it.

The fortnightly cheque of seventy-two dollars we were given was a generous amount at a time when a factory worker with some overtime used to earn less than thirty dollars a week. Straight away we opened an account at a Commonwealth Bank under instruction from Mrs Bailey. The first day of our English course was but a week away so we had time to get over our jetlag and to settle down. It rained in Sydney for the whole week. It was a depressing and nagging drizzle and the days were grey. It was enough to encourage my nostalgia for the Cambodian sunshine. I had not talked much since I had arrived. The four other Cambodian girls in my boarding house were friends from the same school. They provided one another with a safety net of which I was not a part. They were not unpleasant to me but I was conscious I was different, and an 'outsider'. It was this feeling of isolation and vulnerability that stopped me from joining their group. Besides, we had fallen into an arrangement I could not change. From the moment our luggage had been carried into the front entrance hall, the landlady announced she had reserved two adjoining double bedrooms on the first floor and a single room on the ground floor. The four girls from the same school were naturally sharing these doubles upstairs and I went on my own. I was also afraid of rejection.

I was lonely and I missed Mum. I could not speak English well enough to make friends with the other guests. I felt a cold gap in my life, and it did not help in the least that I should be extra-sensitive to the cold weather brought on by the rain, which seemed to seep through the walls of my small room. My scanty wardrobe did not equip me to face the climate. I wore the pink cotton cardigan on top of layers of blouses. I stayed tucked in bed to keep warm and to pass the time.

I needed something to cheer me up. One of the four girls suggested shopping. We all went. The ferry took us to Circular Quay where we asked directions to the nearest department store. We ended up at Coles supermarket, which was bigger than the one we had been in in Singapore. We each had to buy an umbrella, since it seemed to pour continuously in Sydney.

'Upper floor by the escalator,' the shop assistant pointed. None of us could stand on the escalator, on those quick-moving steps, without falling to our knees in panic. We backed off, looked desperately around for conventional stairs, but the place had none. The only way up was the terrifying escalator. One of us had the idea of squatting all the way up. We must have looked like tribal women who were having their first brush with civilisation!

Another instance appears funny now, but it wasn't then. After two months of being in Australia, I was still learning new things. Every so often I caught the bus to Chinatown to buy a box of instant two-minute noodles which I boiled for supper in my room. I had a problem with this particular bus line, which serviced George Street between Central Station and Circular Quay. At each point marked 'bus stop' was a contradicting sign that said 'No Standing Any Time'. I took the sign quite literally and being a law-abiding citizen, I sat on the bench some distance away and waited. The bus driver failed to pick me up many times because I could not run fast enough to wave for him to stop. I was very confused so I asked my teacher, Leslie Zuber. She was a kind lady who, apart from her job at the language laboratory, was also a published writer of short stories. She was to solve my dilemma.

'Why is there a sign at the bus stop which says "no standing any time", Lesley? I do not want to do the wrong thing so I sit on the bench and I nearly always miss my bus. Please tell me what to do.'

Lesley laughed and laughed. 'Poor girl,' she said. 'The "no standing" sign is not meant for pedestrians. It is for cars not to park at the bus stop.' I had not learnt that the verb 'stand' could apply to cars. But why didn't the city council use the 'No Parking' sign instead?

Sydney then was a less cosmopolitan city than it is now. Suburban Chinese restaurants in Cremorne could get away with heaps of chopped celery thrown in their 'chow mien' fried noodles. The most popular dishes on the menu were 'short soup' and 'long soup'. Canned coconut cream was a rarity, perhaps not yet imported, and when we craved Indian curry we had to use dairy cream instead. Many of the students discovered they could eat better if they moved out of boarding houses. They rented small flats and cooked the food they missed.

We spent one beautiful sunny afternoon in Centennial Park, where we picnicked on the lawn under the trees, near a small lake which was home to the ducks. A few Cambodian boys planned to return, not to picnic again but to catch a few of the ducks for dinner. Our supervisors were aghast at this story, and told us that we were not supposed to take the ducks—they were public property. There were such places as public parks in Cambodia too, but we were to learn that in Australia, the attitude was different. Where we came from, if a person could get away with grabbing from the 'common good' it would be silly not to.

A few boys found out that rents varied suburb to suburb. To save, they went to Redfern against the advice of their supervisors. The supervisors did not say that Redfern was mainly populated by the Aborigines and that it was a suburb with a high crime rate. We were students in transit; there was no need for them to reveal to us that Australia had its racial problems. Australia was living the last phase of what the Australian journalist John Pilger called the great 'Australian conspiracy of silence'. Australian conscience was gradually being awakened; it wanted to right the wrongs of the past. At long last, the Aborigines were officially recognised and given official papers to say they were citizens. This had happened fewer than five years before I arrived.

The Asians in the early 1970s were not seen as a threat to most Australians. Long forgotten was the early influx of Chinese migrants to the goldfields. Although attitudes linked to the White Australia Policy lingered, I had not encountered racism. There was some curiosity, which was aroused by us wearing our traditional Cambodian costumes in Sydney. It was the Middle Easterners, the Greeks, and the Eastern Europeans who were receiving the wary glances then.

At the Mel Woods laboratory, on a top floor in Oxford Street, Darlinghurst, English was taught to us with earphones, switchboard and voice monitors. We had a set course which was repeated from one term to the next. The challenge of the first few months wore down to a routine but I was somewhat amazed by the slow progress of a much older student, Shiga. He was a middle-aged Japanese man whose wife was a teacher in our laboratory. A potter by profession, his exquisite work was exhibited at Farmers department store. Shiga told me in English more deplorable than mine that he had been enrolled for three consecutive years in the same laboratory! He was a burly and friendly man whom I remember distinctly for his electric hand heater. He normally held it inside his palms in winter and sometimes shared it with me when he saw me rub my cold hands to keep warm.

Winter or summer, I was addicted to ice-cream. I loved to go downstairs during my coffee breaks to buy gelati. Mr Graham, another teacher at the lab used to comment in the most proper English, with exaggerated stresses put on the right syllables. 'What a cold thing to eat on such a cold day!'

The nine months of our fellowship crept by. I longed to be with my mother and our correspondence left things unsaid. The mail was censored and our dialogue was broken by a delay imposed by distance. How could we pick up our thoughts from two weeks, a month, ago? Despite homesickness, I did not want to go home yet. I had not achieved my goal, which was a university degree. My old dream, which centred on France and my nostalgia for its language, which I had not had a chance to speak, its literature, which had been my intellectual food, came back like an obsession. When I left Cambodia I initially considered the nine-month fellowship in Sydney as my chance to get out legally from Cambodia and once in Australia, I thought I would have less difficulty in going to Paris. But I was no longer certain I could obtain a scholarship in France, although I had kept M. Carpentier's letter of recommendation. I let my commonsense prevail; it was best for me to try to extend my stay in Australia and apply for another scholarship. Mrs Bailey promised she would help.

As our fellowship was about to expire, we had to act with urgency. The Australian Education Department consented to keep some of us and pay our tertiary study expenses. All the students had to be retested, and the best fifteen would stay on. Among the other twenty-five who did not make the mark, some returned to our war-torn country, but a few refused to accept their fate. They grappled with the problem of being sent back home against their wish. They seized the last desperate option to marry or get engaged to Australians.

I passed the test and at last, in front of me, I had not merely a wish, but a solid and clear path I could now take. At the end of it would be a degree I could be proud of. It meant three or four more years in Australia. With the other fourteen successful candidates, I had to undergo a preliminary semester at the University of New South Wales in Randwick. During this time, my new supervisor, Mr Owen, took notes of my projected career. I indicated to him my wish to take up a course of five languages, which would enable me to work as an international interpreter with the United Nations. Such a course of languages was not available at any university in Australia.

My second choice was to study hotel management. This was not available at universities, although it was taught in some institutes of technology. The scholarship by which I was bound was specific on this point: I had to attend a university. Red tape, regulations and conditions were a nightmare. The closest course to what I wanted to study was linguistics. I wrestled long and hard against what the Colombo Plan Scheme approved or disapproved and finally accepted linguistics. It was not exactly what I wanted to do but I figured that a bachelor's degree is a bachelor's degree. My mother had told me that knowledge would never go to waste. I was enrolled at Monash University, the second and newest university in Victoria.

After twenty months in Sydney, Melbourne appeared a slower-paced city where people had more time for friendship. My judgement was, of course, subjective. My better command of English meant I could form relationships more easily and my impression of Melbourne was quickly coloured by the warmth my host, Barbara Charles, brought into my life.

She is a wonderful woman, a friend in spirit and a mother in her concern for my emotional wellbeing. She hosted a group of foreign students like me, and helped to bridge the loneliness of our separation from our families and countries. She understood without asking questions and opened her house during those times we were likely to miss home the most. As the student population around Monash purposefully prepared to head back to celebrate Christmas, New Year or Easter with their families, those of us from abroad with no kin or close friends wondered what to do with ourselves. More often than not, an invitation would arrive from Barb over the phone asking us to share these occasions with her around a generous meal. Thanks to her, Melbourne became a place where I felt more at home.

30

Under Lon Nol

My mother kept a steady flow of letters coming to me whereas my sparse letters to her were evasive, quite reminiscent of those sent home by Uncle Duck's Feet during his student days in Paris. I was conscious of not making my stay overseas sound too exciting, for I knew that my relatives were coping with the suffering of war. My mother displayed a latent writing talent, and her accounts of our family's life, in spite of the war, included only good news.

She told me of my brother Vandy's studies in aeronautical engineering at the Russian Institute in Phnom Penh. After his graduation in 1973, and before he was employed in air traffic control at Pochentong Airport, he treated himself to a vacation in Bangkok. The accompanying letter—one of the very few he ever wrote—was brief and abrupt. He urged me to go home. He was counting on me to take over the responsibility of our mother. I was not impressed that he should be so direct about shirking his role.

My mother talked about our family's excitement preceding Aunt Somalee's wedding. Her future husband was a naval officer who would be living in my grandmother's apartment. I reacted to this news with mixed feelings—my cynicism about marriage made me deplore my aunt's choice and I was tempted to remind her of its snares. Somalee was academically gifted, and I resented her for seeming to forget the pact that we had made to look after our respective mothers. We had agreed that the only possible way for us to do so would be to never marry. I considered her change of direction a personal betrayal. I decided not to write to her and to treat the news of her marriage with a condescending silence. After her wedding in August 1973, I found in my mail a picture of her and Vutha (her husband) dressed in their ceremonial clothes. Somalee looked beautiful but much less so than I recalled in the flesh. The camera could not capture the clarity of her huge eyes and the flawlessness of her marble skin. I admit that at times, at the university hall of residence where the sense of isolation was amplified by the stillness of some nights, and where my real need for affection made me long for companionship, I did wonder whose path was right. At least Aunt Somalee spared herself and Grandma the trauma of separation while I, whatever my plan for the future was worth, had to impose on my mother and myself the physical distance of an ocean.

Before the long summer holidays of Christmas 1973, after three years in Australia, I was entitled to a trip back to Cambodia. I declined, however, to take up the offer. It was a difficult decision. It was likely that the Passport Bureau in Phnom Penh would expect a large bribe, without which it would not issue my return visa to Australia. I decided not to put myself through the ordeal again, and faced another summer break regretting my decision and missing home. The letter my mother wrote during this period revealed her disappointment. She had run into a few scholarship holders from Australia and suggested that I was being over-cautious, implying that I had nothing to fear since my father appeared to be well connected.

She mentioned the better reception he was enjoying in the new government. Because of Dad's demotion under the previous government, Lon Nol's Cabinet assumed that he had harboured bad sentiments against Sihanouk and that it was safe to take him on board. Dad did not hate the old royal regime nor did he side with the new. He seized his good fortune with both hands and Mum boasted that the Minister of Agriculture had given him *carte blanche* to make changes.

What she failed to say was that there was little he could improve. Cambodia was going backwards. The production of rice from 1966 had declined from the previous year. The political unrest, followed by the bombing of the most fertile heartland, had chased the peasants away from their farms. Dad could only reshuffle the administrative personnel, relocating people into positions they deserved due to their academic training. Mum gauged Dad's popularity by the number of grateful visitors who came with presents to the house. In the face of the minister's clear support of his actions, his critics retreated for the time being to a quiet corner. As much as it looked like he had a personal vendetta against Mr Som Ok, whom he demoted and placed behind a desk, Dad was only acting in accordance with the man's true merit.

Toward my third and last year at Monash, the situation in Cambodia deteriorated. My mother's letters persisted in dwelling on good news. By now, I had learned to read between the lines and concluded that life was getting almost impossible. The censorship laws would have meant that any critical reference to politics or one word out of place would see our correspondence go straight into the bin. What my mother did not say painted the true picture.

She wrote about good people, about E, our beloved villager—now a soldier—who looked her up. E came with a last offering when the whole population was being rationed to one kilogram of meat per month per entire household, regardless of size. He remembered that Mum always had to feed many people. He and two of his vegetarian friends donated their share of meat; he had cycled forty kilometres to give Mum three kilograms of beef. He told her his village had been bombed and his parents killed, along with his wife and new-born infant. His relatives were dispersed. He could find no work in Phnom

Penh, and the army guaranteed to feed him. He did not understand whom he was fighting against, and did not hold an ideology. For him, survival was paramount. It was a common story all over Cambodia.

'Tell me, E, have you shot a man?' Mum asked with concern.

He said not yet, and he wondered whether he could. If he were pushed, however, he would. Then he would get used to killing. Until he was desensitised. His gentleness I used to love would be lost.

Did E desert the army? Or did he stick to the gun? Was he a victim or an executioner in the long run? All I could say was that he did not have a range of choices. When I think of my country, I think of E and millions like him. Little people caught powerless in a tragedy beyond their grasp. They are the little ants that get killed when elephants fight.

It was common knowledge that Prime Minister Lon Nol was a hopeless leader. Governed by superstition and reliant on the reading of astrology before he started the day, he convinced his troops to partake in rituals of black magic by which he firmly believed the war could be won. Men went to have their bodies tattooed for protection against injuries by guns; army generals were supposedly capable of marching to the frontline and avoid bullets with the wave of a baton. Many more extraordinary stories of miracles circulated around the barracks. In reality, the army chiefs were cowards, reluctant to face the enemy and preferring to make fraudulent deals. They immediately sold to the Khmer Rouge the equipment and ammunition they received from the government; falsified the numbers of recruits and omitted to report dead soldiers in order to pocket their wages.

Lon Nol was unable to discipline his officers and stop the corruption in his army and administration. The early military offensives against the communists in 1970–71 met with negligible success. The Americans had to keep Lon Nol's republican government on its feet by pouring in funds and by bombing the countryside heavily. Although they succeeded in containing the flow of the communists and keeping them away from important government-controlled areas, mainly the cities of Phnom Penh and Battambang, the B-52s damaged the country-side, killed an estimated six hundred thousand people and rendered many homeless. Cities could no longer cope with the rapid influx of rural migration: Battambang received a quarter of a million refugees and the population in Phnom Penh jumped to two million. As a result, the majority of peasants ran to the forests, which held the promise of a haven when life became impossible in the city.

There is a sad tale, born of the long and turbulent history of Cambodia that tells the plight of two homeless orphan girls who, in order to survive the war, changed into birds and flew into the woods. The harshness of the early seventies saw this legend translate to reality yet again as hundreds of thousands of country folk fled to the maquis where, instead of finding safety, they played directly into the hands of the Khmer Rouge and helped augment its numbers. The Americans who set out to crush the communists ended up creating a situation which, ironically, contributed to their growth. In addition, the political manoeuvres undertaken by Prince Sihanouk lent to the increased importance of the Khmer Rouge.

In exile in Beijing after the National Assembly under the leadership of Lon Nol voted him out of office, the Prince agreed in 1970 to form an alliance with the Khmer Rouge. Sihanouk, the symbol of absolute royalty and the Khmer Rouge, the symbol of communism, were two political extremes that were unlikely bedfellows. They had been old sworn enemies, but their alliance, which was baptised the 'Coalition of Democratic Kampuchea', was born out of the need to use and eventually outplay each other for their own end. What the communists gave Sihanouk was the military backbone he so badly lacked and with which he hoped to regain power. What Sihanouk gave the Khmer Rouge was legitimacy. Their coalition government in exile won representation at the United Nations and the Prince's presence helped the communists gain the support from the peasants who were traditionally loyal to the monarchy. Thus, in their flight to escape from the B-52s, the masses of rural refugees were physically trapped in the enclaves of the forests where they played the only role that they had always been condemned to—pawns of yet another political game. While they let the Khmer Rouge train them in guerrilla warfare, most of these peasants were naïve enough to believe that they were participating in the struggle to reinstate the prince.

In August 1973 the US Congress voted to ban further bombing in Cambodia after the American youth, poised as the conscience of their nation, signed many petitions demanding an end to military involvement in Southeast Asia. Without the B-52s, nothing could stop the Khmer Rouge. They marched out of the forests and closed in on cities where they intended to bring down Lon Nol's republic. From August 1973 Lon Nol and his men barely clung to power. During this time the insurgents concentrated their assaults on the city.

At the beginning of 1975 Phnom Penh had run out of food, medicine and fuel. Mum's letters began to quote details of hardship, the long blackouts and curfews and my father's difficulty in buying medicine. He had to ration his diabetic tablets to one every second day in his attempt to save the little he had left of his medication. In the end he resisted taking it until he was seized by queasiness, the imminent symptom of a coma. For one year, the communists choked supplies into Phnom Penh; they scattered Chinese-made floating mines in the Mekong River.

Food, which used to arrive by convoys from the Delta, could not reach the capital. The United States had to fly it in but their aid funds dried up. Rice could no longer be bought. My mother wrote to me that she could actually count the grains. Because of the shortage of electricity and charcoal, she soaked the rice for long hours to soften it; this allowed her to cut down on the cooking time. She had practically pruned the tree branches around the house and finally lopped the trunks to the roots until she could not find a stick of timber to light her stove. With minimum fuel, the trickiest part was to turn the rice into thin porridge; this was made with lots of water to bloat the stomach and cheat hunger. It tasted more like fluid than starch.

With Barbara Charles, my host mother, on my graduation from Monash University in 1977.

My mother in my garden in Melbourne during her visit in1984.

My mother and her sister-in-law, Saturday, in Maryland, 1994.

My parents and 'Barb' Charles in her garden in 1984. My father holding my eldest son.

With my grandmother Nguen, in Seattle in 1994.

As I am today.

She lived with a nagging feeling of hunger while others who were less fortunate died from outright starvation. Some were poisoned from eating rotting food. Others ate dogs and human flesh. It was a fact that a government garrison not far from Phnom Penh, which was besieged for nine months and refused to surrender, survived on cannibalism. The children and the elderly, who were more prone to disease, were dying in large numbers. In the street where my family lived, a rocket thundered down right next door. At least twenty people were dug out of the debris and many more wounded bodies were dragged to dispensaries. My mother heard scores of rockets whistle pass; she believed that our house was blessed and that god himself was shielding our roof. It was never hit. Statistics revealed that an average of three hundred people died daily. My mother's letters contained distressing facts but in the rapidly advanced phase of the war, censorship ceased to exist or matter.

By the beginning of 1975 American aid had been completely drained. An immediate injection of nearly two hundred million dollars was required but the American Congress refused further handouts. Phnom Penh and Battambang were besieged by the Khmer Rouge; Lon Nol's government was doomed. During its final days, the regime concentrated on minimising its humiliation. As its defeat drew close, many dignitaries, military leaders and rich businessmen absconded. At the beginning of April, cabinet ministers under the guidance of American advisers decided that Lon Nol should leave Phnom Penh to enable negotiations to take place with the Khmer Rouge. Richer by a million American dollars given by the government as a pay-out, the Prime Minister shed crocodile tears when he boarded a plane with his family at Pochentong airport for Hawaii. All those who deserted had invariably a last-minute excuse, a mission or some medical condition that could only be treated overseas. The Khmer Rouge, sure of their forthcoming victory, refused to negotiate with Lon Nol's men and their American mentors. By April 1975 American Embassy personnel were evacuated by helicopter.

In the general panic when almost anyone would jump at the opportunity of leaving Cambodia, Somalee refused to go with her husband to Bangkok in an army jet. Vutha told her that he was permitted, thanks to his high rank in the Navy, to bring one companion because of the limited availability of seats in the aircraft. In offering her the chance to save her own life, he implied that Grandma should be left behind. She packed his suitcase and waved him goodbye outside the apartment, holding back tears, even as Grandma urged her to change her mind.

Somalee shut the door and stepped back into the apartment where her mother, half-blind from trachoma, cried out, 'Oh, foolish daughter! Why didn't you go with your husband and get yourself out of this city?' More than my grandmother could ever guess, Somalee was fulfilling the promise to care for her. The future would unfold to show that Somalee indeed made the ultimate sacrifice. She held her mother dearer than freedom and life itself.

Another army officer also offered to fly my half-sister Nee to Bangkok. After some consideration, she was suspicious that a change of heart and the thought of monetary gain might tempt him to sell her off to some brothel in Thailand. She decided to stay in Phnom Penh.

My mother wrote to me about my half-brother Tha, who was stationed at the airforce base in Battambang where he worked with my aunt Saturday's husband Toum, then a colonel. Mum was particularly fond of Tha who enlisted with Vaan. Tha was proud of the uniform he wore and the promotion he earned. During his short leaves of duty, he spent his time with my mother. His stories became more atrocious and his enthusiasm in defending our motherland passed into disillusionment and apprehension.

'Nobody keeps prisoners, Mother Number Two. Captives were executed on the spot.' His statement made my mother wonder whether it was the shortage of food needed to feed the prisoners or a senseless cruelty that prompted the government and the Khmer Rouge to kill each other so readily. The fact was this: both Republicans and communists, more and more in need of new troops, began to recruit boys younger than teenagers. Children of twelve years and under were entrusted to handle real guns and weapons, and given the licence to kill. They saw it as a game.

Tha was aware of the blatant corruption of some of his superiors who sold guns to the enemies. 'Isn't it absurd?' he asked rhetorically. 'That in this war, I am serving the traitors. Many people like myself are helplessly caught in the middle, waiting for our time to come.'

In hindsight, my mother thought Tha had a premonition that he would never get another chance to confide his fears before returning to his base. 'Pray for me,' he said to my mother. She did, for him and for others and for the whole country.

My father could not leave. Financially he could not afford to fly his large family out of Phnom Penh and was resigned to staying in his native country. He had lived through hectic changes, from Sihanouk's long reign to Lon Nol's republic, to communist domination. He assumed that it would be just another government. In his pragmatism, he did not think that his political affiliations would have repercussions. For better or worse, Cambodia was home. In the meantime, starvation, fear and the feeling of helplessness worsened by the day.

The final showdown to the five years of war came on 17 April 1975 with a deafening shelling of heavy artillery, bombs and rockets that the Khmer Rouge rebels launched into Phnom Penh. Mortars and grenades exploded, sirens whirred, machine guns and rifles hammered in the air. The citizens expected the Khmer Rouge to spill into the city at any moment and they were prepared to cheer them on. After onerous years under the corrupt Lon Nol's administration, the communist victory gave the population a sense of relief. They thought the Communist regime would mark the end of lawlessness and corruption, the end of starvation and the end of killing.

Peace, they thought, was here at last.

31

Communist Victory

I saw the televised pictures of Phnom Penh burning on television in Melbourne the day the communists seized power. The scene was of widespread mayhem. The Khmer Rouge shot their way into the streets where terrified people fled the turmoil; some raced towards the French Embassy—the last foreign power to evacuate, and where many Cambodian civilians hoped to enter and receive political asylum.

That same day, in Battambang, five hundred kilometres away from Phnom Penh, the airforce men of the near-defunct Lon Nol republic put up a last desperate attempt to delay the invasion of their base. My Aunt Saturday's husband, Toum, had anticipated the inevitable enemy victory, but unable to leave his post, ordered a pilot under his command to hurry to Phnom Penh, pick up his wife and their three children and fly them to Bangkok. The moment the insurgents broke the defence line and began to infiltrate the airforce compound, Toum jumped on a plane and signalled for Tha to join him on board.

Tha could not run. Like a pack of hungry wolves, the enemies appeared from nowhere and blocked him. Toum took off, leaving Tha at the mercy of his executioners. They swarmed in around Tha and hacked at his neck repeatedly with their rifle butts, until he dropped face down. The fear he had expressed to my mother about dying a senseless death had proven to be prophetic. The Khmer Rouge did not wish to kill him quickly, they did not think of wasting a bullet on him. What did my little brother do in his time to deserve such an excruciating end? The years that have passed since I learnt of the horrific way he died have not lessened my grief at having lost him.

Up in the air, Toum tried to forget about Tha. His survival instinct was stronger than his will to save my brother. Had he attempted to help, he reasoned with his conscience, they both would have died. The colonel owed it to his family to stay alive. He assumed that Saturday and his three children were also flying out of Cambodia. He did not know that Phnom Penh was caught in such turmoil that Saturday was scared to stay home. The pilot whom Toum had sent to fetch her missed her by minutes. He drove back to the airport and flew to Thailand. In Bangkok, he met up with Toum and apologised for his unsuccessful mission.

Saturday had reasons for wanting to leave her house in a hurry—if these victorious troops came to her door and looted her place, they would discover her husband's uniforms, and she would be as good as dead. She rummaged through her kitchen for leftover rice, which she put in the fold of a towel she tied around her waist. She hoisted her youngest on her back, a two-year-old boy, who began to cry. She hushed him and gave the order to her children to act dumb. 'For God's sake, don't tell anybody who your father is for they will kill us.' She took them by their hands and disappeared from her house.

The promise of peace in Cambodia quickly gave way to confusion. On the same day of their victory, the Khmer Rouge demanded an immediate evacuation of Phnom Penh. Anyone who dared to disobey their orders was to be shot.

By mid-morning, my mother crawled out from under the bed. She was shaking uncontrollably when she went to answer the door on the orders of a young soldier. He asked for the key of the Mercedes, which belonged to Uncle Ho. She eventually found it charred a block away. My brother Vaan sneaked out to Rue Charles de Gaulle in an effort to round up Grandma, Somalee and Uncle Chea so they could evacuate together. He dodged blockades and checkpoints. Everywhere, trigger-happy armed troops seemed to shoot at any moving target.

He finally reached my grandmother's apartment and found the door ajar. On stepping into the lounge, he could see the floor, furniture and walls sprayed red. Uncle Chea lay sprawled in a fresh pool of his own blood, he was peppered with bullets. Grandma's body was curled up, her head was broken and her eyes were wide open, clouded with tears, which had not yet dried. Aunt Somalee was stripped naked; she had been raped and butchered. The sight made Vaan's head spin, he fell into a chair and could not stop retching. Slowly, he took a hold of himself and left the apartment and struggled to walk away. He remembered that he had lifted Grandma's head, still dripping with blood, and rested it on a pillow. He covered Aunt Somalee's naked body with a bedsheet. He promised himself that he would come back with some help to bury them properly at the first opportunity. He was now sure that the communist changeover was the start of a barbarous period. To him, the killing had begun.

My grandmother's prophecy of a Cambodian apocalypse was indeed shaping into brutal reality. How could she know then that her blood would be shed at the foot of our hill? I kept asking myself why. 'What could prompt someone to attack an old, half-blind woman like her? What threat could she possibly present?'

I found the answer in one frightening conclusion. In Cambodia, at that time, and from that time, humanity had gone out of our race. From that day on, nobody could afford the time or the luxury of burying the dead. The living themselves were being whipped through the gates of hell.

At one o' clock, on the same afternoon, the members of my father's household reluctantly locked up and left. Mum took family photographs, vital documents such as birth and marriage certificates, the title of the house, light clothes and each person carried their own blanket. Vandy's dogs followed him down the stairs.

In front of our gate, he turned around and told them to stay. 'You cannot come with me. You will be trampled to death out there. Just look after yourselves until I come back.' He, like his dogs, detected the finality of that goodbye. He bent down to embrace their heads in his arms. He could not tear himself away as they licked the tears on his face and yelped.

My mother had to pull him up and tell him that it was high time they went. 'Son,' she said, 'I am afraid that your tears are needed more for the humans.'

Outside our gate, our street was overflowing with evacuees pushing their bikes, which were loaded with bags, blankets, cooking utensils and whatever else they valued. A neighbour struggled to take with him a heavy television set; in the past it had been the means for him to make a living. He had turned his lounge into a home theatre where people in the community paid an entrance fee to watch their favourite programme. In the panic of the evacuation, few could think rationally. My mother noticed that some tried to shift big furniture on trishaws and wheelbarrows; they seemed to treat the evacuation as if they were moving house.

When she reached the main street, Mum could not believe what she saw. On Boulevard Monivong, which was a long, straight, wide stretch of a road, she could not tell where the human procession began or ended. An endless trail was heading out of the city. At one intersection where a Chinese hospital was situated, patients were being rolled out in their beds, needles still stuck in their veins and bottles of serum dangling upside-down above their heads. Out came the invalids in wheelchairs, the walking wounded with bandaged heads, bandaged arms, the lame in plaster limping on crutches, the women who had just given birth, their newborn babies crying or sucking at their breasts. There were old folk on walking sticks, toddlers dragging to keep up with the mad pace. And everywhere there were the soldiers, shouting in tow, edging them on at gunpoint.

It was madness on an incredible scale. This exodus from Phnom Penh struck my mother as one of biblical magnitude. She was with civilians who were pressed to flee the city of Phnom Penh where corruption condemned it as a modern version of Gomorrah to be punished, reduced to ashes by American bombs.

'The US are coming!' shouted the Khmer Rouge. This was the reason they gave for evacuating Phnom Penh. The unfounded threat was used to scare and force millions of Cambodians out of their homes. Whether or not people believed that the Americans were flying in to blast Phnom Penh to smithereens, they had to leave. Within a week, the capital and other cities were ghost towns. Within a week, the whole population in Cambodia was homeless.

Aunt Saturday found herself drifting among the crowds who walked north toward Kompong Cham. She saw a man trudge next to her. At one point, he slumped on his backside and rested. Immediately, an irascible boy poked the gun at his head and told him to get up and move. He stayed seated and looked up beseechingly. The sound of a bullet echoed in the air and from the man's temple, crimson blood spurted all over Saturday. Too petrified to react, she dug her hand in her belt and hid in her palm a lump of rice which she shoved in her children's mouths. It had gone slimy, but it was food.

On the second day, at some ten kilometres out of Phnom Penh going south, on the highway to Prek Neak Loeung, my mother saw people dropping by the roadside after struggling on an empty stomach with swollen feet and tired muscles that refused to carry them further. The soldiers shot many who gave up walking, but they did not have enough bullets to fire at everybody. Many were left to die in the sun. The communists were sure that the April heat, thirst and hunger would soon claim their victims. On the third day, almost everybody had shed most of their possessions. The tiredness was crippling but at the first crack of dawn, people were woken up for another long day's march. Aunt Tam's three young children were able to ride on my two brothers' shoulders some of the way.

My father was panting and fighting against his dizziness. He did not have a single tablet left to control his diabetes. In the face of death, he was one of those who could call on a hidden reserve of energy to carry on. Not everybody had it. My mother noticed a young couple trailing along with two children and a newborn baby. On the fifth day, the wife tottered and collapsed. The husband panicked around her. He reached down to lift her up but he was too weak. My mother moved closer to help, and for the next few hours, a number of people took turns to help the woman until she begged to sit down. The soldiers came to bully her and fearful that she might cause others to get shot because of her, she asked to be left to her fate.

'Take our two children with you and go!' She whispered to her husband. She waved him off, almost getting angry at him for being so indecisive. My mother watched the man leave his wife. Their two young children continued to turn back to look at their mother holding the newborn baby, who was too dependent on her milk to go with the father. The irony of the situation was that the mother was probably too exhausted to produce any. Moved by the scene of this separation, my mother lacked the courage to look at the man's face. Had she seen the distress in his eyes, she risked coming to the awful conclusion that god did not exist.

On the eighth day, they passed Prek Neak Loeung. In the first village out of this township, they came to a temple, which straddled the halfway mark to our family's lands in Prek Dek. Dad was in a familiar area but could not recognise it. The place was disfigured. On the first evening, after they had been warned to stay put, the refugees fell to the ground and collapsed in sleep. There was not a hut in sight. Human shelters had been demolished in this expanse of rural landscape where communities of peasants had once lived and grown their crops. Their vegetable patches and their clusters of fruit trees had disappeared. Its desolation was proof of systematic destruction. Other than the devastation inflicted by the B-52 bombers, which in six months had dropped over the Cambodian heartland a load four times the size of that which hit Hiroshima, the Khmer Rouge had eroded the countryside further.

Not a banana bush stood to bear fruit, nor a stalk of corn had escaped the thorough Khmer Rouge policy to end the civilisation that pre-existed them. In one of the first broadcasts that they issued, they made a solemn statement: 'Today, we have ended two thousand years of history.' They proclaimed a new beginning for Cambodia and marked it Year Zero.

During the relentless evacuation march, it was already clear at that early stage that the new communist rule was more hellish than the years under Lon Nol. The evacuees were ordered to leave their homes and were simply told to take up 'special duties' in the countryside. They were not aware of, nor were they told about, the Khmer Rouge's master plan to transform Cambodian society into an agrarian society, and the entire population into unpaid collective agricultural labourers. The social engineers of this new era fostered the survival of the peasants. They were prepared to sacrifice the educated class and the bourgeoisie who were too set in their leisurely ways to grow crops and to conform to the radical changes without a challenge. City dwellers, among them my family, were earmarked as the most 'disposable' people of all. Many of them, unless they had already perished on the highways, struggled under perilous conditions only to advance into a totally unknown future.

32

Man Plans, God Laughs

A few weeks before the invasion of Phnom Penh, Mum's letters stopped. I followed the developments in Cambodia through the media. The last foreign journalists had left and the Khmer Rouge cancelled all diplomatic ties with the outside world. I was in my third year at Monash University. Within a few days after the Khmer Rouge's victory, reports from Cambodia ceased to be accurate. They were repetitive or the same reports were reissued without added facts. It dawned on the world how little they knew about the Khmer Rouge.

In April 1976, a year to the day after they took control, they proclaimed their new constitution and named their new Prime Minister, a man called Pol Pot, of whom the world had no knowledge. He was presented as an elusive 'rubber plantation worker'. Where was he born? Where was he educated? How did he rise to the rank of leadership? By that time, a few escapees from Cambodia began to give their testimonies of forced labour, torture, execution and death, but their stories were so extraordinary that they sounded grossly exaggerated to the outside world.

My country was sealed behind an impenetrable wall of secrecy and silence. The speculation and uncertainty expressed by the media as to what was happening inside made me increasingly restless. The Cambodian students at Monash grouped to console each other. Each of us had different ways of reacting to and coping with the lack of news from our families. Our supervisors kept close checks on us. From a meeting once a month, I had to see my supervisor Mrs O'Day weekly. I bombarded her with questions, harassed her to tell me what she knew, the facts I suspected she must possess in her official function as an Australian public servant. She admitted that the situation in my homeland was grim.

What had become of my mother? It was obvious to me that she had not escaped, otherwise I would have already received word.

By April 1975 I was very close to attaining my goal and at the end of that year, under normal circumstances, I would graduate. But the circumstances in April were far from normal. The absence of news from my mother became unbearable. I expressed the wish to go back to Cambodia and search for her. Mrs O'Day reminded me that commercial planes had stopped going to Phnom Penh, and even if I got there, she assured me, off the record, that the Khmer Rouge were killing educated people. She asked me to 'get on with life' and to accept the political refugee status Australia was offering me. And by a further gesture of goodwill, the Australian government paid my allowance until I finished my degree.

I was in a state of lethargy and distress, and unable to concentrate on my studies. I had no reason to want to. I was almost certain that Mum was dead and I had no country to go back to. I had never contemplated that I would stay in Australia forever and had not quite learned to live for my own sake. My passionate duty towards my mother had kept me wanting to live, and it was with her and for her that I had wanted to fight for a better life. Without her I could not imagine living. I was severely depressed and felt guilty for having failed my mother.

The latest events in Cambodia suddenly dismantled the scaffolding of my dreams. At twenty-three, I was still dependent on my mother as my sole purpose in life. I could not even cry on Mrs O'Day's shoulders, I was like a zombie, sedated with sleeping pills that could not put me to sleep but numbed and drowsed my pain. I remember telling her I wished I could sleep for a long long time.

The heavy doses of sleeping tablets gave me hallucinations. I felt one of my fingers growing monstrously big, so big I could not lift up my hand, or else some other part of my body, one of my eyes, for instance, would grow and grow until I thought I heard it pop in my head.

My birthday in May, two weeks after the fall of Lon Nol, was a sorry day. I cried for having been born. I was angry for not having the cowardice or the courage, whatever it was that I needed to end it all. Consumed by depression, I spent my birthday alone. I bought a bottle of wine, and drank myself silly in my room. I hated the taste, but I drank for the effect, for the oblivion. Some memories rushed back in spite of my conscious efforts to push them away. They were memories of the little butter cream cakes, which Mum bought and halved on occasions like this. My childhood and my home life in Cambodia, which I had always thought to be sad, seemed suddenly sweet and better than the emptiness of the present.

Although I was far from coping with my problems, I decided against psychiatric help, afraid of any treatment that might be tried on me. I began missing lectures and lost motivation, dozing off in the morning when other students went to breakfast and woke up when they came back from lectures and tutorials in the late afternoon. My cycle was helplessly reversed; I tossed and turned in the company of ghosts who inhabited my nights till dawn.

I stopped believing that God cared. He had been an old friend, through loneliness, through uncertainty and fear. With his help I had come a long way. He had aided me this far, now six months before graduation, he dropped me without warning. I believed he was laughing at the lofty plans I had made and I felt betrayed. I had searched for God in Sydney, in a church in Darlinghurst where the Baptist

Reverend Mitchell plunged my head in a pool of water and baptised me. The congregation who gathered around to congratulate me claimed victory for having drawn a lost child to the Baptist faith. They were told of my mixed religious background, which was a cross between a Catholic mother and a Buddhist father. To confuse them even more, I told them that my grandmother was an ancestral cult worshipper! Sometime after my baptism I began to feel an uncomfortable competition among people who drew strength from comparing their faith. In my final analysis, I found God was more in the solitude of the heart and in the peace of a public garden. My shift to Monash University gave me a convenient excuse to break away from the Baptist church. But suddenly God vanished from my life completely, and I was alone.

For two nights I followed the flight of a mosquito in my small room. I watched it cling to the wall, hover in the air and when it disappeared into a dark corner, I started to panic. I got out of bed and looked for it. All the care I had for the living world was concentrated on this minuscule insect. I was relieved when it fluttered back up the wall. Then it dropped on the carpet, stiff and lifeless. At that very moment, I stared at its mortality as if it were my own, and felt that I was losing my mind. I could see a line, a beam of light and beyond it, an abyss of darkness, the endless pit I was scared of as a child. An inner voice warned me that once I crossed that line, I would have surrendered my sanity.

At three o'clock in the morning I chose to live. I crawled out of bed, had my shower and nibbled on a bar of chocolate.

I buried my mother. I buried Cambodia.

I had to start another future without them. There is so much grief stored in the depths of my subconscious where it waits, like an undetonated bomb, to explode at the oddest times. One night, a few months after I lost contact with my mother, she appeared in my dreams without a face. I woke up shaking and reassured myself that I could remember what she looked like, that it was all a nightmare. I lay awake and tried to picture Mum. I saw nothing.

I had wished to forget the past, but I also wished to retain the ability to recall my memories at will. My mind refused to obey. With the same effort that I had previously used to wipe out my memories, I now tried to summon them back. I leafed through my family album, reread Mum's letters and reconstructed my childhood. One by one, the expressions of my mother's face showed themselves again in my mind. There was her smile that I love and there was the wisdom and the tenderness that shone from her eyes. I promised that I would one day write about her, a personal record in which she would be immortalised. I was thankful for the privilege of being born to this very ordinary woman, who, by the way she lived, had become extraordinary in my eyes.

I picked up my studies and thought that I had finished my degree in the first semester of 1976. To my disappointment, I still had to complete a first-year subject to obtain the right number of points to graduate. I had a first-year subject left. I had skipped first-year French because I was a 'near-native French speaker' but the French department refused to credit me for the first level. I was too tired to argue with the bureaucracy and besides I now saw no real purpose to be the holder of a degree. My major in linguistics had made me quite unemployable in Australia unless I was prepared to study further for a diploma of education, which would allow me to teach English as a foreign language. The prospect of an academic career was not appealing. I deferred my degree and discontinued my scholarship. I accepted the status of political refugee, became an Australian resident and I went out into the workforce. I got a job as a salesgirl in a jeans shop and lived a bohemian life, without care or focus, packing up and changing addresses many times on a whim. In doing so, I unintentionally made it impossible for my mother's letters, if she were to write, to ever reach me.

3 3

The Reign of Terror

Although I presumed my mother dead, she was in fact still alive. In Cambodia, she battled to survive. She had jotted my address at Monash on a worn piece of paper, folded it and tucked it tight against her bosom like a second skin. Alas, this address was not current, but it was her only link with the outside world if and when she could escape from Cambodia.

In the third week at the village outside the town of Prek Neak Loeung, she stumbled on a tomato seedling. The sight of an edible plant sprouting after the rain was as exciting to her as someone discovering a precious stone from the mines of Pailin. My mother religiously watered it and transplanted it away from sight. One day, she would pluck fruit from it and start a tomato bed. However, a soldier angrily discovered her nurturing the seedling and squashed it under his feet.

'No plants without permission!' he yelled.

The distribution of food to the refugees was sporadic and scanty. People fished and ate whatever they could forage on the uncultivated grounds: sweet potatoes, wild bamboo shoots and reeds. They gathered logs, broken pieces of timber and began to build shelters instead of sleeping under willows. They were drenched to the bone when it rained at night. The temple, no longer a place of worship, was turned into headquarters where soldiers lived and stored guns.

The supervision of the area where my family was changed frequently. The refugees themselves were forced to move on, and not allowed to stay for long in the same place and become familiar with the area and grow attached to a group of people. These changes helped the Khmer Rouge confuse, divide and control the refugees. The whole society was disrupted. Cultural ties, community and family obligations, blood bonds and security were obliterated. Members of the same family were forcibly separated; siblings from each other, children above seven years of age from their mothers, sometimes husbands from their wives. Aunt Tam and her three young children were sent to another village farther south. Our relatives from Prek Dek who had joined the family went east toward Prey Veng. Due to some inexplicable oversight on the part of the Khmer Rouge, my parents, my two brothers, my father's de-facto wife, my half brother No and my half sister Nee were in the same village.

Vandy and Vaan used their shirts to snare fish in the shallow water of the prek which had previously been dug by villagers to irrigate their fields. One day they caught a decent quantity of fish. They were about to bring them to my mother to grill over an open fire when the soldiers stopped them and took the best of their catch. They were left with a miserable handful of bait, but restrained themselves from displaying anything other than acceptance of this injustice.

Privately, Vandy told my mother that he could not see himself lasting much longer in this environment, 'I can live without freedom perhaps, but I certainly cannot live without food'. The next morning, two senior communists came to look for my brothers, and handed them a proper fishing net with a faint smile. 'We will make sure you keep your catch from now on.' It was their way of apologising, a singular gesture of human consideration worthy of mention among countless other abuses of power. Vandy and Vaan made their way to the river and returned with more fish than they could carry. They shared the catch with other refugees and barbecued and filled their own bellies. What was left they thought they would consume the following day. Unfortunately, the fish, cooked without salt, became coated with worms overnight.

In those early weeks, the Khmer Rouge chiefs in the surroundings where my family camped allowed the Vietnamese back to Vietnam. On and off, fishing boats arrived and fishermen received a fee in gold in exchange for a trip to the Mekong Delta. My mother was tempted to go but she also had her suspicions. She was not sure whether it was a ploy to identify and isolate the Vietnamese, to take them by boat somewhere and rob them and execute them afterward. Since Vandy continued to tell her he would rather risk death on these boats than live in a state of permanent starvation, Mum changed her mind.

When she saw a few boats on the river, she jumped to the foreground and said in her usual unrefined accent: 'I am Vietnamese! Please let me go back to Vietnam!'

A soldier stopped her short in her tracks. 'Listen! You and your family are not Vietnamese! Who are you trying to fool?' It was ironic. In the past, the problem with our family had been quite the reverse. We could not get complete acceptance for being Cambodian. Those boats were the last that were allowed to anchor on the riverbank. When they left, Vandy's hopes of leaving were gone.

The civilians were ordered to state their origins, and based on this information, the Khmer Rouge officials assured them that they would be repatriated accordingly. Many believed in this promise and hoped to return soon to their homes. Those who revealed that they were born and bred in cities were putting their names on a blacklist. Already the communists had established a network of spies whom they secretly recruited among people; it was a network that had 'eyes like the pineapple' that saw and knew everything. To toady to the authorities, and perhaps to live a day longer, friends betrayed friends, and relatives turned their backs on other relatives to avoid guilt and punishment by association. The social fabric, normally woven with loyalty and trust, was being torn apart; each individual was driven by the necessity to save his neck first. My father, without any real intention of lying, declared that his place of origin was Prek Dek. He believed that survival would be less difficult in his ancestral village than in Phnom Penh. Close to the land, he could at least grow his own food. His claim of a rural background spared him from scrutiny.

The officials began to get better organised. They grouped and herded the refugees out to the fields and subjected them to hard physical labour. Without exception, even children of seven years had to join in and work like adults, for fourteen hours a day. Hundreds of civilians were forced to dig a network of canals and hundreds more to plant rice. By maximising the labour force everywhere in Cambodia and pushing the people to their limits of endurance, most of the time without adequate food, the Khmer Rouge intended to double the yield achieved in the best years before 1966.

The programme was overly ambitious, the task mammoth and the technology to implement it non-existent. Heavy agricultural machinery had become useless, due to missing spare parts or lack of expertise to repair it. Or the machines had been vandalised by communist troops during the war. Like all other motor vehicles, they had been destroyed because they had been seen as symbols of capitalism.

Soldiers surrounded the workers and kept watch on the young and the old. Under fear of punishment, civilians worked without protest. It worried my father that the canal he helped hand dig might damage the land instead. Such major earthwork should not be conducted before the topography of the place had been properly studied. It irked him even more that so much sweat and loss of human life went into shovelling dirt. Two weeks after the project was commenced, many men standing close to my father simply fell because of insufficient food, dehydration and despair. Dad himself was on the verge of giving in but the rage he felt towards this regime would not let him. He could not accept such gross misuse of human resources.

The situation worsened the day the regular change of guards brought in yet another new rural cadre. It marked the onset of a bloodbath in the camp. The replacement team was boisterous; its members giddy with power as they brandished their rifles. They aimed at an onlooker and hit him in the chest—the poor victim had committed the unforgivable mistake of staring a soldier in the face. Such insolence was considered to be a capital crime just as it had been under the absolute rule of Cambodian kings in the past. His corpse bloated in the heat and was ravaged by maggots. A handful of refugees hesitantly crept up and pulled it into a shallow grave.

Rampant disease arising from famine, lack of sanitation and lack of treatment or medicine took its toll. Execution in the hands of those now in charge was arbitrary and the number of casualties escalated. It became blatantly obvious that educated people attracted the wrath of the commanders. A friend's sister, who lived through the communist reign and who survived to tell her story, related how she had to throw away her glasses to make herself less conspicuous. Reduced to crawling on her hands and knees to feel her way around because she was very short-sighted, she remembers having to wade out at night to go to the toilet and many times landing on top of a decomposed body. She claimed that in the starless evenings, although her eyesight was bad, she could see small fluttering lights hovering low among the bushes. She believed that these were the souls of the dead who, having met a violent end, floundered between two worlds. The foul smell of rotting human flesh was overpowering.

My mother was rightly concerned that somebody would remember the incident on the riverbank when she had revealed herself to be Vietnamese. My father might be recognised for having been a ranked civil servant in Lon Nol's cabinet. However hard they tried to conceal that they were educated, my family fulfilled the three criteria that would condemn them to the death penalty.

One day my father was walking out to the fields when the guards dragged him to a cart to which they yoked his trunk in the manner that a beast is yoked to a plough. A couple of these men jumped onto the cart and whipped him. For a whole day, my father was made to pull the cart around the village. He winced and heaved, weak and dizzy from exhaustion and his untreated diabetes. When he stopped to catch his breath, a volley of shots was fired around his feet, making him jump, jerk and pull the carriage ahead. That night the guards removed the cart and dumped him inside the temple hall. His hands were tied behind his back and his four limbs were tied together so tightly they throbbed. He wriggled to ease the pain and ended up on his stomach. All night, he fought against the intolerable itch in his groin from his urine. He begged for a drink and a soldier came, not to give him water, but to throw a thick drape over his head. He had not been told what crime he had committed to be given this treatment. Inside the lofty temple where once the sounds of prayers had echoed, Dad experienced a glimpse of hell.

My father's de-facto wife and her two children kept as far away as they could from my mother and my two brothers to avoid being found guilty by association. Sitting under the low straw roof, my mother wept in the dark and listened to Vaan telling her and Vandy of the murders of Grandma, Uncle Chea and Aunt Somalee. He had kept his knowledge a secret and would not have talked about it if he had not felt a desperate need to influence my mother to leave Cambodia.

'We must escape from here,' he begged. 'My premonitions are accurate. The communists are insane.'

Vandy was really quiet. When Mum touched his face, she felt it wet with tears. 'Don't cry, son. Pray hard. From a pure heart like yours, maybe God will hear us this time,' she said.

'They are killing my father!' Vandy cried softly, his head buried between his bony knees. Before she could stop him, he slithered out of the hut. She was paralysed with fear for his safety. She ordered Vaan to follow him but Vaan came back and told her that he had lost sight of Vandy. It was so dark outside that he could not see his outstretched hands.

Mum lamented and sobbed, saying repeatedly to Vaan that the end was near, 'By tomorrow, we will all be dead. They must have executed your father already. And Vandy must have gone to the temple to see whether he could help. What kind of courage is his? Oh God!' She shook her head and beat her hands on her lap. She let her imagination run ahead of her. She calmed down eventually but she was convinced that by sunrise, she would have lost her husband and son. Vaan did not have the will to contradict her. He had seen enough death in the camp not to have any faith left.

Vandy reappeared just before dawn was about to break; his clothes were dripping, clinging to his skeletal body. My mother had the impulse to whack him. Somehow, his silence stopped her short. She suddenly realised that he was a fully grown man and not a disobedient little boy who had been on an escapade. He had come back from the mouth of death. She opened her arms wide for a hug and again burst into tears. 'I was so afraid! Where did you go?'

'To the river. I had a long swim across it.' Vandy wrung out his shirt, he turned to Vaan and gave him instructions. 'Before we go to the fields today, go and tell No, Nee and their mother to meet us here at nightfall. My task is to save Dad before we leave this damned place. A fisherman has a boat, he will take us all out of here.'

Vaan went to relay the message to Dad's second wife. She shook her head. It was too perilous to risk an escape. Vaan was concerned that any indiscretion on her part might jeopardise their plan. He said to her: 'Our escape is dangerous indeed, Aunt. If we get caught, they will torture us in public. We will not blame you for denying that you are related to us in any way at all. However, if we are fortunate enough to get out of here safely, please remember that my mother did make you the offer to come with us.'

The sun had risen; Dad was fastened to the cart for a second day of torture. He broke into loud sobs, pulling his load of laughing soldiers. He exhorted them to kill him but they smirked and laughed, 'Old man! Don't be impatient! We can't kill you yet!'

Dad's desire for them to execute him had the reverse effect on them. They toyed with him until dusk and then left him harnessed to the cart while they returned to the temple for the night. It began to drizzle.

Vandy squirmed toward Dad, who was bent double in order to sleep on his feet. He whispered, 'Dad, it's me, Vandy!' He undid the knots and released the rope. Slowly he steadied Dad towards the river where Mum and Vaan were waiting. Vandy took off his shirt, rolled his pants up and swam to the other bank. My father was too feeble to ask what was happening; he closed his eyes and moaned. After a long while, Vandy came back in a boat with a rower who had idled furtively along the river waiting for an opportunity to take clandestine passengers out of Cambodia. His fee could not be anything less than gold.

My mother took out from her undergarment a two-ounce chain of twenty-four-carat gold, the last piece of jewellery she had hidden for an emergency. 'It's all I have, please!'

The fisherman nodded. Straight away, Vandy jumped out of the boat to give Vaan a hand. They hoisted Dad in while my mother groped on the edge and lifted herself on board. The man quietly raised his oars and the boat bobbed and sculled noiselessly on the Mekong, its bow heading south, toward Prek Dek.

In the deep silence of this first leg of the escape, Dad sank into delirium. His fever peaked and stayed high, he lost the control of his bowels, and he retched, soaking in his own discharge and perspiration. My mother rolled him on the side and raised his head on her lap to stop him from choking. She silently repeated the same prayer until the words were empty of meaning; she could hear the throb of her own fear beating madly at her temples. My brothers' eyes scanned the dark in dreadful anticipation. Their lives were hovering between freedom and recapture. At the slightest irregular noise, other than Dad's groans and the patter of drizzle on the water, they bent their heads low, holding their breath.

Just before dawn, they came close to a river island. The rower leaned on one oar trying to feel the bottom of the river and guided the boat into the mangroves. 'We have to rest during the day,' he said simply. The place looked like the same river island Vandy, Vaan and I had discovered during our many idyllic holidays in Granddad's native village. Indeed, when Vaan gazed across the water, he was almost certain that Prek Dek lay on the other side. Under the morning sun, nature had a way of conveying composure. Vaan knew it to be only an illusion, because at that very moment, in the whole of the Cambodian countryside, he knew that people were held prisoners by their own government, forced to become a hungry mass of state slaves. So much for the egalitarian society communism professed to establish. In Cambodia, the Khmer Rouge's application of its principle took the country back to feudal times.

Something about the stretch of landscape in front of Vaan filled him with sadness, something that was different from the mornings of child-hood when he woke up to village life in Prek Dek. It suddenly struck him that it was the absence of normal sounds—the mooing of cattle, the clucking of fowls, the sound of children playing and especially the absence of birds chirping in the trees. Vaan sat next to Mum and said, 'Children are robbed of their childhood and even the birds have taken leave of this country.'

'Don't waste your time thinking of the birds! We are not out of the danger zone yet. This is no time for poetry! Help me build the fire, the logs are wet from the rain!' My mother was more worried about the practicalities of the moment. She had to boil water, cook some rice and try to bring Dad's temperature down and eat while they could. The boat's owner was equipped with dented aluminium pots, stale rice that had been sun-dried, a small bag of dried salted fish and a supply of pills that had outlasted their use-by date. Two of them looked like painkillers. Mum took a gamble and put them in Dad's throat, and forced him to gulp them down with the warm water that she had boiled. She stripped and washed him, then threaded her way through the mangroves to rinse his dirty clothes, too involved in her task to dwell on the immediate dangers and uncertainties. She managed to stabilise Dad's temperature. He had at least kept down the fluid she had been making him drink. She stayed by his side, her hand constantly checking his forehead and she drifted into a heavy sleep while sitting with her back against a tree.

At dusk, they reboarded the boat and drifted through the night. They crossed Cambodian waters before dawn and landed on the bank of Tan Chau, Grandma's native village in Vietnam. My brothers carried Dad to a dirt track and rested him on the grass. They watched the dormant village stir to the wake-up calls of farm animals. There, by the road, came an ice-cream man on an old bike, ringing his bell. Vandy beseeched Mum to buy him a treat and sobbed like a child when she swore she did not have a cent to her name. The merchant stopped in front of them.

He looked at my brother and spoke to Mum, 'Is he your son? Is he all right?'

'You would not believe that a twenty-six-year-old man would cry like this, would you? This is my son. He has just saved his father from the Khmer Rouge. Without his courage, we would have been dead by now.' She pointed in the direction of Cambodia and confided, 'A lot of blood is staining the land next door. You cannot guess how many people have died!'

The man was amazed at my mother's account. In a spontaneous gesture of kindness, he gave my brothers two sticks of ice-cream. 'You should officially report your arrival,' he said.

Like Cambodia, Vietnam had recently been taken over by a communist government. Contrary to what was happening in Cambodia, the peace in Vietnam was a straightforward changeover from the war. Its army had laid down its arms and the peace process had begun. Tan Chau exuded a harmony that made it hard to believe that it had ever been disturbed. My family went to the local authorities and presented their identification. Because they spoke fluent Vietnamese, they were classed in the category of repatriated citizens and their papers were stamped without fuss. Free at last, but still helpless and hungry, my family found it necessary to beg for the first time in their lives. Pride had less to do with the act of stretching out one's hand, opening one's palm and pleading. It required a tremendous amount of courage on my brothers' part and they felt a loss of self-esteem. They offered themselves for work in return for food and somewhere to stay. My father slowly recuperated and regained the capacity to think. While the boys were busy with the local farmers, he leaned on my mother and asked around the village whether anybody remembered the old Tan Chau patriarch who used to own a lot of land in the region. Before long, my parents were given the name of a woman they should visit.

They entered a farmhouse and were received by a well-preserved woman. Her hair was gelled back in a bun, not a strand was out of place. The neatness of her house was also impressive; the ground was wide, paved and clean.

'Oh yes,' the lady said, 'although she had never met my grand-mother Kim, she knew of her by reputation and she was honoured to extend a welcome to her descendants.' She recited a lengthy and complicated family genealogy and declared that she was a third cousin to Grandma. She sent a boy to fetch my two brothers and ordered an abundant meal of chicken, fish, meat, rice and vegetables be prepared for her unexpected guests. Vandy and Vaan feasted to excess. My mother was embarrassed to count eleven bowls of food, which they devoured. Their hostess laughed benevolently and assured her that they did credit to her hospitality. She invited my family to treat her house like their own and two weeks later, at the risk of outliving their welcome, they told her that they had to move on to Saigon. Before they departed, she gave them enough money to last them through their journey and to stop them from refusing her offer, she looked at my father: 'Your mother used to give generously to many people in the village. What they owed her is now returned to you.'

She sent them off in a cart pulled slowly by a pair of water buffalo. On the dirt road out of the village, my father recognised the unmistakable long bamboo hedge that fenced the Tan Chau compound. He decided to take a nostalgic walk over his mother's ancestral land. The last time he had been there, he remembered holding his mother's hand and watching her sorrow as she stood in front of the charred frame of her grandfather's house. A stream of tears rolled down my father's cheeks, and my mother heard him say, 'My poor old mother could not have lived through the evacuation. There must be a kind of doom upon my family and an even worse curse upon my country. How many of us are still alive, do you know?'

Mum kept the knowledge of Grandma's death to herself. Some things were better left unsaid.

34

Tree Bark and Weeds

Saturday and her three children were stationed in a camp off the main route going north, on the west side of the province of Kompong Cham. She concealed the fact that she was the wife of an airforce colonel under Lon Nol. She claimed that both her husband and her brother had fled to the forest to join the communists. At the time when not a single person was left untouched by the tragedy of death and the brutalities inflicted by the Khmer Rouge, Saturday's story of separation from a communist husband did nothing to attract sympathy from the refugees. However she gained small privileges and leniency from the local cadre and received rice on a more regular basis.

From the start, Saturday contemplated fleeing to the border. She was petrified by the hazards, and had considered gathering a group to break away from the camp. But whom could she really trust? Who would not divulge her intention? Anyone was a potential enemy or a secret spy. Besides, having posed as the wife of a Khmer Rouge, who would trust her? She realised that she should not stay in the same camp; the longer she remained, the more she risked getting trapped in the web of her own lies. The communist supervisors were still disorganised, but soon someone in authority might start investigating her husband. There was no doubt what would happen if the truth were revealed. She had witnessed the severity of punishment for the least breach of discipline, which was always followed by an arbitrary killing spree. Refugees who ventured further from the temple into the fields to gather food seldom returned. They either stepped on landmines or were shot because they were accused of trying to escape. Human life was cheap. Although she had succeeded in buying salvation by deceit, because of it she was compelled to stay one step ahead before fate caught up with her. Her children were young and gaunt, and she wondered whether they could cope with the journey. She tried not to think of what would happen to them if she were to die on the way. In preparation for the next move, she hinted that she wished to search for her husband.

She made a cross of twigs and clipped it close to her chest, praying for a sign of the right time for her and her children to sneak away without attracting attention. She normally tucked her children snugly against her at dusk and stayed alert even when she closed her eyes, never allowing herself to fall too deeply asleep. One night a scream pierced the dark silence. Somebody was calling out to a thief and within a few minutes, people on the opposite side of the compound were awakened by the uproar. From inside the temple, the guards raced out, firing into the air. Saturday woke up her children, and without wasting time, grabbed her two-year-old son and gestured the two older ones to follow her. They bent low and slipped between the bushes, sidling further and further into the dark. When they were at the point where the sound of bullets and human voices could not be heard, they stood up and ran, faster than they had ever run before. Saturday had no idea how much distance they had covered; her back had gone numb from carrying her small son. They stopped, slumped on the wet ground, and breathed in the atmosphere, heavy, humid, almost suffocating. The light of dawn filtered through the canopy of tall trees and Saturday was swept with a feeling of isolation. They were lost in a forest, cut off from any hint of human life. She did not have a watch, nor a compass nor an ounce of food. She urged her children to get up and they travelled by instinct in the direction of Vietnam, moving toward the place they believed they had seen the sun rise. They left the forest and found themselves in the flat lands. The children showed a stamina beyond their age, even the youngest one, less than three years old, tottered on his own bare feet. The four of them walked until the children limped and finally could move no more. Saturday bent down to pull up some weeds. She put a stem between her blistered lips and chewed. 'If cattle can live on grass, there is no reason why humans can't,' she reasoned. She gathered some more weeds, handed them to her children and assured them they were edible.

They struggled on, to the point where Saturday lost all notion of time. She could not explain where they found the strength to continue under the hot sun, and sometimes rain. The nights were cold and they endured a hunger that would not go away. For Saturday, her faith in God and the hope of being not too far from a village allowed her to persevere. Some weeks later, they sighted smoke rising in the distance and trudged into a camp. She presented her case to the rural communist chiefs. She relied on the same previous lie—her quest for a lost communist husband and again cheated her way into a short reprieve, during which her family regained their strength and renewed their courage before moving on.

Kompong Cham is a relatively new province. At the beginning of the century, its plateaus of tall grasses, its mountains and dense forests hosted abundant wildlife, mostly boars and tigers. An active programme to clear the trees and gain more arable land during the fifties saw a rapid growth in human population in the province. In Chup, tobacco and rubber plantations, mostly French-owned, turned it into an area rich in revenue and the city of Kompong Cham became the third largest after Phnom Penh and Battambang. Its cultivated fields were abandoned during the war and east of the city were vacant spaces where man had failed to conquer. These areas were unforgiving and potentially dangerous to the likes of Saturday and the children. The region of Kompong Cham generally receives the highest rainfall, its clay soil stores large puddles of water where mosquitoes breed and spread malaria. For all its harshness it offered water to drink, and Saturday and the children were able to quench their thirst.

On their second exit into this wilderness, even more difficult than the first, Saturday and her children found their hunger more unbearable and the distance between two villages increasingly longer. From one village to the next, they were trapped in a vicious cycle. They either faced the risks of living among the Khmer Rouge or the risks of wandering in the bush. By the time they left the fifth and last village behind, it was the struggle against nature that really crushed Saturday's willpower and demoralised her. At every step she made, her feet ached where deep cuts had turned into open weeping wounds. During one section of their journey, her children were hungry and she could not find even green grass with which to feed them. She had to pluck from the trunk of a tree some bark which she gave them to eat. They struggled to swallow the wood. Saturday was seized by such anger and helplessness that she screamed and cursed toward the sky, but her voice came out weakly, sounding more feeble than a whisper. She bent her head to the ground and wept in front of her children. It was at that moment that she felt she could no longer protect and deceive them with her outward show of courage and endurance. They grouped around her and cried together. Slowly, the tempting thought of giving up crept into her mind. She wished they could all die. In many other moments, she found herself thinking of ways to kill herself. But always the quiet stamina of her children pulled her back to reason. Day by day she became more attracted to the idea of death, unable to justify the pointless sufferings of a journey that appeared to lead nowhere. Despite the fact that their bodies were covered in sores and their feet scarred by thorns, Saturday's children remained pillars of tenacious strength. It was they who took over the role of leader and reminded her that they would struggle to survive in order to see their father again.

Saturday did not realise that they had come to the end of their journey and had crossed the border into Vietnam. They thought they were dreaming when they heard a cock crowing early one morning. The sound brought back the remote memory of a normal rural life they had forgotten existed.

They had spent ten months travelling before they reached the border. It would be another three months before they made it to Saigon. All in all, one woman and three very brave little children covered the extraordinary distance from Phnom Penh to Saigon on foot. They would never again take freedom for granted.

35

The Dust of Life

In Melbourne, it was not enough for me to merely accept that I was an orphan. Deep within, I needed to know how my family had met their deaths so I could begin to mourn properly. Whoever has lost a close relative without the trace of a body and the benefit of a conventional funeral can perhaps empathise with how I felt. My grief was unresolved and I was in a state of limbo; a state halfway between disbelief and acceptance. My moods swung between depression, suicide and the illusion of false hope and left me exhausted. My efforts to trace my mother's letters were in vain. I realised that I could no longer handle the uncertainty. It was perhaps at this stage, after one-and-a-half years of silence, that I wanted my mother to be truly dead. I had this inexplicable urge to burn her letters. With the benefit of hindsight, I see it was my way of cremating the past and closing a chapter. The destruction of my mother's correspondence haunted me with shame and guilt but I also experienced a sense of relief. Whether this played a part in allowing me to drop my guard and look to forming other relationships, I could not say. At least I was beginning to lock away my past, to the point of denial.

I met a Lebanese migrant who studied electrical engineering part-time and worked in a knitwear factory full-time. In 1970, at seventeen, he had arrived in Melbourne with five dollars in his pocket. He had wanted to go to America to flee the war, which was starting to divide the Middle East, but his mother had said that she would rather he go to Australia to where his older brother had migrated. Together they lived frugally in order to send money to Lebanon to support their widowed mother and three unmarried sisters.

Despite putting in a solid ten-hour working day for six days a week at the factory where he packed boxes of wool and acrylic, he found time to squeeze in lectures and tutorials in the evenings and graduated as an engineer. He had sound conservative values, the nobility of caring for his family, the courage to work hard and he wanted a good education. His dream echoed mine, and I found myself loving him for it. He encouraged me to go back to university to do that one subject I had passed up, and I graduated in 1977. That year, we got married over a cup of coffee and a tray of Arabic sweets coated in thick sugary syrup. He knew only the broadest facts about my past. I did not intend to hide from him but neither did I feel it necessary at the time to tell him the details.

At the time I destroyed my mother's letters, my family arrived in Saigon. It was a bleak place to escape to. Saigon had fallen to Vietcong forces less than two weeks after Phnom Penh fell to the Khmer Rouge. The two cities, which the Americans had tried their utmost to spare from the Communists, fell out of their control in the same way two blocks tumble in dominoes. In April 1975, the Americans airlifted their staff, foreign war correspondents and some Vietnamese dignitaries from the lawn of their embassy. On 29 April, American helicopter pilots worked non-stop. Back and forth, they picked sixty to eighty people on each shift and deposited them on the deck of the aircraft carrier. By the next morning, American marines locked the embassy doors, sprayed tear gas behind them and ran to the rooftop where they jumped on the last rescue flight. Hundreds of hopeful locals, stranded inside the embassy grounds, were left waiting in vain to be evacuated. Outside its walls and gate, secured by armed Vietnamese retainers, thousands more civilians clambered to get in. The surrender to the Vietcong delegates took place on the first of May, ending a war that had lasted for thirty years. The gunshots stopped, but the fear and the suffering continued.

Vietnam was on the verge of famine. Crop cultivation, disrupted by years of fighting, had dropped, due to floods. The situation got worse because the United States stopped food aid and ceased trade with Vietnam. Saigon, which had enjoyed imported consumer goods, soft drinks, canned food and crisp cold cash brought in by the Americans, was suddenly without a patron. A spate of city people whose livelihoods had in the past relied on the American presence were now thrown into disarray. The mass of soldiers of the now-defunct Army of South Vietnam, the fourth-largest military forces in the world, sponsored by the United States to combat the Vietcong, was subjected to a punitive 're-education' programme under the new Communist government.

The city was packed with refugees like my family. Orphans, street children, prostitutes, poor and bankrupt people begged and stole in the streets. These were the downtrodden that the local Vietnamese referred to by an almost poetic name—the 'dust of life'. The search for food, shelter and survival for many people was a long, hard battle. For the newly established Communist government, there was more to do than just unify the country. The rubble of such a long war lay deep, way deeper than the visible destruction of buildings.

In this overwhelming mess, my father felt fortunate to be employed. He was paid minimally by a state storehouse for doing menial chores. He was a coolie—he repaired jute bags, swept the floors and ran errands. After a chance encounter with a Vietnamese official who had previously known of him in Phnom Penh and who certified that he was an agricultural engineer, my father was promoted to supervising the quality control of Saigon rice mills. His improvement in responsibility did not come with an increase in wage, most of which he had to spend on his medical treatment. His diabetes had been aggravated by emotional stress, and medicine was available only at a formidable price.

Once in Saigon, my mother tried to write to me but her letters were lost. Had she been able to contact me, our destiny may now tell a different story. After writing many times without a response from me, Mum gave up. She could not afford the cost of postage.

Since Dad's meagre income could not buy food, she and my brothers made cigarettes. The boys moved around the city undercutting the price of the established brands, and pooled their money to buy food. Mum was grateful when they came back from their black-market activities. There was no other alternative but to take such risks and they faced terrific difficulties just to see each day out, but my mother would say with her unrelenting courage that they were 'lucky'. At least they did not have a gun pointing at their heads and were living with the hope that they soon would fly off to the security of Paris. They were able to get in touch with Duck's Feet, who was willing to sponsor them to France, and the Red Cross, in principle, agreed that they fitted the category of foreign refugees. My family was waiting for resettlement. It was only a matter of time.

It was in Saigon where Vaan finally met his biological father, Leng. Leng was engaged in the Communist cause which, in the pre-independence years, was formed to fight against French colonial rule. The PCI (Indochinese Communist Party) dissolved in 1951 for tactical reasons, only to be reformed as separate national groups. Leng stayed with the Khmer Communists, who were condemned to a long period of obscurity, while their Vietnamese counterparts succeeded in winning the battle of Dien Bien Phu and negotiated with France in 1954 in Geneva. In this Convention, the Vietnamese did not mention their old Cambodian comrades—an omission that confirmed to the Cambodians that they could not trust the Vietnamese. A rift occurred. Because of his mixed parentage Leng was personally affected. He defected from the Cambodians in 1955, rejoined the Vietnamese ranks and fought with the Vietcong forces against the Americans until 1975.

In 1976, he sipped tea in the company of his grown-up son whom he did not raise but wanted to impress with his heroism.

Vaan asked his father, 'What made you leave me before I was even born?' Leng told him that it had been in search of freedom.

'For you, because it certainly was not for my sake. The absence of a father throughout my life has robbed me of the "freedom" that is so dear to you.'

Vaan then asked his father, 'Would you like to know where your mother is?'

Leng was perplexed.

Vaan replied, 'I found her in her apartment in Phnom Penh. The Communist bastards bashed her head and broke her jaw. They killed my grandmother. As far as I am concerned, it was as if it had been you who killed your own mother. Your involvement in this war does not warrant any glory for you to gloat about.'

That was the only meeting father and son had.

The cross-reference of information on refugees collected by the Red Cross informed my father about Saturday's whereabouts. She was also applying for humanitarian aid. Dad searched for her and brought her and her three children to live with him. My parents stayed in the back shed of a widow's house whose name was recommended to them by the kind-hearted matriarch from the village of Tan Chau on their first stop across the border. Their landlady was the wife of a South Vietnamese army officer who had failed to return after the fall of Saigon. She was financially well off with the funds her husband had accumulated from his 'phantom soldiers'. He kept them officially alive on his records in order to collect their wages from the Americans during the war. Chances were that he had escaped with the American staff. His wife declared herself a widow and avoided trouble with the new government. When she knew that my family was eligible to go to France, she was too shrewd not to detect a good opportunity. If she played her cards right, she could use my father to legally exit Vietnam. She became extremely obliging in accommodating Saturday, insisting that she stay in the big house. And after Saturday, she was even more considerate toward anyone my father wished to bring home.

It was at this point that my mother heard about Tam, who was spotted in a refugee camp out of Saigon. For the second time, and against her better judgement, Mum went and rescued Tam from another horrific situation. Tam was reduced to just skin and bone, barely able to breathe. She dragged herself on her knees at the excitement of seeing my mother enter the camp. Her thinning hair was clumped with lice and the camp officers had shaven her head. Her two daughters had died. Only her son clung to her side, a stunted scrawny ten-year-old who looked half his age in size but who bore the face of an old man who had suffered an intolerable life. Mum helped Tam to her feet and supported her by the waist back to the shack. She nurtured her back to health and with her regained vigour, Tam reverted to the opportunist she was. She soon sided with the widow in her plot to get rid of Mum.

The widow gave my father a blunt ultimatum. She would let him, Tam and her son and Saturday and her three children stay in her house on one condition—my mother and two brothers would have to go. She was masterminding a divorce between my parents in order to marry Dad. Once his legal wife, she could automatically get out of Vietnam. My father had on countless occasions cheated on my mother but never in the past had he meant to desert her totally for the sake of another woman. The widow's demand put him in an unprecedented dilemma. To refuse her ultimatum meant that all of his family would be out in the streets. He thought of his sisters and their young children, and he was also bound by duty—if not love—to my brothers and my mother. As always his care for my mother came with far less consideration than he showed to others. He decided not to turn his back on the widow's free accommodation; his small wage could not pay rent elsewhere. He was not the family provider he once was.

The widow chased my mother out of the house while Dad was at work. My parents had a confrontation in the street where Mum insisted on knowing where she stood.

'Am I still your wife?' she asked. 'Are you moving out of the widow's place?'

My father gave her a defeated look. 'I can't do much for you any more. I am, however, still useful in helping my sisters and their children. By staying at the widow's place, I am keeping them off the streets where they are too young to survive. I am the last resort they have. You have the alternative of staying with your mother and your brother Ho.'

My mother stared at him in disbelief. 'How about your sons?'

He simply said, 'They are grown-ups.'

Mum was numb with silence as he slowly walked away from her life. It was the ultimate act of betrayal. Even in his most philandering moments, he had never left her without a roof over her head. What made it worse was the knowledge that he had abandoned her because the widow had money. Her Christian heart ran dry of forgiveness.

She refused to ask Uncle Ho and Grandma Nguen to take her in. She could not stand them to tell her that they had been right about my father all along. For a few weeks she slept around the market places where my two brothers guarded her and took turns to sleep. Finally they found a shed to rent. Saturday was the only person who came to visit Mum.

Mum was at her lowest ebb. She pined for me and oscillated between the longing for me to share her pain and anger against me for being so far away from her. My brothers felt frustrated and helpless as they watched her sink into a deep depression. Through the rough deals that life had handed her, they had never seen her drift into such a state.

Vandy, in particular, was furious with my father and me. He and Vaan visited the Red Cross office daily to follow up the progress of their application.

Toward the end of 1977, a few months after I had married in Melbourne, I received a letter from the Red Cross. The hall of residence to which it was sent re-addressed it to the university's central office. By pure chance, it was at this stage that my student's record was revived because I wanted to finish the one subject I needed to graduate.

The Red Cross conveyed the extraordinary news about my family. The message arrived in registered mail from Paris—brief, official, impersonal and concise. It notified me that funds were tight because of the overwhelming number of war refugees who begged to be relocated, and that my family's passage to France had been put in a queue.

Words failed me. I was incredulous. It was my husband who rejoiced at the news whereas I could only fake my reaction. I had mentally and emotionally buried my family. Now to hear they were still alive was too much of a shock. I woke up in the middle of the night weeks later and the impact of the letter hit me like thunder. The layer of numbness that had protected me from so much hurt, had started to peel away. A window into my old life in which my mother had occupied such a vital role was suddenly burst open. The pain of the previous years came flooding back. I longed to see my family.

I approached the Red Cross, requesting my parents' address in Saigon. Because of the volume of their paperwork, my request was met with silence. I wrote to Uncle Duck's Feet, who failed to reply. Finally I heard from Saturday. The Red Cross prioritised servicemen's wives and she was the first in my family to leave Saigon. During her stopover in Berlin, before she flew to Maryland to be reunited with her husband Toum, she poured out her excitement and recounted to me her story in a long and moving letter. For reasons I found odd and which became obvious to me years later, she only gave me sparing details about my parents' life in Saigon.

Saturday ended her letter on a note of gratitude in memory of Granddad, and I quote, 'For many months in Cambodia, I saw people die like flies. Why I had been spared was not coincidental. I now thank my father for his generosity to the poor and his abstinence from greed. I resented the deprivation he used to impose on us, our family was potentially well-to-do, but we lived with so much lack I used to feel ashamed. Right now, I appreciate his foresight to bank with karma. At the time when man-made currency was worthless, his goodness bought back my life.'

Her second letter, dated four months later, informed me of what had happened to her in America. Her husband Toum rushed home from work, she said. His hair was sprinkled in flour dust from the bakery where he kneaded dough. He spent the first night crying with joy, with disbelief that they were reunited. He kept the children in his arms but after a few days, he still dwelled on the past whereas Saturday wished to get on with life. Toum seemed to torture himself for longer than he should and despaired for their future. 'I cannot bear losing you again!' he said. Saturday had to reassure him that the worst was behind and that they should start living a normal life. She would find work. There would not be a war in America to split them again.

She spoke too soon. Toum confessed that, having hoped against all hope that his family was still alive, he came to grips with the more likely scenario that they had died. He had accepted a companion, a Cambodian refugee, who had a similar toll of losses to bear from the war. She was about to give birth to a child. Saturday was shattered by the revelation but admitted that Toum's relationship was not a case of disloyalty or adultery. She visited his de-facto wife in hospital when the latter gave birth to a boy. In other circumstances Saturday would consider this woman her rival. But in this twist of fate, she reached out to her like a friend, held her hand and they both wept. After much thought, Saturday came to a decision. She told her husband to go to the new wife.

'She and you', she said, 'should stay together to provide for an infant. My children are much older, they have been to hell and back and I think we can survive without you. Leave us with my blessings.'

Toum continued to bake his bread and never progressed in life. His children by Saturday turned their backs on him. They felt betrayed and resented the fact that he had given up waiting for them so quickly. In the many years that followed, the ex-colonel concluded from his experiences that he would rather have died on the battlefields. The war claims its worst victims among the survivors.

Saturday told me my parents would leave Vietnam by September. My husband withdrew his life savings and bought two tickets to France for October. He timed our trip to coincide with my parents' arrival. I sent letters to Duck's Feet, urging him to tell me whether he had heard from my parents. Again he did not bother to reply. My husband and I prepared for our journey. We were full of anticipation; he was looking forward to meeting my parents, and I was exhilarated at the thought of being with my mother after six turbulent years.

36

Paris

There it was, the Paris of my many dreams. It was the city where I had hoped to study. Instead it turned out to be the place where I came to search for my lost family.

My husband and I dropped our luggage at the hotel and looked up the metro route to see Duck's Feet and to obtain from him my parents' address. We were under the assumption that they must have arrived. My husband was concerned if we had caught the right train while I wondered if one of the apartments that flashed past our window could well be where my parents actually lived. We knocked at Duck's Feet's door, and a teenager with sweeping hair greeted us. She was my cousin, the baby I had nursed and sometimes bottle-fed in Cambodia more than fifteen years before. Her brother was now a tall adolescent. They were surprised to see us and did not know who we were. We introduced ourselves and I asked them about my family. They had no knowledge of them. Their mother was not due to return for an hour or so. During this time, I tried to break the ice and brought into my conversation a lot of nostalgic incidents of their childhood in Cambodia. I was slightly taken aback by their lack of response but I put it down to the possibility that they could not remember their lives in Phnom Penh. I found out later that they could not give a damn about anything relating to their past and to their father.

When Jacqueline finally showed up, I could hardly contain my impatience. After a hug, I fired a barrage of questions. Where could I see my parents? To this, she merely shrugged her shoulders and said, 'Don't you know they are still in Vietnam?' These words uttered with such casualness threw me off-balance. I would have wept with disappointment had I not been so equally furious. 'You and my uncle were the only people I depended on for accurate information about my parents. I wrote to my uncle but he did not reply. Where is he, by the way?'

Jacqueline tensed and curtly delivered the news that she and Duck's Feet were divorced. He lived elsewhere. This explained in part his silence to my letters. Jacqueline assured me that she had forwarded them and my uncle would later claim that he had not received them. Neither Jacqueline nor Duck's Feet understood the importance I had attached to my family reunion.

For the rest of the afternoon, my husband and I half-listened to Jacqueline telling us the many reasons for her divorce. We tried to be patient. My husband could not understand a word of French, while I was distraught and forced to follow the account of a nasty divorce. Jacqueline had discovered Duck's Feet's bigamy when Ying, the first wife, came to Phnom Penh to check the rumours that he was living with a French girl in Cambodia. Ying reacted calmly to the truth and asked him to go to Saigon, where she would grant him a divorce. He made the mistake of taking Jacqueline with him. On her home ground, Ying was less amicable. Apparently she was provoked when she caught Duck's Feet and Jacqueline behaving amorously in the streets of Saigon. She took off her high heels and in front of many amazed witnesses hit him on the head. It was a scandal, and the gossip columnists had a field day. Instead of agreeing to a divorce, she laid bigamy charges against Duck's Feet, who fled with Jacqueline out of Saigon.

Back in Phnom Penh, the problem of bigamy was still pending. Jacqueline proceeded with a formal separation but found herself pregnant with their second child. They stayed together under duress until they went back to Paris in 1970 and for another seven tedious years. Jacqueline accused him of a string of affairs and they divorced in 1977, just two weeks before we arrived in Paris.

My uncle came to our hotel the following day where we heard his version of the same story. He was keen to show us the culinary delights of Paris, and tried to take us to restaurants that didn't list their prices on the menu. Those places did not look affordable and I assured him that we were not in the league of dining with an open account.

My husband was working out whether we had the funds to stay in Paris but decided that we could not afford a three-month wait until my parents' arrival. Neither could we afford to return in the near future. We had already stretched our budget to the limit, curtailed our expenses to one meal a day, and downgraded our accommodation. From a rather comfortable three-star hotel, we went to the Latin Quarter where we stayed in a renovated pension. Our tiny room was squalid and the armoire had one leg missing; it rattled and swayed at every footfall.

Our trip was a total disaster. My husband had partly meant for it to be our honeymoon! I was not in the right frame of mind to be romantic nor was I in the right frame of mind to be a tourist.

Four months after we left Paris, my parents and my two brothers arrived. Dad had met up with Mum on the plane. He had checked in with four full suitcases, purchased and filled by the widow, who had kept him well fed and well dressed. Her plan on leaving Saigon as Dad's new wife met with resistance from Duck's Feet, who refused to change his sponsorship in favour of any woman other than my mother. He declined to even sponsor his own sister Tam, who was left with the widow until Saturday established herself in America and eventually sent for her.

On the flight to Paris, my parents and two brothers could not find a word to say to each other. A whole year had passed since my parents had parted company in a street in Saigon. Having assumed that she and my two brothers had lived in the relative safety of Uncle Ho's household, Dad had therefore been able to negotiate with his guilt. But my mother found it difficult to forgive him; his behaviour was the death knell of their marriage. Suddenly thrown back in my father's presence, flying with him towards the same destination, she wondered if she could ever share the same life. In spite of her anger, the church and Asian tradition, both of which disapprove of a divorce, always carry the most influence with my mother. She decided to give my father the chance of reconciliation.

Till the moment Dad boarded the plane, the widow held him to the promise that he would find a way for her to leave Vietnam. He never did.

It was Saturday who did so. Before she applied for the woman's exit visa to America, she sought my mother's approval. Saturday apologised for her gesture and explained in her letter to Mum: 'It would be wrong of me not to help the widow. She did feed my children and me for a few months when we were caught in Saigon. I cannot stand in judgement of her bad treatment of you. I am obliged to pay my personal debt to her and in doing this I am acting in conflict with my respect for you. The gratitude I owe you is beyond repayment. You did not give me birth, but you were a mother to me for many long years. I hope you forgive me.'

Mum's reply acquitted Saturday, 'I would not discourage you from listening to your conscience. The widow treated me shabbily in Saigon. I did hate her then. Now that I have had time to think it through, I realise wars and necessity do influence people to behave badly.'

My family landed in Paris in winter, in the post-Christmas weeks when charitable organisations were especially active in administering to the destitute. They distributed second-hand warm clothes, blankets, plates and cutlery and cooking utensils. My family was put in a bachelor's studio, heated but otherwise unfurnished. Duck's Feet, recently divorced, was too disorganised to provide the day-to-day support, though his social contacts were useful. A friend of his owned an Asian restaurant and offered instant employment. Mum became the cook, Dad was the dishwasher and my two brothers waited on tables.

I followed their lives from one continent away. They were migrants starting from scratch in a new society, and each letter from Mum filled me with guilt. She did not complain or accuse me for not helping. The guilt I bore derived from the failure to live up to my own promise to care for her.

After the grand plans I had made in my childhood, I was in the position I had so hoped to avoid. I was a wife with no personal income. Along with a wedding band, I also slipped around my hands an invisible handcuff that impeded me from providing my mother with the financial assistance she so desperately needed. Having said this, I could only blame myself and not my husband for putting pride above need. My pride stopped me from asking him to help. My husband's regard for my pride stopped him from offering. To him, merely by being in strife does not mean that one needs charity. In his Arabic culture, pride is valued more than currency, and charitable deeds are done anonymously to enable the recipients to preserve their pride. The price of my parents' self-esteem exceeded the money my husband could spare. I hid my frustration and watched them struggle unaided.

Epilogue

In 1981 my husband and I travelled back to Paris. Our trip proved to be a challenge because it included a third party, our ten-month-old baby boy. The weeks that preceded the trip had kept me busy, for which I was glad—it allowed me to push to the back of my mind the reality of seeing my mother again. I had lived, hoped and prayed for such a reunion to take place. Yet, when life was kind enough to bring us together for the three short weeks we planned to spend in Paris, I felt almost frightened. The time had come for me to deal with my sense of guilt and of failure. I remembered all too clearly how, in order to survive I had wished my mother dead and how, to free myself from her memories I had burnt her letters. It was a guilt from which I had been trying to run away and which I now had to face.

Ten years before, I left Mum and Cambodia with the promise of going back and making a difference. Although I ended up with a university degree in my drawer, I realised with some bitterness that I was in no better position to help her than I had been as a child. I ask myself in those moments of conscience whether I had needed and used the quest for a higher education abroad as my excuse to escape, because without this excuse I would never have been able to tear myself away from a mother I so dearly loved.

Had it all been a big deception on my part, hidden beneath a show of strength? It was a lie I was the first, if not the only, person to believe. I thought of my young Aunt Somalee, who stayed by her mother and was subsequently butchered with her. Her death was full of eloquence whereas I was left alive to question the sincerity of my own daughterly love. I defined it in terms of obligation and duty and without the fulfilment of both, I felt I had proven nothing of my deep care.

I came to dread arriving at my destination. Soon I would have to look into my mother's eyes. Because circumstances had altered my destiny and all my plans had gone away, I wondered whether I could tell her how much I had missed her. Although I was myself already a mother, cradling my little boy close to my chest, I failed to grasp at that time that a mother's love is always unconditional.

During the eighteen-hour journey to Paris, I coped with the demands of my baby who had low tolerance to air pockets, air pressure and the space restriction in his cot or on my lap, while my mind was in a whirl. I counted down the hours before I would throw my arms around Mum's shoulders and hear her voice. I attempted to guess how she had changed and aged, but my thoughts brought back a picture I had mentally stored from a past long gone. She was thirty-three on the night she had worn a strand of pearls around her neck . . . Somewhere I heard my husband's voice asking me whether I was all right and my mind awoke to the present. He had no idea of the extent of turmoil inside my chest, but he knew that I must be experiencing an unbearable suspense.

My family would be at Charles de Gaulle Airport to greet us. From the moment I stepped out of the door into the area where they were waiting, and recognised them from a distance, my whole body was seized by a sudden numbness. I reached for the handle of the baby's pusher, taking quick breaths, but I could no longer keep the tears inside.

Ten steps away, I saw my mother. I had half-expected her not to be at the airport. But there she was, struggling to breach the short distance between us, supported by Vandy. It felt like a dream happening in slow motion, unreal, too wonderful to be true.

I remembered closing my arms around my mother's small frame, her head hardly reaching my chin and the familiar smell of her hair so close made me burst into sobs. 'Oh God, it's been such a long time!'

Mum looked up at me and she echoed my remark. 'Yes, Naree, it has been a lifetime!'

Unlike the tears of separation which she had preferred to shed in private by choosing to stay home on the day I departed for Australia, Mum was not embarrassed to show her tears of happiness at our reunion. She had westernised her appearance and manners. She was in her home-tailored pantsuit and she sprinkled her conversation with French expressions, which she pronounced with a confident Parisian accent.

We stayed at my parents' apartment in a group of housing blocks occupied mainly by a non-French community. My husband Raafat ventured out into central Paris on his own and left me to catch up with my family. The few pointed questions Vandy asked me related to the circumstances that made it impossible for Mum to reach me in Melbourne. His words implied that I had forgotten my family, and that I should have tried harder to find out if they were still alive.

The force of his blame was something I had not quite expected. The war, alas, continued to damage people's lives well after its ceasefire. Vandy could not bring himself to forgive me for the pain I had caused our mother. Like many of us who have escaped the physical dangers of war, I found myself apologising for not being there. I could not tell him about my near suicide in Melbourne. Had I dared disclose my lonely battle for survival, it would have sounded to him self-indulgent and incidental. However much I felt I suffered, it could not compare with the Cambodian killing fields or with my mother's suffering in Saigon.

To my brother, who told me that I was lucky, I had to acknowledge I was. My conversation with him left me feeling like a deserter.

Mum had more than forgiven me. She was only glad for the little borrowed time we spent together. She did not ask for any justification but wanted to know whether I finished my university studies.

'A first and most basic degree.' I replied.

'What do you mean?' she asked. 'What is its equivalent in the French system?'

'I guess it must be similar to a French *licence*.'

She asked me whether I had brought a photocopy of it in my luggage, and disappointed when I told her that I kept the original in a drawer and did not think of making copies of it.

'It makes you the highest academic achiever in your father's family. You have to hang it up in your lounge.' I protested and said that so far it had not served any purpose.

'But it will! To begin with, it will inspire your children to achieve the same, if not better!' Her mind wandered off in silence. Slowly she began to speak again, but her voice was almost like a whisper. 'Pol Pot meant to eradicate people like you. Your degree might seem inconsequential to you now. However, from your studies, you will retain the ability to write one day about what happened to Cambodia.'

And then, my mother started to speak about the cruelties of the war. They were personal stories, and stories of a whole people. I did not realise it then, but she had already begun sowing the seeds of a book that one day I would be compelled to write. It would have to be essentially about Cambodian suffering, but the idea was initiated by my Vietnamese mother. Considering that the two races are hereditary enemies, I now know that inside each one of us, we carry a humanity that has no skin colour.

At fifty, my mother was building her independence and was on an equal footing with Dad. From her wages she contributed toward the rent, the phone bills and the food. She left the restaurant kitchen for a job in a clothing factory, which allowed her to bring home piecework and for the same hours, she was able to earn more. She was officially accepted back into the Catholic church and absolved from the anachronistic sin of marrying a non-Catholic. The feminist movement had far-reaching implications that benefited her. Church leniency made further allowance for ancestral worship and Mum can now light joss sticks in memory of Dad's ancestors. In exchange, my father accompanied her on her pilgrimage to Lourdes where St Bernadette had witnessed the appearances of the Virgin Mary.

I was blessed during my brief stay in Paris to find my parents respectful of each other. After three decades of being married, my father confided that 'it had not been easy to live next to a model of perfection'. Now an adult, and with my own luggage of mistakes and failures, I was less judgemental of my father's weaknesses and more drawn to accept and overlook the sufferings he created during my childhood. Was he not a prisoner of life's circumstances like all of us? Perhaps more than trying to forget the pain he brought, I needed to forgive him before my own healing could resume.

My mother travels often to the United States to visit Saturday, her favourite sister-in-law. My aunt had moved up in the world. She owned a beauty salon, had bought a house and put her three children through college—two were doing law and one, medicine.

From Aunt Saturday in Maryland, Mum flies north-west to Seattle to stay with her family. The Nguens had more or less progressively regrouped in the United States after the fall of Saigon in 1975. They are typical hard-working migrants, and had secured their future in less than a generation. Two Nguen children are now chartered accountants and one is training to be a medical doctor. They do not like to remember the past and the American-born generation has put such cultural distance between them and Vietnam that they cannot tolerate the smell of fish sauce. This is like saying that an Indian cannot stand the smell of curry spices or that an Australian cannot eat Vegemite.

Yesterday's millionaire in peaceful Cambodia, Uncle Ho, lost his wealth in Saigon where he invested in freehold he could not sell. The diamonds he had smuggled out of Phnom Penh inside cans of powdered milk packed in the boot of his car disappeared in a Saigon street riot. He wasted his time persuading his relatives of business opportunities in Seattle; nobody in the Nguen family was game enough to risk investing their hard-earned savings in Ho's dreams.

My mother was optimistic. 'Who knows?' she said. 'Ho's son might take up his father's advice and one day, somebody will make it big in America!' Who knows indeed?

Vaan went on from the restaurant to work with a wallpaper manufacturer. He packed and dispatched heavy boxes which, by his keenness to impress the management, he carried unaided from the factory floor to the delivery trucks. The weight of these boxes crushed the lower disks of his vertebra. This injury is operable but surgery, besides being costly, gives unpromising results. To this day he prefers to wear a permanent girdle and put up with the back pain. He has had to sleep on his stomach and in the cold of the worst winter months, which are unkind to bone sufferers, he lies on the hard flat surface of the floor to keep his spine straight. During the periodic attacks when the disks collapse and pinch the nerves, which control the movement of his legs, he continuously slaps his thighs to stimulate some physical sensation into his temporarily crippled lower limbs.

My visit to Paris coincided with a time that Vaan could not move. As I walked into his apartment and saw him lying on the floor, his huge eyes looking up, I decided to mask my shock with a misplaced joke, 'I waited all these years to play hopscotch with you!' The start of his laugh brought a squeal of pain instead. His wife rushed to flip him back into a straight position while Mum scolded me for teasing.

Vaan married a Cambodian-born Chinese girl. He used to dislike the Chinese when we were living in Cambodia and I teased him that he should end up loving one. I reminded him of a Cambodian proverb, which says that whatever a person dislikes most will eventually get 'spilled over their head'. Vaan's wife is exuberant and speaks two Chinese dialects fluently, Cambodian, Vietnamese and French and she possesses the characteristics of her race—hard-working and adaptable to change. She was a nursing aide; her compliance and patience with old people gained her a well-paid position in the nursing home. She lost this job with a change of ownership and bridged the gap by working as a cleaner for a few months without losing her cheerful smile.

Vandy's aeronautical qualifications from the Russian Institute of Technology in Phnom Penh were not fully recognised in France and he was advised to go back for a course to update his degree. He felt too old to study again and works as a mechanic. My brother's hands have the hardness of rock; they are stained with oil and grease. 'This job does me just fine,' he assured me.

I look at him with sorrow and regret that he has had a hard life. He never wanted much for himself and never boasted of the noble ambition of caring for Mum. Yet, it was he who was there for her and will be there in the years to come whereas I, with all my planning and my dreams, was only 'visiting'. Quietly and modestly, Vandy was carrying the role of the eldest son.

After he had washed dishes for one year in a Vietnamese restaurant, a job my father bore with a fatalistic acceptance, he entered the organisation CEEMAT, an acronym for Centre d'Études et d'Expèrimentation du Machinisme Agricole Tropical. Dad poured his energy into his work, and belonged to a team that experimented on the production of fuel from crop residues to substitute firewood in Egypt. He travelled extensively around Europe to deliver papers, and exchange opinions and results with other bodies of scientists. Due to his expertise in tropical agronomy, part of his activities included regular missions to tropical countries and to former French territories.

Following the visit in March 1989 to Paris by the Cambodian vice-minister of agriculture, Mr Chea Song, France agreed to offer more

active assistance to Cambodia. In conjunction with the French government, CEEMAT chose my father to head a delegation to Cambodia. His
familiarity with this region was invaluable in assessing the kind of
agricultural aid Cambodia would need to re-establish the proper infra-
structure that had been obliterated by Pol Pot.

At that stage Dad had taken up French nationality and changed his
first name to Gerard. Officially, nothing could indicate to the people in
the Cambodian government that they were about to receive one of their
old colleagues at the airport. Thirteen years after he had escaped to the
border like a common criminal, my father was ceremoniously received
back in his native Cambodia. On 8 June 1989, he landed in Phnom
Penh where a Cambodian official party lined the red carpet for their
French visitor's arrival at the airport. To their surprise, instead of a
Frenchman, my father stepped out of the plane.

The first note of the French anthem resounded for his delegation.
Cambodian by birth, he now represented France. He was standing on
the land he loved, but he belonged officially to another. In his mind, his
whole life was condensed into those few minutes, during which he saw
in rapid flashback his long career in Cambodia.

He owed his loyalty to France for nurturing his professional ability,
now his countrymen were paying him the accolade he once used to
dream about. Dad had waited throughout his working life in Cambodia
for a hint of appreciation. Nepotism, prejudice and absurd politics had
stood in his way and many more capable men like him had been deprived
of the chance of developing their skills. When he stood listening to the
'Marseillaise', the honour he was receiving at that moment might have been
sweet revenge. However it only heightened the awful confusion of allegiance and the profound sadness he felt for his native country.

In 1989 Cambodia was not free. To explain the control Vietnam had
over it, I have to go back to the years under Pol Pot.

In stark contradiction to his Communist stand, the Angkorian
empire seduced Pol Pot. He was quoted as having said, 'If the Khmer

people could build Angkor, they could do anything.' He drew from Cambodian ancient history a misplaced sense of arrogance and directed his efforts to chasing the mirage of a glorious past. He launched against Vietnam a military offensive aimed at reclaiming the old territories of Prey Nokor, which a Cambodian king lost by consent in 1620 to a Vietnamese civil settlement. Three-and-a-half centuries later, the Khmer Rouge raids, which started in 1977, rendered half a million Vietnamese peasants homeless.

Hanoi retaliated, and with the same strength that had stood up successfully against France and the United States, its army defeated the Khmer Rouge forces in early 1979. It installed two Cambodian Communists, Heng Samrin and Hun Sen—who both defected from Pol Pot's rank in 1977—at the head of a new government in Phnom Penh. The international press condemned Vietnam. In response to world opinion against its occupation of and its patronage over Cambodia, Hanoi was quick to lift the curtain of secrecy, and revealed the atrocities committed during the Khmer Rouge era. For the first time, after four years of speculation, the media could enter Cambodia.

The first journalists who went on location to file their reports fell on their knees and wept. They were the first to witness the gruesome horror of another holocaust. In some ways, the Cambodian holocaust was worse, because it was 'auto-genocide'. More deranged than Hitler, Pol Pot had orchestrated the mass murder of his own race. Phnom Penh smelt of the dead. Nearly two million people had died, or one in every eight.

Schools were converted to places of execution; human skulls and bones were piled up to the ceilings. Records of tortures were meticulously filed, photographs and names of the victims—children, women, elderly folks—displayed on walls. Mass graves were found everywhere around the countryside, and these were countless testimonies to lives lost when people were ill-fed and forced to work as state agricultural slaves across the wide green fields. The survivors of the war were traumatised to the extent that a high percentage of women of child-bearing age stopped menstruating. Not one person was spared from the death of a close relative. Everybody was mourning somebody.

The military offensives against Vietnam prevented the rice harvest in 1978–79. In the wake of the Khmer Rouge defeat came famine. Charity organisations, alerted by the first batch of journalists, promptly raised funds and flew in food and medical supplies to alleviate the famine and to start saving lives in Cambodia. They could not find one stretch of road that was smooth enough to travel on, nor one decent truck capable of distributing goods to remote places.

In 1989, after ten years of Vietnamese control, Cambodia was still in dire straits. Everywhere my father toured on his mission, the vastness of the damage to the land by the Khmer Rouge was obvious. The network of canals, dams and ditches for drainage had been manually dug by the enslaved population. Pol Pot had the ambition of doubling the production of rice but his schemes were not based on technical research or on any understanding of the topography of the sites. The massive works undertaken resulted mostly in high human cost and provoked either excessive drought or floods. The rectification of this damage was slow. The majority of agricultural experts had either been killed or migrated overseas. There were few reference manuals to guide the corrective program. Agricultural staff relied on their memory, and much of their efforts were by trial and error. They were uncoordinated and handicapped by a shortage of funds and technical skills.

It was, and it remains, impossible to estimate how many educated people met their deaths during the four years under Pol Pot. Without taking into account the tolls in the hands of the Khmer Rouge, after 1979, Cambodia lost a further two hundred thousand of its educated citizens through migration. To many of them, the prospect of remaining in their country was no longer viable. Vietnam, in defeating Pol Pot, had certainly halted the killing, and for this reason, it was claimed that it saved Cambodia, but in another way, because Cambodia was now in

Vietnamese control it revived bad memories of previous Vietnamese occupation and the humiliation the locals suffered in the early 1800s. Worse still, Vietnam installed in 1979 another Communist government to replace Pol Pot's Communist regime, which made many feel the ongoing risk of persecution.

In the absence of skills to help rebuild the country, Cambodia found it hard to recover. Its difficulties also stemmed from the politics inflicted from outside. The alliance of big powers, namely the United States, Britain and China, decided to punish Vietnam for having won the Vietnam War and imposed a trade embargo that meant Vietnam was reduced to depending on Russian development aid. As Vietnam struggled to get back on its feet, so Cambodia was also punished indirectly, by association.

The American government now endeavoured to nurture the survival of the Khmer Rouge, the only forces that could be used by the United States to exact revenge on Vietnam. They set up refugee camps along the border between Cambodia and Thailand where Khmer Rouge troops, hurt by the Vietnamese retaliation in 1979, regrouped and recuperated. These camps were recruitment centres for the Khmer Rouge whom the American authorities housed, fed and armed. So much so that, after their full-fledged genocide, the Khmer Communists now had full foreign backing and better means to strike, intimidate and murder innocent Cambodian civilians throughout the 1980s.

In the aftermath of the Cambodian holocaust came famine and an epidemic break-out of disease, notably malaria, dysentery, dengue fever and tuberculosis. Official aid assigned by the United States and Britain to help Cambodia did not reach the majority of victims. Instead it found its way to the refugee camps where it sustained Pol Pot's troops and their families. The Khmer Rouge formed another government in exile, called CGDK, an acronym for Coalition Government of Democratic Kampuchea, joining forces with Sihanouk and Sonn San. They were officially recognised by the United Nations. Their main aim was to chase Vietnam out of Cambodia. They commanded a combined military force of forty thousand troops who placed landmines all over the countryside. The Cambodian government of Hun Sen in Phnom Penh also proceeded to plant more landmines in its attempt to impede the Communist advance.

Mostly unaware of the sinister game of politics that was being played by their governments, the private citizens of the world looked on, sympathised, cried and reached out to help Cambodia. Many became desensitised by so much misery, and by a tragedy that seemed to stretch for too long.

During my father's visit, Phnom Penh had a population of between five and six hundred thousand. Once a beautiful city, the blows of the war had left many physical scars. Bridges were not yet repaired; temples, buildings, shops and private houses bore traces of heavy artillery; a big empty space exists where the cathedral close to my old school once stood. What stirred my father deeply was the poverty in the streets, which were crowded with young victims of landmines. When the sun set, the city was enveloped in silence and darkness. There were severe electricity shortages; street lamps were not lit and power was switched off early at night. Next to the Royal Palace, where Sihanouk used to hold his annual congress, a makeshift shanty cluster of tin roofs housed a community of country folk. It was putrid with litter, with the smell of excrement mixing with that of cooking.

In his second week in Phnom Penh, behind ministerial doors, Dad was invited to come back to Cambodia permanently. His visitors wished their identity to remain confidential. It was possible that they spoke on behalf of people in Hanoi who deemed him to be an excellent choice since he was half-Cambodian and half-Vietnamese, and could be trusted to report directly to them. The attempt to recruit Dad contradicted with the official promise by Vietnam that it would withdraw its tutelage from Cambodia by the end of 1989. A top position in agriculture was tempting to him, not for the prestige attached to it, but for the contribution he could make. Yet he was reluctant to involve himself in politics.

Back in Paris, Dad compiled his assessments and his recommendations in a report, which was bound in a book and a copy stored at the library at CEEMAT. In the one he gave me to keep, I could feel his contained emotions as he struggled to write with a professional detachment. He was silent on the offer to work in Cambodia. He was not certain of the motives behind the invitation and he did not want to leave France, a country that had offered him a new chance at life.

I have had the opportunity to head back to Paris many times since the initial reunion with my family. Although visiting Thailand on two occasions, I have not been able to go back to Cambodia. To visit would open up old wounds that have not properly healed. They never will, until peace is fully restored.

By September 1989, Vietnam withdrew, as promised, all of its thirty thousand troops from Cambodia, which had become too expensive to maintain. A further glimpse of hope for a peaceful settlement came with the American decision to stop recognising the official status of the Coalition Government of the Khmer Rouge, Sihanouk and Sonn San.

In 1991, the United Nations sponsored a general election to take place in Cambodia. Despite billions of dollars spent to maintain a peacekeeping force there, democracy remained unattainable. Hun Sen, whose government had been installed by Vietnam back in 1979, was re-elected. Sihanouk re-entered Cambodia and is now king. His son, Ranarith, shares power with Hun Sen. By and large, an attitude of mistrust between them cripples the running of the government.

Leading up to the general elections, people were frightened, their voices fell silent and their choices were not perhaps reflected in the ballots in spite of the guarantee given by the United Nations troops that they should vote in the spirit of freedom. 'Freedom' was an empty word. Asking the Cambodians to feel free was to assume that they had human rights and that they knew of equality. They had never experienced any of these to conceive of them.

If the world at large truly wants to help Cambodia, let it send teaching staff and develop education. Let my people understand that their long overdue freedom comes from learning and then and only then will they have a chance to make choices.

In 1998, Pol Pot was reported to have died. Early in 1999, he presented himself at a trial, which was really a mock trial. Later that year, he was supposed to have died a second time and a body was shown while his ex-commanders—now enjoying immunity from prosecution by the government and some of whom are back in power—staged a press conference in which they admitted to responsibility for the countless unspeakable crimes against the people.

For the time being, and without any foreseeable change, the majority of Cambodians are very poor and helpless. Since schooling was stopped under Pol Pot, children's literacy, which in the 1960s reached 86 per cent, is now very low. Hundreds of male children and young men whose traditional responsibility it is to tend cattle in the fields continue to die or to have their arms and legs blown off by landmines every week. Poverty is such that child malnutrition and infant mortality rates are among the highest in the world. The birthrate is low because many young women have stopped menstruating. Child prostitution has shifted into Phnom Penh and AIDS is rampant. Mental illness is also high. Various diseases that are usually curable and preventable in the world become killers in Cambodia.

The protracted miseries of my people are beyond the scope of my book. Only the research and scholarly writings of historians such as Professor David Chandler can give accurate accounts of Pol Pot's legacy. I wonder if there is hope? According to Andrew Morris, head of the Cambodian health services of UNICEF, the future of Cambodia 'cannot depend on this generation. At best, it may rest with the generation of children not yet born'.

I cannot stop crying for Cambodia, for the fate it has endured and for the people whose lives mingled with mine during my nineteen years there. I long for the opportunity I could never have to meet friends at school reunions, for instance. To allow myself to wonder about any of them is to invite ghosts to haunt me.

But I am luckier than the six million Cambodians who are still living there. I am now a citizen of Australia, a country that was quick to adopt me. To be honest, for the first ten years or so, I accepted living here by default. Australia then was just a place where my destiny happened to have swept me. Perhaps I had learnt the hard way, and had given up wanting to belong. Having not been fully accepted by my own race, I must have thought it would be more difficult for me to pass for an Australian.

Australia felt like home only when I had the chance to travel abroad in 1981. Before then, I did not think I had any deep attachment towards this country. It had slowly grown in me, in secret ways that I was not aware. Coming back after four weeks away was the first awakening. How very true to say that a human being is like a tree: where it gets planted and drinks the water, it becomes a part of the landscape.

Twenty-nine years in Australia have made the adult in me an Australian. This country has educated me, shaped my maturity, and provided me with security. I have raised my three children to be a part of this country. I hope they will participate in its future. I have avoided burdening them with my past, but it occurred to me that one day, curiosity will lead them to ask me questions about my heritage, which I initially did not wish them to know. Why, for instance, do they have cousins in France with whom they can barely communicate? What brought—and keeps—me here? How will I be able to sit them down and explain the long story of a dismembered and scattered family?

I conceived five years ago the idea of writing for their sake. What started as a personal diary slowly transformed into a book. If it is informative for my children, it may well be of interest to others.

I believe it is crucial to speak up on behalf of those who, more than having their lives cut short, have also been deprived of all dignity. In writing this book, I have recalled them with the respect I owe to martyrs. In light of their suffering and loss, the living among us might hear their plea. Lest we forget; we cannot afford the same fate to befall future generations.

For the lucky few who escaped Cambodia, we find stability else-where. But wherever we might settle in the world, we carry the burden of guilt for those who died and those who are left behind. We have been uprooted and transplanted, and like the sunflowers that turn towards the light, our spirits will forever bend toward the land of Angkor Wat. For the rest of my life, the voiceless victims of the killing fields will continue to haunt me in my dreams.